Salesforce Data Architecture and Management

A pragmatic guide for aspiring Salesforce architects and developers to manage, govern, and secure their data effectively

Ahsan Zafar

BIRMINGHAM—MUMBAI

Salesforce Data Architecture and Management

Copyright © 2021 Packt Publishing

Group Product Manager: Alok Dhuri

Publishing Product Manager: Kunal Chaudhari

Senior Editor: Storm Mann

Content Development Editor: Nithya Sadanandan

Technical Editor: Pradeep Sahu

Language Support Editor: Safis Editing

Copy Editor: Safis Editing

Project Coordinator: Deeksha Thakkar

Proofreader: Safis Editing

Indexer: Pratik Shirodkar

Production Designer: Joshua Misquitta

First published: June 2021

Production reference: 1240621

Published by Packt Publishing Ltd.

Livery Place

35 Livery Street

Birmingham

B3 2PB, UK.

ISBN 978-1-80107-324-0

www.packt.com

To my parents for instilling the belief that I can do anything that I set my mind on, and to my wife for her immense support and keeping our young kids busy so that I could think and write uninterrupted.

- Ahsan Zafar

Contributors

About the author

Ahsan Zafar is Salesforce Technical Architect. He is 15x Salesforce certified and is a Salesforce Certified Technical Architect (CTA) candidate. He has spent around two decades working with different aspects of data, including data architecture, master data management, and data migrations. Ahsan has also had stints as a Business Analyst, Project Manager, and Salesforce consultant on various projects that gave him a unique understanding of how data is perceived by different roles. He has also worked as a developer and as a technical lead, spending almost a decade implementing Oracle ERP systems that typically involved migrating significant volumes of data from legacy systems.

About the reviewers

Ali Najefi is an enterprise architect with 18 years of experience, of which 13 years has been in Salesforce. He is a Salesforce CTA with a track record for delivering complex digital transformation projects on the Salesforce platform.

Experienced in leading Salesforce architecture and design authority teams, he was responsible for ensuring all Salesforce delivery teams adhered to Salesforce's best architecture and design principles. He has a significant interest in cybersecurity, identity and access management, digital data management, MDM, analytics, and AI, where he has worked on several enterprise clients both directing the architectural domain and delivering solutions that have proven to be secure and scalable for millions of customers and thousands of enterprise users.

Ram Iyer is a certified Salesforce application architect and system architect with 20 years of overall experience in enterprise architecture, solution design, data architecture, business analysis, and project management. He has over 12 years of architecture, design, and development expertise in Salesforce.com, Lightning, and Einstein Analytics. Ram has been a guest speaker at Dreamforce (2016, 2017) and is an evangelist for enabling continuous integration and delivery capabilities in large organizations. Passionate about technology, Ram has worked extensively on API design, application integration, business intelligence, DevSecOps, Agile, and Waterfall models of software development, with proven leadership abilities in managing large, complex projects.

Table of Contents

3

Understanding Data Management

Section 2: Salesforce Data Governance and Master Data Management

4
Making Sense of Master Data Management

5
Implementing Data Governance

6
Managing Performance

Section 3: Large Data Volumes (LDVs) and Data Migrations

7
Working with Large Volumes of Data

8

Best Practices for General Data Migration

Assessments

Preface

Data is becoming more and more valuable to organizations as they realize its true potential and how it can help them to achieve their business objectives. The reason for this is that data can be turned into actionable intelligence that organizations can leverage to keep their internal and external customers happy while maintaining their competitive edge.

The key here is actionable intelligence derived from data otherwise it takes up storage space and is an expense to the organization. The Salesforce Platform facilitates turning unactionable data into actionable intelligence, but for this to happen on an on going basis, the data architecture must be properly designed and allow scalability. Data modeling blunders include creating roll-up summary fields on an account record that have the year hard coded in them to show account revenue and require the roll-up summary filter to be updated every year. Blunders also include worse situations where a lookup relationship may have been used for an application, but a parent-child relationship was created, leading to a tightly coupled relationship. The sole reason for choosing this type of relationship would be due to it providing the roll-up summary field capability.

In this book, we will start with the very basics of understanding what data architects are expected to do and how you can be a successful Salesforce data architect. You will then learn about data modeling and data management. Once we have the basics covered, we will delve into master data management, data governance, and how we can ensure performance for our applications.

Data keeps on growing at a fast pace and knowing how to design solutions effectively involving large volumes of data is a crucial skill set. Therefore, we will extensively cover Large Data Volumes (LDVs) and what we can do as architects to effectively manage them while keeping scalability and Salesforce governor limits under consideration.

I have included questions at the end of each chapter to ensure you have clearly understood the concepts discussed in the chapter. Moreover, there are extensive examples and diagrams throughout the chapters to ensure that a firm understanding of the concepts is developed.

When all is said and done and you have reached the end of the book, you will have gained a solid understanding of data architectural skills and best practices that you can apply immediately within the context of Salesforce. The content covered in this book is also very relevant to the *Data Architecture and Management Designer* exam and the data architecture domain that is tested in the Salesforce *Certified Technical Architect (CTA)* exam (`https://trailhead.salesforce.com/credentials/dataarchitectureandmanagementdesigner`).

Who this book is for

This book is for both aspiring and experienced architects, Salesforce admins, and developers who want to learn more about the core architecture of the Salesforce platform in the context of data management and architecture. Whether you are just starting off in the Salesforce ecosystem as an admin or a developer, or whether you are an experienced architect with several years of experience under your belt, this book has something for everyone to benefit from.

To get the most out of the book, you will have had experience with data migration and integrations in large, complex technology landscapes consisting of disparate systems. You will also have had to deal with data with privacy regulations and topics such as master data management to further manage data in your technology landscape. Salesforce professionals that have large orgs with millions of records who are concerned about performance will also benefit from the book as scalability and performance have been at the forefront when writing.

Although the book covers a multitude of topics that overlap different Salesforce certification exams, Salesforce professionals specifically preparing for the *Data Architecture and Management Designer* exam or the Salesforce CTA review board will find the book helpful as supporting material for these exam preparation.

What is this book covers

Chapter 1, Data Architect-Roles and Responsibilities, describes the role of a data architect and the core skills and experience that are required for it. It will also go in to detail on what soft skills are required to be successful in the role. You will also get to have a look at a day in the life of a data architect.

Chapter 2, Understanding Salesforce Objects and Data Modeling, will take you through the unique architecture of the Salesforce platform and how it is optimized for read access rather than write operations traditionally seen in relational databases. Data modeling concepts, how they get applied in the context of Salesforce, what de-normalization is, and why it is important to spend the time designing your data model properly will be discussed. At the end of the chapter, Salesforce objects and how they are created, different types of fields on them, and their use cases will be covered.

Chapter 3, Understanding Data Management, will explain data management, what it is, and why it's important. The different aspects of managing data, including the data lifecycle, will also be discussed. With Salesforce's discontinuation of data recovery services, data backup and archiving have come to the forefront, so we will discuss that in detail as well. At the end, some tools that are available to manage data effectively will be reviewed.

Chapter 4, Making Sense of Master Data Management, will discuss the key attributes of master data, what the Golden Record is and why it is so important for organizations. We will look at how to align your MDM and CRM strategy with a discussion on Salesforce's Customer 360 and its key components. MDM is a platform-agnostic concept that can be used within the context of non-Salesforce landscapes as well. The chapter is concluded with a brief discussion of the Common Information Model (CIM).

Chapter 5, Implementing Data Governance, covers the importance of enterprise data governance, the relationship between data governance and data management, and how to assess the current state of data governance. Two major privacy protection laws, the GDPR and CCPA, will also be covered in detail. To conclude and firm up understanding of the content, a sample case study will describe a hypothetical scenario and the solution approach to solve it.

Chapter 6, Managing Performance, will explore foundational aspects of performance on the Force.com platform, how to use the Query Plan tool to determine performance-impacting queries, and query costs when using indexes versus full table scans. The chapter also covers the various tools that can be used to monitor the platform for performance and auditing changes. Multiple code blocks will be used to drive the point home of how performance can be determined and optimized. Performance testing is critical especially when dealing with large volumes of data, so an extensive discussion around aspects of performance testing will be covered, followed by a discussion on monitoring the performance of the Salesforce org.

Chapter 7, Working with Large Volumes of Data, will introduce you to the concept of relational and non-relational databases. LDVs, which are becoming more and more relevant in the Salesforce ecosystem as orgs generate or consume lots of data, will be discussed extensively, from identifying LDV scenarios to managing LDV orgs and integrating data into these org types.

We will look at some options in cases where large volumes of data don't necessarily have to be brought into Salesforce, but the data can still be made available to users. We will cap our discussion with Big Objects which is yet another way to deal with very large data volumes.

Chapter 8, Best Practices for General Data Migration, will introduce you to data migration - how to assess, plan, and execute data migrations. Considerations and best practices related to data migration will also be discussed. Close to the end, we will discuss some commonly used tools that can be used for data migration. We will cap our discussion by discussing the different APIs that are available in Salesforce within the context of data migration.

To get the most out of this book

Theis book has multiple SOQL query code blocks throughout the chapters, and you are strongly encouraged to follow along and try them in a Developer Edition of Salesforce. For chapters that may appear to be theoretical in nature, for example, ones on data governance, I would encourage you to think of your own current or past organizations and try to apply the principles learned in the chapters, including the practical aspects of these topics, for example, metrics or KPIs for data quality.

The book assumes an understanding of basic Salesforce functionality, so at times, advanced topics may be challenging to grasp in the absence of the required knowledge.

Software/Hardware covered in the book	OS Requirements
Salesforce Developer Edition (`https://developer.salesforce.com/signup`)	Windows, macOS, or Linux (Any)
Workbench (`https://workbench.developerforce.com/`)	Windows, macOS, or Linux (Any)

Download the color images

We also provide a PDF file that has color images of the screenshots and diagrams used in this book. You can download it here: `https://static.packt-cdn.com/downloads/9781801073240_ColorImages.pdf`.

Conventions used

There are a number of text conventions used throughout this book.

`Code in text`: Indicates code words in text, database table names, folder names, filenames, file extensions, pathnames, dummy URLs, user input, and Twitter handles.

Here is an example: "Changing the criterion to `LastModifiedDate` will fix the issue."

A block of code is set as follows:

```
SELECT Id, Name, Description, LastRunDate, LastModifiedBy.Name
FROM Report
WHERE LastRunDate < 2019-06-01T00:00:00Z
ORDER BY LastRunDate DESC
LIMIT 50
```

When we wish to draw your attention to a particular part of a code block, the relevant lines or items are set in bold:

```
SELECT Id, Name, Description, LastRunDate, LastModifiedBy.Name
FROM Report
WHERE LastRunDate < 2019-06-01T00:00:00Z
ORDER BY LastRunDate DESC
LIMIT 50
```

Any command-line input or output is written as follows:

```
ping -f -n 25 -l 1200 na111.salesforce.com
ping -f -n 25 -l 1300 na111.salesforce.com
ping -n 25 -l 1400 na111.salesforce.com
```

Bold: Indicates a new term, an important word, or words that you see onscreen. For instance, words in menus or dialog boxes appear in **bold**. Here is an example: "In **Developer Console**, click on the **Logs** tab."

> **Tips or important notes**
> Appear like this.

Get in touch

Feedback from our readers is always welcome.

General feedback: If you have questions about any aspect of this book, email us at customercare@packtpub.com and mention the book title in the subject of your message.

Errata: Although we have taken every care to ensure the accuracy of our content, mistakes do happen. If you have found a mistake in this book, we would be grateful if you would report this to us. Please visit www.packtpub.com/support/errata and fill in the form.

Piracy: If you come across any illegal copies of our works in any form on the internet, we would be grateful if you would provide us with the location address or website name. Please contact us at copyright@packt.com with a link to the material.

If you are interested in becoming an author: If there is a topic that you have expertise in and you are interested in either writing or contributing to a book, please visit authors.packtpub.com.

Share Your Thoughts

Once you've read *Salesforce Data Architecture and Management*, we'd love to hear your thoughts! Scan the QR code below to go straight to the Amazon review page for this book and share your feedback.

https://packt.link/r/1801073244

Your review is important to us and the tech community and will help us make sure we're delivering excellent quality content.

Section 1: Data Architecture and Data Management Essentials

By the end of this section, you will have understood the role of a data architect and the skills that are required to be successful in the role. You will understand what data modeling is, how to apply data modeling concepts in Salesforce, and how they relate to objects and fields in Salesforce. Concepts related to data management and the different aspects of data management will be discussed. Backup and archiving strategies and some tools to use to manage data will also be discussed with hands-on exercises.

In this section, there are the following chapters:

- *Chapter 1, Data Architect – Roles and Responsibilities*
- *Chapter 2, Understanding Salesforce Objects and Data Modeling*
- *Chapter 3, Understanding Data Management*

1
Data Architect Roles and Responsibilities

In this chapter, we will first define the term **architecture** in order to establish a baseline understanding of what the term means. This will help us to establish what it is, bring other stakeholders on the same page, and prevent scope creep in roles and responsibilities. We will then look at the types of architects, their roles, and why it's important for them to work together in order to both produce a cohesive architectural strategy and to deliver value to an enterprise. Often, people may mention needing a solution architect, but in reality, the work they need to do may be more suitable for a data architect because the skill set required is different. So, understanding the different types of architects is important.

In this chapter, we will also look at the responsibilities of a data architect and the soft and hard skills needed to be successful in the role. Covering these topics will help you to communicate with architects more effectively in order to engage the right resources for your project. Understanding this from the beginning will help you to see the overlap that sometimes exists between the skills that data architects and solution architects have and understand when a task may require the skills of one role more than the other.

We will conclude the chapter by discussing a typical day in the life of a data architect, which will allow us to understand the work they do and the potential challenges they face.

In particular, we will cover these topics:

- Defining architecture
- Exploring architecture roles
- Why is data architecture important?
- Data architect responsibilities
- Data architect skills
- A day in the life of a data architect

Defining architecture

Architecture is a broadly used term and can mean different things to different people. Therefore, it is important to first define it so that we can establish a common understanding of this term before proceeding further. The term *architecture* is defined as the practice of designing systems, buildings, or things. In the context of technology, it refers to the practice of designing structures or systems with individual components with the intention of optimizing the function, cost, and performance of the overall structure.

Thinking in physical terms, a construction architect designing a home will architect how large each room is going to be, as well as decide on the number of windows and their placement in the room. This may also include planning where each room should be located to maximize the use of space and what direction the windows should be facing to maximize sunlight. In a nutshell, a building architect aims to maximize the use of space while keeping optimal functionality and costs in mind.

Similarly, a technology architect designs solutions by making use of the available components, considering the pros and cons of each component, overall costs, and the overall performance of the system. Of course, the desired functionality needed from the overall system and its ability to meet the business objectives will also be a critical factor in determining what individual components to use for the system. The key difference between physical and technology architecture is that most technology architecture used to be based on the waterfall methodology and, as such, required extensive upfront planning, requirements gathering, and documentation. The waterfall methodology is a linear project methodology where a project is broken down into phases, and in most cases, the next phase cannot start until the previous phase has been completed with deliverables signed off. With the advent of Agile and other methodologies, the focus has now turned toward designing solutions that are scalable and can be quickly adapted to changing market conditions. This is important because in order for a business to stay competitive in the global economy, they cannot afford to spend weeks and months updating their systems.

For enterprises, architectural needs vary depending on the needs and stage of the issue the enterprise is trying to solve. Over several years, technology professionals have realized this and have delineated architecture into multiple domains. Since our discussion topic is the role of a data architect, it would be prudent to discuss the various domains of architecture because they are interlinked and exert constraints over each other.

In the subsequent sections, we will look at why data architecture is important as well as explore the different types of architects, their roles, and some of the deliverables they are responsible for producing and maintaining. This will give us a greater understanding of the differences in responsibilities and an appreciation of how the type of architect fits into the architectural puzzle of an enterprise.

Exploring architecture roles

Architects have been around for as long as business systems. They may have had different titles over the years, such as systems analyst, technology analyst, and the like, but fundamentally, they have always designed systems that are scalable and efficient. Today, the titles have become more refined and there are multiple types of architects specializing in their own domains. Understanding each of these is important because it will help us have better communication with them and enable us to bring other stakeholders on the same page as well.

Business architect

Business architects are concerned with identifying how value can be created for internal and external stakeholders of the enterprise. This usually involves producing strategy documents, process maps, capability maps, and commonly used business terms within the enterprise or the industry in which the enterprise operates.

Data architect

Data architects are the key topic of this book. Of course, they are mainly concerned with data: how data is organized, how it is moved internally or externally, and how it can be made accessible to users when it is needed. Data architects create data models and make decisions on how data will be stored, consumed, and archived. Some data architects will also analyze and communicate how insights and intelligence can be derived from data that can be useful to stakeholders. Typical deliverables include data models, data definitions, the flow of data, and integrations.

Solution architect

A **solution architect** is concerned with designing systems that deliver business value to stakeholders. Working closely with **Business Architects (BAs)**, they ensure that the solution will provide the business value that the business requires. One of the key responsibilities of solution architects is to identify the most optimal technology that will meet business requirements. This can include packaged software such as Salesforce or designing custom solutions from the ground up. Deliverables for this type of architecture include functional and technical design documents, system landscape diagrams, and the actual software that's delivered in line with the design that the architect puts forward.

Domain architects

These are architects that have expertise in a particular domain of technology. For example, **Information Security (IS)** architects, technology architects, and cloud architects have very specific expertise in their respective areas and are considered domain architects. A **Salesforce Certified Technical Architect (CTA)**, although required to have a broad knowledge of certain areas, are experts in implementing Salesforce solutions.

Information security architect

The IS architect has been becoming more important as data integrations between systems become common and cybersecurity becomes critical for enterprises to protect their data and, by extension, their reputation. IS architects are responsible for designing, implementing, and maintaining security solutions that can protect the organization's network and hardware. They regularly conduct different types of testing to identify vulnerabilities and proactively fix them before a security incident materializes. In cases where the organization's security is breached, they work on a root cause analysis and identify fixes to remediate those vulnerabilities.

Technology architect

A **technology (or infrastructure) architect** is concerned with the physical infrastructure needed to enable organizations to deliver their software applications to their stakeholders. Servers, networks, and cloud-based **Infrastructure as a Service (IaaS)** fall into this category. Their responsibilities include the following:

- Designing and implementing the infrastructure solutions needed by organizations
- Supporting the hardware needs of projects in an enterprise
- Monitoring production environments to ensure that they are running optimally by monitoring certain attributes such as throughput, latency, and redundancy, among others

Deliverables include network diagrams, server-to-server diagrams, and others. With the advent of the cloud, another type of architect that's gaining traction is the **cloud architect**.

Cloud architect

These architects are mainly concerned with an enterprise's cloud strategy and its implementation. Like technology architects, they are concerned with implementing cloud solutions that can support software that runs on the cloud. The key difference between technology and cloud architects is that traditionally, the former has been more focused on on-premises systems whereas the latter has been focused primarily on cloud solutions. Salesforce, for example, runs entirely on the cloud and although customers don't have to be concerned with how that cloud is implemented, maintenance schedules, and security patches, Salesforce has internal resources that focus on maintaining the cloud infrastructure, ensuring that it can meet the needs of its customers. Cloud architects are also change agents as they must be able to effectively communicate the benefits of using the cloud and be knowledgeable enough to address the questions and concerns that people not so familiar with cloud technologies have.

Let's look at why data architecture is important and what its benefits are.

Why is data architecture important?

A common mistake that rookie software developers make is to jump in and start writing code, thinking that the design can be modified later to fit requirements. Sometimes, they may refer to this as *Agile thinking and approach*. However, this is a fallacy as the data model, once defined, will be used as the foundation upon which other required business functionality is built; it is usually not straightforward to make changes to it quickly.

Let's take an example of an integration that pushes data from an external webinar system into a Salesforce `Campaign Member` object. Here, the webinar system takes the amount of time a person watched the live webinar and records it as a percentage. The developer has created a custom field of the number type called `Webinar % Attended` on the `Campaign Member` object. This field will only accept a number and therefore rejects any letters or special characters.

When the integration is run for the first time, it errors out because the webinar system is sending the percentage attended with the special character, %, and Salesforce therefore rejects it. This is a simple example to demonstrate how the data model needs to be well thought out and designed, not only considering the business requirements, but also understanding system functionality and limitations. In this case, the business doesn't need the values in the **Webinar Completed** field to make any calculations, so changing the field type to **Text** will work. In most cases, though, a change like this would require a thorough analysis of impacts on existing functionality and integrations and this can be a time-consuming effort.

Moreover, owing to the large number of systems that are now used in an organization, the sharing of data between these systems (that is, integration) has become crucial. Proper data architecture can avoid costly mistakes such as integrating two systems only to find out at a later stage in the project that there are technical limitations on how often the data can be moved between the two systems.

> **Important note**
>
> In architecture, decisions made earlier affect decisions made later. For example, should a Team Member-related list, intended to record team members working on the lead, be a lookup or a master-detail relationship? These are important design decisions to consider upfront as a change during build, or worse, when the application is in production, can be costly. For example, a decision to change from a multi-select picklist to a single picklist when the app is in production can lead to data loss. Consequently, our earlier decision affects decisions we will have to make surrounding the subsequent data loss.

Another consideration for data architecture is **data security**. Nefarious individuals or state-sponsored actors understand the value of data, and they look to exploit vulnerabilities for their own advantage. Data architecture ensures that the proper security processes and techniques are applied to the data when it's at rest or in transit. Modern data architecture also needs to conform to data protection regulations such as **General Data Protection Regulation (GDPR)** and **California Consumer Protection Act (CCPA)**.

Organizations recognize the value of data and derive insights from it. Moving data from one system to another is not done in vain, rather, there are clear business objectives that are to be achieved. The most common of these objectives is decision making based on hard data. Proper data architecture will take into account how data from a multitude of systems can be brought together to meet the operational and analytical requirements of the business. An intense topic of interest these days, which we will discuss in the upcoming chapters, is how to achieve that single, unified view of the customer commonly referred to as Customer 360, and data architecture plays a key role in that.

The benefits of data architecture

Having discussed the importance of data architecture, let's look at some of the benefits it offers:

- **It sets the stage for discussion and easy communication with different stakeholders**: Creating a data architect diagram can facilitate discussions with solution architects and **Business Analysts (BAs)**. It also facilitates getting approval from security teams that are concerned with how data is utilized and the boundaries it's going to cross; for example, a multi-national organization that has multiple legacy **Customer Relationship Management (CRM)** systems will want to address how data is going to move and be stored across continents in consideration of compliance with the **General Data Protection Regulation (GDPR)**.

- **It plays a vital role in driving non-functional requirements (NFRs)**: NFRs are related to the quality of the system being designed, such as performance, usability, and maintainability. Considering maintainability, for example, if the architecture is well defined, we will be able to enhance our application with relative ease compared to when the architecture has major flaws and in certain situations may require a complete redesign of the application, which is a costly and time-consuming endeavor.

- **It enables change management**: Change is inevitable. Now more than ever, internal and external forces are driving change at a rapid pace. Internally, enhancement requests, new business processes, and technological changes drive this change, whereas externally, raw market forces such as competition, geopolitical changes, and regulatory policies can drive this change. Having a well-defined data architecture that is properly documented and uses commonly understood language and standards enables stakeholders to respond to change quickly.

- **It enables fast ramp-ups**: Part of the change that we discussed in the last point also applies to changes in resourcing, meaning people in the company come and go. Having a good architecture established can be very helpful in training new personnel. Take the example of a new hire who joins the support team of an AppExchange partner that sells a popular recruitment app. Having the data model and reviewing it with the new hire can cut short the time needed to ramp up the resource to provide quality support to their customers.

- **It is reusable**: If an architecture was used once for an application and it was successful, it can be easily adapted by other areas in the enterprise or used for similar-natured projects in the future. Architecture work is intense and time-consuming and for large projects, it requires a lot of collaboration with multiple stakeholders. Reusing architecture eliminates or reduces the need to put in the same level of effort as the first time and this alone can translate into hard dollar savings for an enterprise.

    There is also the quality aspect: when you are reusing your architecture the second or third time, you will be thinking of further improving it rather than rethinking the architecture from scratch. Over time, this cycle of continuous improvement can lead to an architecture that will start to be accepted in the company as a reference architecture. More and more, projects will start to adopt it, or the **Enterprise Architect** (**EA**) may mandate it as the starting point for designing other projects.

Having learned about the importance of data architecture and its benefits, we will next discuss in detail a data architect's responsibilities in the next section.

Data architect responsibilities

Enterprise architecture is the highest level and the starting point from where guidelines, best practices, and overall enterprise parameters are set. For example, all integrations, whenever possible, will use the enterprise middleware and tightly coupled point-to-point interfaces will be avoided. Alternatively, when integrating two systems, the receiving system must pull data from the sending system rather than the sending system pushing data into the receiving system on a set schedule. This impacts the data architecture directly because, when designing interfaces, the data architect will need to be cognizant of these constraints set by the EA. Similarly, the solution architect would need to consider what other integration options are available if a system cannot be directly integrated using a point-to-point design (the point-to-point integration pattern is generally discouraged and should not be used when other viable options are available).

In this section, we will focus on the responsibilities of a data architect. However, it is important to understand the goals of data architecture before discussing the roles and responsibilities of a data architect. In any enterprise these days, usually there are volumes of data generated or flowing into or out of the enterprise. The data architect's goal is to design blueprints to facilitate the short-term and long-term data needs of the enterprise securely. This requires understanding the long-term vision of the enterprise (business strategy) so that the data architect can propose and implement processes that will align data management with the business strategy and maximize the ROI in the enterprise's data initiatives. The responsibilities of a data architect include the following:

- **Understanding, assessing, and documenting the current state of the organization**: This is the first and probably the most important step for a data architect, ensuring that they understand the current state thoroughly. This helps in identifying current issues in data flows and integration pain points as well as in formulating a plan for the future. Furthermore, documenting the current state aids in communicating with other stakeholders, such as EAs, solution architects, and business architects. This helps in securing project funding from the executive leadership.

- **Developing a dictionary for data across the organization**: Data architects define and maintain data dictionaries. A data dictionary is an inventory of data items that are used to convey information about data, such as metadata.

- **Aligning data architecture activities with enterprise architecture**: The data architect works closely with the EAs to ensure the initiatives that the data architect takes align with policies and guidelines established by the EA.

- **Developing a data requirements plan for the long-term storage, archiving, processing, and transmitting of data**: On an ongoing basis, data architects work on ensuring that the organization's data remains viable over a long period of time. They also need to anticipate industry and technology changes to ensure initiatives taken today will not obstruct the future use of newer technologies and that the organization can continue to evolve to face new marketplace realities.

- **Guiding domain architects and external partners on optimal ways to access data**: Data architects assist and provide guidance to domain architects and other stakeholders that may be trying to access the organization's data. They are expected to provide guidance around integration design as well to ensure that they align with EAs' policies and guidelines.

- **Evaluating applications**: Often, data architects are asked to participate in evaluating **Commercial off-the-Shelf (COTS)** applications from the context of data. They will look at data flows and how the new application would interact with the data. What changes, if any, need to be made before the application can work with existing data or data that is getting produced by the organization?

- **Data governance**: The data architect is also an integral part of data governance activities in the organization. They are responsible for documenting and maintaining processes related to technical data governance and data models for master data subject areas and reference master data.

- **Coaching and mentoring**: Lead data architects may also have team members that specialize in certain domains reporting to them. These individuals, as well as individuals or architects from other teams, may need coaching and mentoring with respect to matters pertaining to data architecture.

- **Being the primary contact for vendors**: Data architects also act as the primary technical contact for vendors pertaining to data, particularly **Master Data Management (MDM)** solutions or other data-focused applications within their portfolio.

- **Delivering innovative solutions**: With the rapid increase in the volumes and sources of data, regulatory requirements, and policies, organizations require innovative solutions to solve their data-related business problems. A data architect is required to maintain an extensive knowledge base of industry trends, best practices, and the available tools in the marketplace to propose optimal solutions.

- **Compliance**: Compliance is another area where data architects will spend a considerable amount of their time. To be clear, many organizations will have data privacy officers that understand the privacy laws and develop requirements to adhere to those laws. The data architect, on the other hand, is responsible for the technical implementation and ensures that data flow, storage, and retrieval are in line with these laws and organizational policies.

Now that we have looked at the responsibilities of data architects and their role in an organization, let's review the soft and hard skills that data architects need to be effective in their roles.

Data architect skills

A combination of **technical** and **soft skills** is required to be successful in a data architect role. Both sets of skills are equally important; it will be difficult to become a successful data architect if either set of skills is lacking. But don't worry, these skills can be learned, and once practiced, they will, over time, make you a very productive and successful data architect. In this section, we cover the skills required to become a successful data architect. Let's start with technical skills.

Technical skills

We will now discuss some of the technical skills that are needed to be a successful data architect. Keep in mind that these are high-level and this is intentional because otherwise, we would need to list individual skills that are needed:

- **Data modeling**: The ability to define data models is a must-have skill to be successful as a data architect. This forms a very handy tool to communicate with different stakeholders in projects or in the general day-to-day operations of the organization. Knowledge of well-known and commonly used data vendor models, application models, and industry reference models is also an asset.

- **Data integrations**: The ability to design effective, secure, and scalable integrations using a multitude of tools, as well as knowledge of various integration concepts, such as pub/sub, request/replay, batch processing, and fire and forget.

- **Data processing**: Understanding and designing flows that take in data and output meaningful information is a skill that is becoming more and more important for data architects. With the advent of huge volumes of data that organizations have been storing over the years, knowing how best to make use of that data to provide insightful wisdom to decision makers is key for data architects.

These are some of the high-level technical skills needed by data architects but typically, they are required to have programming skills such as working with Python or another language, experience in data mining and modeling tools, and an understanding of operating systems.

Soft skills

In this section, we will talk about the character attributes of an exceptional data architect. There are many others that may not be listed here but these are some of the key personality attributes that a good data architect should have:

- **Problem-solving**: A multitude of data issues are faced by data architects. Therefore, they must be able to apply a beginner's mindset in order to solve these problems. Communication skills including active listening and clear articulation of the problem and what the approach would be to resolve them are also characteristics that help in shaping a successful data architect. Knowing how to solve problems using systems thinking is also a very valuable skill to have. In a nutshell, systems thinking is the understanding that individual parts in a system behave differently compared to their behavior when they are by themselves. Utilizing systems thinking, along with the ability to model systems in a way that they have enough detail and convey the intent of the modeler, is a key advantage to have when solving problems.

- **Storytelling**: This is an essential skill that makes it easy to communicate with different technical and non-technical stakeholders. The ability to communicate to audiences using stories and metaphors that make the subject matter easy to understand for a non-technical audience can help to build rapport with stakeholders quickly.

- **Objectivity**: The ability to think and act objectively while keeping emotions in check and out of the decision-making process is an important skill for a data architect. Often, you will be interacting with other technical resources that may prefer one solution over another. The ability to objectively analyze each option and make a recommendation after considering each option will earn your stakeholders' respect and trust.

- **Strategic thinking**: Data is not something that is around for a month or two, but rather one of the most critical assets of a business and it needs to be treated as such. This requires understanding current and future business needs and the direction an organization is taking. It also involves anticipating the future trends of the industry and its best practices.

- **Adaptable**: A data architect should be flexible; they should be able to adapt to changes and operate in a fast-paced environment. Many organizations do not have the discipline and the necessary governance processes in place, resulting in a very chaotic environment from a data perspective. The data architect must be able to sift through that, understand what's required, and deliver on what will add value to the business.

- **Leadership**: As an architect, you will be expected to be responsible for designing and developing an optimal solution, which is all fine and dandy if you were doing all the work yourself, but that's not how the real world works. In many projects, you will be working with a team of architects, developers, BAs, and other stakeholders. Your decisions may be challenged and the rationale of certain decisions questioned. How do you deal with that? Using your technical or positional authority to push through your decisions? That may work in the short term, but in the longer term, you will face more challenges from the team and may also lose respect in the process. Having leadership skills that influence people to follow your decisions by inspiring them to do the right thing is a better longer-term approach. This requires establishing trust by *walking the talk* and being transparent with your peers. Keep in mind that you don't have to have an official title to be a leader; rather, you can still influence people regardless of the position or title you hold in the company.

- **Analytical**: Data architects need to be observant and have the ability to investigate a problem and find an optimal solution in a timely and efficient manner. This skill is very important because the ability to collect data from various sources, sift through non-relevant information, and analyze the rest to get to the root cause of a problem, can mean the difference between suggesting a solution that will solve the problem versus wasted time and effort.

One of the things that I want to drill down further is **communication**: the **barriers to effective communication** and the **famous seven Cs** that can be used to efficiently communicate. The importance of these cannot be stressed enough because unless you are an efficient communicator, your mileage with being a successful data architect will vary and you will face challenges. Now, let's look at these in the next section.

Barriers to effective communication

From the time we wake up to the time we go to bed, most of us are communicating with the people in our lives. Communication is not only verbal but can also be via body language or even social media these days.

The PRovoke Media, a reputable PR firm, estimated that a staggering $37 billion dollars were lost among 400 companies (100,000+ employees) surveyed in the US and UK and, according to the report, this may just be the tip of the iceberg – the actual losses may be much more. Let's look at some of the major barriers to communication. Recognizing these will help you to be cognizant and more careful next time you are giving a presentation, conducting a global team call, having a discussion with your children, or coaching a direct report at work.

Physical barriers

These are barriers to communication that are caused by physical conditions, for example, if your car breaks down on the highway and you are speaking with the tow-truck driver. Unless you are speaking loudly, you might be telling the driver to tow your car to your house, but they may hear it wrong and tow it to the garage. Another example is when you have an important presentation to give and your boss emails you 5 minutes before the presentation asking you to remove a slide but doesn't mention which one. You try to send them an instant message, but the service is down. Thinking they must have meant the slide with too many diagrams, you remove that slide but find out after the meeting that it was in fact a different slide.

This type of barrier is especially felt when people cannot have face-to-face interactions; for example, during the COVID-19 pandemic, people were reduced to communicating through phone, text, email, or on-camera meetings. Although on-camera meetings can be very effective, important information related to non-verbal cues, such as body language, eye contact, and gestures, can still get lost, all of which form an integral part of communication.

Psychological barriers

This is the type of barrier where communication cannot be effective due to psychological issues. A somewhat common manifestation is when you notice your co-worker is not performing their job well and you find out that they are going through debt issues or, worst yet, a divorce. Or, when you are in a meeting and one of the attendees appears to be absent-minded and feels slightly embarrassed when they are asked a question. Speaking with them afterward, you find out that they witnessed a horrible accident that day when driving to the office.

Language barriers

This type of barrier is related to the language of the speaker and the listener. Let's say the speaker is a native English speaker whereas the listener is not well versed in English; the speaker might say one thing and the listener may understand it to be something else. This could also be affected by different dialects, so the language may be the same but the dialects may be so different that speakers of one dialect may have a hard time understanding speakers of another dialect.

Semantical barriers

This barrier is related to the meaning and interpretation of words. It's important that the speaker and the listener have the same understanding of the words or terms used. If a school counselor is counseling a student and they say, *you need to turn a new page in your life*, unless the student knows what that idiom means, the intent of the speaker by using this idiom will be lost. Another common example is the use of buzzwords or phrases, which are especially prevalent in technology. Using the phrase *eat your own dog food* means using your own software internally that you sell to customers. Unless properly explained, this may sound disgusting and abhorrent to a listener who is not aware of this phrase. That's why you should avoid the use of buzzwords and idioms as much as possible to ensure your listeners are not confused and communication is not lost.

Information overload barriers

This type of barrier happens when the information processing demands placed on a person exceed their capacity to properly process them. Many of us can relate to this when we are getting emails, Slack messages, text messages, and meeting reminders and we feel we are drowning in work. This also happens in projects that are not very well organized and the BA, for example, is sent similar requirements through email, a meeting that just happened, instant messaging, or verbally by someone stopping at their cube for 2 minutes. This can lead to important pieces of information being either dropped completely or mixed up with another requirement.

Cultural barriers

These barriers relate to different cultures, and with increasing diversity in workplaces, you will likely be dealing with people from different cultures. That's why it's important to recognize these barriers to ensure your communication is understood and effective. Some examples of cultural barriers include following strict org hierarchies and reservedly answering questions from your manager's boss because the cultural norm at your previous workplace in a different country was to have all communication upward or downward come through your immediate manager. Another example is how in some cultures, anyone higher than you in rank should be addressed with either *Sir* or *Ma'am*. A third example, in some cultures, is that it is rude to make eye contact when talking with the opposite gender, whereas in some cultures, it would be considered rude not to make eye contact and could be construed as lying or trying to hide something.

Now that we have looked at the barriers, let's look at what constitutes effective communication that can be used to mitigate these barriers and have our message easily understood and acted on.

The seven Cs of effective communication

The seven Cs of communication give us a way to effectively communicate and have something tangible to evaluate ourselves on whether we are communicating effectively or not. The seven Cs are also an effective tool to manage the barriers to communication discussed in the last section. Think of these as a checklist to ensure your next presentation, speech, email, or even a simple text message to your kid is understood. Remember, the most important goal of communication is getting your message across to the audience.

Clarity

Have a clear goal and purpose for your message. It can be helpful to think of a quote by Steve Coveys: *begin with the end in mind*. Think about what you want your listener to do at the end of your message. Given that the human mind can comprehend a limited amount of information at a time (think of the information overload barrier discussed earlier), try to break down your message into parts that the listener can easily understand.

Conciseness

Keep your message concise and short. If you have written an email with 3 paragraphs and 19 lines, could you convey the same message in 1 paragraph and 5 lines? Here are some examples of wordy sentences:

The pandemic caused a great deal of anxiety and frequent mental health problems in society.

The poverty usually suffered by children in inner-city neighborhoods caused Anna to deeply think about how she could change things for the better in her neighborhood.

The following are examples of concise sentences:

The pandemic caused intense anxiety and health problems in society.

Seeing the suffering of kids in inner-city neighborhoods caused Anna to think of ways in which she could improve her neighborhood.

Concreteness

This relates to how precise the message is that is being delivered. Avoiding ambiguity helps your audience understand your message and act on it. This is where you can also provide facts and figures to ensure the message is understood. Take this example: *according to the research firm IDC, Salesforce and its ecosystem will create 4.2 million new jobs between 2019 and 2024.* Providing this research reference is better than saying there are going to be lots of jobs generated in the Salesforce ecosystem in the next few years.

Coherence

This relates to how well the beginning, body, and ending of a message are aligned with each other. This is probably one of the reasons why communication trickling down from top management in companies is intended to be something else, but by the time it gets to the bottom, it can be easily misconstrued because the original message is not coherent and there are contradictions in it or the ideas are not connected with each other.

Courtesy

Showing respect and being polite in your communications will help you get your message across smoothly and make your audience more perceptive to receive and accept your message. They will be more willing to act on or approve your proposal. Try to be inclusive in your communication and use words that reflect inclusivity and are deemed culturally acceptable.

Completeness

This relates to how far the message is complete. Does it have the information the audience requires to act? Are you jumping from topic to topic, leaving the listener confused on what the expectation is of them?

Consideration

Consider your audience and present your material accordingly. Try to understand your audience beforehand: what are their viewpoints, opinions, or constraints? Try to put yourself in their shoes and try to be empathetic. This can help you craft your message so that it is more easily understood and accepted by your audience. Many people struggle with the right amount of information to present. The ladder of abstraction is a mental framework that can be used to determine the right amount of information to present. As seen in the following diagram, the higher up the ladder you are, the more abstract the idea is, and the lower you are on the ladder, the more concrete the idea is:

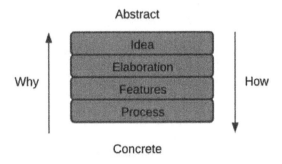

Figure 1.1 – The ladder of abstraction

The diagram depicts how you can move on the ladder of abstraction and tailor your message for your audience. Typically, C-level executives want to understand the *why* and leave the implementation details to their direct reports.

Let's look at an example:

- **Idea**: We want to improve our customer service.

- **Elaboration**: Provide an omnichannel experience to customers. Customer **Service-Level Agreements (SLAs)** must be met and the system should facilitate meeting the SLAs. Product development teams need to know the nature of cases coming in to understand where break/fix efforts should be directed.

- **Features**: A feedback survey is sent to the customer regardless of which channel they used to contact support. Cases can be created directly from social media applications such as Facebook. The system should be able to store customer entitlements and send reminders and escalation notifications at appropriate times. Product development teams can run reports and dashboards to gauge the nature of cases being opened and the average time spent on resolving issues.

- **Process**: The customer can send an email or fill out a form on the website to create a case. That will create a case in Salesforce and assign it to the relevant team using case assignment rules. The entitlement process assists in ensuring that your team is following a methodical process to solve customer cases and are meeting their SLAs.

We have looked at the seven Cs of communication and the ladder of abstraction to tailor our communication so it is more effective. In the next section, we will look at the path to becoming a data architect.

Becoming a data architect

There can be different paths to becoming a data architect and it is hard to define a fixed set of steps to become one, but the following is the path that most people take on their journey toward becoming a data architect:

- **Education**: A large majority of data architect jobs require a bachelor's degree in computer science or information technology with a focus on courses related to data analysis, data modeling, and analytics. Internships while studying can be extremely beneficial and help in launching your career as a data architect. A master's degree in business intelligence and analytics can further deepen your understanding of the subject matter.

- **Experience**: This is perhaps one of the most important components required to become a great data architect but it can be challenging. The reason is most companies require some level of real-world experience before you get a job as a junior data architect or an analyst. An analogy can be made with which came first, the chicken or the egg? If you don't have experience, most companies will not consider you, and if you don't find work, you won't have experience. This can be alleviated to some degree by doing as many hands-on projects as possible during your college years and getting into co-op programs.

- **Training**: Enrolling in training programs that focus on data-related functions can also help strengthen your understanding of the subject matter. Attending training courses or seminars conducted by **DAMA (Data Management Association)** can provide a good foundation for advancing your career or making an entry into the data field.

- **Certifications**: There are many certifications available for data architects, but since this book is mostly for Salesforce data architects, the data architecture and management certification exam can be really helpful in understanding the foundation of Salesforce data modeling and design, managing data in Salesforce, data migrations, and various other data-related topics. I will suggest, though, writing the *Sharing and Visibility Designer* exam first as it has data-related aspects that can be helpful and will help ease you into broader and deeper topics that are covered in the former.

In the next section, we will look at a day in the life of a data architect.

A day in the life of a data architect

In this section, we will explore a day in a data architect's life. As we stated in the introduction, this can help us understand and put into context some of the things that data architects do. It also helps us to translate their responsibilities in a practical way. Keep in mind that this is provided just as a general idea of how data architects spend their day and shouldn't be taken as an exact sequence of how they go about completing their duties:

The morning may look as follows:

- Document the proposed data model for an enhancement project related to order fulfillment. Prepare a presentation for the enterprise, IS, and integration architects and other technical stakeholders.

- Participate in a weekly meeting with EAs and other domain architects to align on existing policies and guidelines and new ones that may be under consideration.

- Participate in a project meeting with an integration architect and a **System, Applications, and Products (SAP)** solution architect looking to integrate work orders and invoicing with SAP and Salesforce.

The afternoon may look as follows:

- Analyze requirements from operations requiring access to Opportunity and Opportunity Products data in a data warehouse for reporting. Opportunity data is more than 5 million rows.

- Work on a request to archive Opportunity and Opportunity Products data. Look into the pros and cons of using big objects, Heroku, or other available options.

- Understand the capabilities of Einstein Analytics and explore its use cases and how it could meet the organization's analytics requirements. Also, explore Salesforce Tableau and its capabilities for reporting needs that are challenging to meet using the native reports and dashboards functionality.

- Present the proposed data model for the order fulfillment project. Field questions and seek feedback from the team.

In this section, we looked at a data architect's day to gain a better understanding of the role, the interactions they have with other stakeholders in the organization, and a glimpse of the research and prototyping that is required to be successful in the role.

Summary

In this chapter, we have reviewed the different types of architects and then focused on data architects, their responsibilities, and the technical and soft skills that are needed to be successful in the role. I hope you have gained a much greater appreciation of what data architects are and how critical their role is in organizations these days. We also reviewed some of the benefits of architecture, which will have convinced you, if you weren't already, that having a proper architecture for a project is a key ingredient for success.

We then reviewed the barriers to effective communication and the use of the seven Cs of communication to help us be effective in our communications. This should give you an objective way to formulate your responses and evaluate the areas where you can improve your communication skills. From my experience, a key challenge that technical folks face is tailoring their communication depending on their audience. The ladder of abstraction is an excellent tool to help you understand your audience so that you can tailor your communication to increase its understanding and acceptability. Remember, the end goal of communication is to convey the information the way you intended it and have it accepted by the audience that is being communicated with.

The role of a data architect is increasingly important and exciting and comes with a lot of challenges and growth. I encourage you to join your local chapter of DAMA, which is a global not-for-profit organization that is committed to advancing the concepts of information and data management. They are vendor-agnostic and cover a variety of topics that influence data.

In the next chapter, we will review fundamental concepts related to objects in Salesforce and the different field types and relationships. Next, we will review data modeling in Salesforce and why you should *unlearn* some of your learnings if you have worked with relational databases before. At the end, we will take a look at the Salesforce architecture and the different components that work together seamlessly to deliver an optimal user experience.

Questions

1. Precision Printing (PP) has been expanding exponentially in the last few years. With the expansion has come a growing list of systems that are used in the enterprise and actionable insights are becoming more and more challenging for business users. The Enterprise Architect (EA) office, consisting of business architects and a lead architect, has been tasked to fix the analytics problem. On an immediate basis, what type of architect should the EA office hire?

   a) Cloud architect

   b) Technology architect

   d) Data architect

   c) Business architect

2. The data architect should define the security standards for all the data in the organization, including compliance with the data-related regulations that the organization is subjected to (True/False).

3. Cobalt Space Exploration Inc. is hiring for a role to help them with putting standards around data governance to improve data quality and data management. What role can help fulfil the stated objective:

   a) Solution architect

   b) Business architect

   c) Cloud architect

   d) Data architect

Further reading

- *The Cost Of Poor Communications,* `https://www.provokemedia.com/latest/article/the-cost-of-poor-communications`

2
Understanding Salesforce Objects and Data Modeling

In this chapter, we will look at data modeling and the concept of **normalization**. This will give us a foundation for understanding how Salesforce is different from conventional relational databases that we may have experience of working with in the past. We will review why Salesforce goes against the convention of data normalization and why data is **de-normalized**, along with the benefits of doing that on the Salesforce Platform. We will also cover the different types of relationships in Salesforce and other features of Salesforce that are associated with data modeling. Having a solid understanding will lay the foundation for upcoming chapters when we discuss APIs and **Large Data Volumes (LDVs)**.

> **Salesforce Platform**
>
> Throughout this book, at various places I will be referring to Salesforce as the *Salesforce Platform or Platform*. When I do that, I am referring to the core Salesforce services including hardware and software that is used by the Sales Cloud or Service Cloud. This is important because there are other Salesforce services that are provided on different infrastructure such as Heroku, Mulesoft, and others.

In this chapter, we will also review the Salesforce Platform architecture. What we will have learned in this chapter will help us understand why the Platform architecture is the way it has been designed. Understanding this is crucial if we want to utilize the Platform in an effective, yet scalable, manner.

At the end of the chapter, we will review the different types of objects that are available in Salesforce and when they should be used, along with a review of the different field types that are available for use. This will provide an understanding of the deeper capabilities of the Platform as far as objects and fields go, as well as the relationships that can be defined on the Platform.

To summarize, we will look at these topics in particular:

- Exploring data modeling
- Understanding the Salesforce platform architecture
- Introducing Salesforce objects

Let's get started with understanding data modeling.

Exploring data modeling

Data modeling is the process of analyzing data requirements that are needed to support business requirements in the information systems of an organization. This involves analyzing the various data objects and the relationships between them. Data modeling provides a visual representation of data and how data elements associate with each other. Let's look into what a data model is in more detail as well as the different types of data models and the benefits of data modeling.

What is a data model?

A **data model** is a visual representation of data elements, their relationships, and the properties they have; for example, a laptop is a data element, a motherboard is another data element, RAM is another example, and so on and so forth. Whether the laptop has one or more than one RAM stick would be defined as the relationship between the two. In most laptops, there is one, and only one, motherboard, which is another relationship between the motherboard and the laptop, but also a constraint that is stating that one laptop will only have one motherboard. In the following diagram, we have three objects that are related to one another:

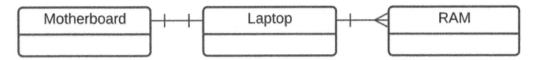

Figure 2.1 – Example of a 1-to-1 and 1-to-many relationship

The motherboard and laptop have a 1-to-1 relationship with each other, whereas the laptop and RAM entities have a 1:M relationship, meaning a laptop can have one or more RAMs.

Data models are important and help in communicating with stakeholders, but let's take a deeper look at the benefits of data models. I offer a word of caution in that the benefits mentioned here are generic in nature and may not fully apply to Salesforce. This is because Salesforce has its own sophisticated way of managing databases, which we will touch upon later:

- **Estimating complexity**: A data model provides a good way to estimate complexity in software and valuable understanding in estimating the effort and associated risk involved in developing or enhancing an application. Consider an application that has 5 database tables versus one that has 35 tables. It is reasonable that the application with 35 tables will be more complex and enhancing it will require a cautious approach and some analysis to reduce the risk of introducing regressions in the finished product.

- **Optimal design**: Data models also help in building applications that respect system boundaries. System boundaries here refer to designing the component with items where they most optimally fit; for example, a developer may attempt to enforce uniqueness on a field using code in the application, whereas using a data model, you could easily enforce that at the database level. This results in less code and system maintenance.

- **Standardization**: Data models provide a standardized way to document your applications that can facilitate long-term maintenance and assists in training new personnel.

- **Risk management**: Data models reduce the risk to the enterprise in situations where a few people with long tenures have a more in-depth knowledge of the application and its database structure. Having an up-to-date data model can keep the enterprise competitive and respond to change quickly.

- **Costs**: Data models reduce costs by capturing errors and issues that will manifest later in the finished application. During the software development life cycle, it always costs less and is easier to fix issues early on, rather than later when the application has been developed. Once an application has been developed, fundamental changes to a data model can be very costly, time-consuming, and requires intense periods of impact analysis to ensure that existing integrations and functionality will not break.

- **Quality assurance**: Data models result in applications that are high in quality because it avoids the typical mistake of jumping into coding straight away, which is the source of many software projects failing. A well-thought-out data model provides an opportunity to consider the different ways in which entities can relate to each other and design an optimal data model.

- **Solution buy-in**: A well-defined data model that is collaboratively developed with different stakeholders creates buy-in and trust within teams that directly impacts team engagement and motivation. Everyone involved feels they have a stake and take responsibility for their tasks, which also results in higher-quality work.

- **Time-to-market**: Data models can reduce the time to market for new applications. During the COVID-19 pandemic, many software companies that develop healthcare applications rushed to develop applications that could be used by health authorities for contact tracing or to enable companies to facilitate a return to work for their employees. Time to market was a clear differentiator, and if an application was developed but without a sound data model, it would run into many issues and cause the company to miss out on revenue opportunities.

- **Facilitate integrations**: As companies grow, the number of systems they use grows and, as a result, the need to integrate these systems also grows. Having a data model can drastically cut down on the time it can take to integrate these different systems.

As seen above, there is a multitude of benefits associated with data modeling that can help organizations remain responsive to changing market conditions. Communication is a constant challenge within organizations and data modeling can help alleviate some of that, along with providing a platform that can be used to create buy-in from different stakeholders.

In the next section, we will look at the different types of data models and their purpose.

Types of data models

There are three **types of data model**, each of which has its own distinct features and purpose:

- The conceptual data model
- The logical data model
- The physical data model

Understanding these can help us determine which level to use to optimally serve our needs. Let's look at these one by one.

Conceptual data model

This data model is the most abstract visual representation of the entities and relationships between them in an application. It is commonly used to communicate with business users as it is straightforward and is not associated with any specific database or technology. Using the recruitment app example introduced in *Chapter 1, Data Architect - Roles and Responsibilities*, an entity represents the `Job` or `Candidate` object and the relationship defines how the entities relate to each other. In our example, the `Candidate` entity is related to the `Job` entity via the `Applicant` object. `Applicant` is a `Junction` object that we will discuss in later sections. A conceptual data model showing a `Junction` object is shown in the following diagram:

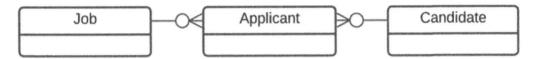

Figure 2.2 – Example of a conceptual diagram showing a junction object

As can be seen in the preceding diagram, in a conceptual data model, just the names of the entities are listed.

Logical data model

This is the next level to the conceptual data model in that it has more details, including attributes and their types. For example, using our recruitment app example, the `Candidate` entity (object) will have **Name, Email, Phone**, and other attributes for each candidate.

Similarly, the `Job` entity can have **Job Description, Job Title**, and **Grade** as attributes. Sometimes, the data type and length of each attribute are also defined; for example, **Name** can be 100 characters, **Phone** can be 10 characters in length, and so on. This is also developed by a data architect or business analyst sometimes and can be used to communicate with business stakeholders easily. Like the conceptual model, this type of data model is also database-agnostic. The following diagram shows an example of a logical data model:

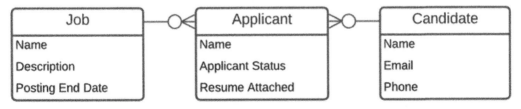

Figure 2.3 – Example of a logical data model

As can be seen in the preceding diagram, the logical data model has more details, including the names of the attributes (fields in Salesforce). Sometimes, the data type and length of each attribute are also listed.

Physical data model

This is the most detailed level in data modeling and is primarily used for the actual build of the database. At the physical level, entities are really tables and attributes are columns in those tables. When visually representing this type of data model, the convention is to use the actual database names of the tables, and columns along with the data type of each attribute. This level also includes **indexes**, **triggers** (different to the triggers we build in Salesforce, although the idea is similar), and **constraints**. I won't present examples of this type to avoid causing confusion because when you create an object using the frontend in Salesforce, you are really sending a command to create a table in the database with its column, primary keys, and constraints. We will look at how all that works later in this chapter. Here is an example of a physical data model for our recruitment app:

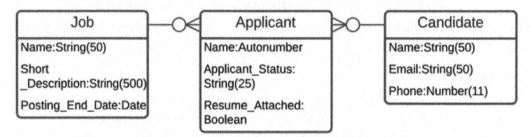

Figure 2.4 – Example of a physical data model

The physical data model, as shown in the preceding diagram, shows the actual attribute (field) names as well as the data type and length of each attribute. Now that we understand data models, let's look at the concepts of normalization and denormalization.

Normalization

Normalization is a database technique for organizing data where large tables are divided into smaller manageable tables while linking them using relationships. The reason this is done is to maintain data integrity and eliminate data redundancy. The theory of normalization covers the different normalization forms starting from 1 Normal Form (1NF), 2NF, 3NF, up to 5NF, but a detailed discussion on normalization is beyond the scope of this book.

However, I want to look at a few examples of why this is used extensively, and most applications will achieve optimal normalization at 3NF. Understanding this will give you a solid understanding to dive into the Salesforce architecture and appreciate the power of the platform.

Normal forms

Repeating data in a database is inefficient, causes the size of the database to increase, and can cause data inconsistency during database operations such as insertion, deletion, and so on. Database normal forms are the answer to this problem and at its core, attempt to minimize data redundancy in the database.

With normal forms, the idea is that a fact is in one place and that the fact needs to be inserted once, and then updated or deleted at a single place without duplicating it across the database.

3NF (Third Normalized Form) is a database design approach in which the goal is to reduce data duplication and achieve data integrity. The 3NF approach defines that any attribute in the table should not be dependent on a non-primary key. To read more about 3NF, refer to the *Data Management Book of Knowledge (DMBOK)* or search on the internet.

To understand this example, we will need to look at it in a non-Salesforce context so we can apply some of the normalization principles. Using our recruitment app example, imagine you have the following Job table, which has details of the job that is posted:

Unique ID	Job Title	Hiring Manager	Hiring Manager Telephone	Hiring Manager Location
123	SQL Architect	James Murthy	(232) 232-2323	Chicago
345	.NET Developer, Technical Lead, Lead Consultant	James Murthy	(232) 232-2323	Chicago
897	UI Developer	James Murthy	(232) 232-2323	Chicago
231	Business Analyst	Grant Simpson	(301) 545-4454	New York

Figure 2.5 – An anti-normalization example

As can be seen in the preceding table, values for **Hiring Manager**, **Hiring Manager Telephone**, and **Hiring Manager Location** are repeated for the first three records. This is data redundancy and undesirable in an optimally normalized database. It will also cause anomalies related to insertion, updating, and deletion, with a real risk of causing data loss. Let's look in more detail at these different anomalies and understand why they are undesirable in a normalized data model:

- **Insertion anomaly**: Let's say in the preceding example that another job was posted for James Murthy, but a new recruiter didn't enter the hiring manager's telephone and location. Unless these fields are mandatory at the database level or application level, you will now have a row with two columns blank. Also notice, if James had 20 new postings, we would be repeating the last columns (Hiring Manager, Hiring Manager Telephone, and Hiring Manager Location) 20 times, which is a clear waste of resources.

- **Update anomaly**: Assume that James Murthy leaves the company, and so now we will need to update 23 records with the new hiring manager and their details. If we miss any records, we will have data quality issues.

- **Deletion anomaly**: If we were to delete records from the Job table after 7 years, we would lose not only the job detail data but also details pertaining to the hiring manager.

We have looked at normalization and why it's used. Let's now spend some time understanding denormalization and why it's used in Salesforce.

Denormalization

If you have worked in a relational database, you know that data redundancy is not desirable, and the normalization forms are used to ensure that databases are free of redundant data and anomalies that we discussed earlier. By way of contrast to that, **denormalization** is the process of improving the read performance over the write performance in a database. As we will see later, this is done by adding redundant data to the database in an organized manner to improve the read performance.

As an example, an email for a customer is going to be stored once in a table and then, using what's called a **join**, it will be meshed up with rows from other tables. However, in Salesforce, the **Email** field is replicated across objects. This is intentional because Salesforce is optimized for read operations, so when you run a **Salesforce Object Query Language (SOQL)**, open a list view, or open a contact, these are querying the database. Designing for read operations primarily results in quick loading of the data, whereas normally, other databases are optimized for write operations. And because read operations on a 3NF database would require a lot of joins that are costly in terms of performance, Salesforce has a flat database structure.

The characteristic of a flat database is that you will have data elements duplicated – a clear violation of normalization principles. How Salesforce achieves this is truly impressive, but we will defer that discussion to a later section in this chapter.

Picking up our example of the **Email** field, you will see in the following screenshots that it is present on the `Lead` object, then another individual **Email** field is on the `Contact` object, and yet another individual **Email** field is on the `Campaign Member` object. But this should all make sense now because remember that we want to read data quickly, and for that to happen, joins between tables should be avoided as much as possible and flattening the database like this is an efficient way to do it. In the following few screenshots, we will see how the **Email** field is replicated across multiple objects – a clear violation of normalization principles:

Lead Fields

Help for this Page

This page allows you to specify the fields that can appear on the Lead page. You can create up to 500 Lead custom fields.

Note that deleting a custom field will delete any filters that use the custom field. It may also change the result of Assignment or Escalation Rules that rely on the custom field data.

Set History Tracking

Lead Standard Fields   Lead Standard Fields Help

Action	Field Label	Field Name	Data Type	Controlling Field	Indexed
	Address	Address	Address		
Edit	Annual Revenue	AnnualRevenue	Currency(18, 0)		
Edit	Campaign	Campaign	Lookup(Campaign)		
Edit	Clean Status	CleanStatus	Picklist		✓
Edit	Company	Company	Text(255)		✓
Edit	Company D-U-N-S Number	CompanyDunsNumber	Text(9)		
	Created By	CreatedBy	Lookup(User)		
Edit	D&B Company	DandbCompany	Lookup(D&B Company)		✓
Edit	Data.com Key	Jigsaw	Text(20)		
Edit	Description	Description	Long Text Area(32000)		
Edit	Do Not Call	DoNotCall	Checkbox		
Edit	Email	Email	Email		✓

Figure 2.6 – Email field on the Lead object

Notice that the `Lead` object has the `Email` field on it. In the following screenshot, the `Contact` object also has an `Email` field:

Contact Fields

This page allows you to specify the fields that can appear on the Contact page. You can create up to 500 Contact custom fields.

Note that deleting a custom field will delete any filters that use the custom field. It may also change the result of Assignment or Escalation Rules that rely on the custom field data.

Set History Tracking

Contact Standard Fields   Contact Standard Fields Help ?

Action	Field Label	Field Name	Data Type	Controlling Field	Indexed
Edit	Account Name	Account	Lookup(Account)		✓
Edit	Assistant	AssistantName	Text(40)		
Edit	Asst. Phone	AssistantPhone	Phone		
Edit	Birthdate	Birthdate	Date		
Edit	Clean Status	CleanStatus	Picklist		✓
Edit	Contact Owner	Owner	Lookup(User)		✓
	Created By	CreatedBy	Lookup(User)		
Edit	Data.com Key	Jigsaw	Text(20)		
Edit	Department	Department	Text(80)		
Edit	Description	Description	Long Text Area(32000)		
Edit	Do Not Call	DoNotCall	Checkbox		
Edit	Email	Email	Email		✓

Figure 2.7 – Email field on the Contact object

The `Contact` object in the preceding screenshot has an **Email** field. By now, you will notice that the **Email** field is duplicated twice. In the following screenshot, the **Email** field appears yet again, this time on the `Campaign Member` object:

Campaign Member Fields

This page allows you to specify the fields that can appear on the Campaign Member page. You can create up to 500 Campaign Member custom fields.

Note that deleting a custom field will delete any filters that use the custom field. It may also change the result of Assignment or Escalation Rules that rely on the custom field data.

Campaign Member Standard Fields   Campaign Member Standard Fields Help ?

Action	Field Label	Field Name	Data Type	Controlling Field	Indexed
Edit	Campaign	Campaign	Lookup(Campaign)		✓
Edit	City	City	Text(40)		
Edit	Company (Account)	CompanyOrAccount	Text(255)		
Edit	Contact	Contact	Lookup(Contact)		✓
Edit	Country	Country	Text(80)		
	Created By	CreatedBy	Lookup(User)		
	Created Date	CreatedDate	Date/Time		
Edit	Description	Description	Long Text Area(32000)		
Edit	Do Not Call	DoNotCall	Checkbox		
Edit	Email	Email	Email		

Figure 2.8 – Email field on the Campaign Member object

The `Campaign Member` object in the preceding screenshot has yet another field for email. So far, we have seen three **Email** fields on three different objects – `Lead`, `Contact`, and `Campaign Member`. Repeating the **Email** field three times would be considered unacceptable in a normalized database, but because Salesforce is tuned for read operations, it makes sense to have redundant fields, so a minimum number of joins are needed to return the query results and improve the query performance.

Another advantage of denormalization is that although duplicated, data is there for you to report on. Think of the example of the lead mapping process. In a nutshell, we have the data on the `Lead` object, which is mapped over to `Account`, `Contact`, and `Opportunity`, so when a `Lead` record is converted, data is copied over from the `Lead` object to the `Account`, `Contact`, and `Opportunity` objects. This gives the ability to report on data in the `Lead` object. For example, what `Lead` sources (ad words, website, blog, and other) of `Lead` records returned the highest revenue on opportunities? How effective are the marketing qualification and sales qualification processes? And so forth…

Design principles for data modeling

Design principles form the rules that you must adhere to and should not be violated unless there is a clear and compelling reason to do so. This is because they form the foundation that you design your system on. They are typically based on industry experiences, best practices, and learned experiences and provide a solid foundation on which to build your data model. Since Salesforce is optimized for read operations, understanding design principles will help us to deliver scalable and maintainable solutions in the long run. Here are some key principles to consider when designing the data model.

User experience

You want your users to use the application you designed or built. If the user finds that they have to navigate to five different screens in order to retrieve one piece of data, that may impact buy-in from your customers and reduce system usage. A common mistake is to create too many fields on the object and place them on the page layout. You want to design your data model in a crisp manner and create fields that are needed. If you truly need many fields on the object, consider using record types, which we will talk about later. You can also use dynamic forms to control fields that appear on the UI when specified conditions are met.

Analytics

Reporting is an important requirement and you want to make sure that your data model can support performant reports, dashboards, and list views. Since you cannot do joins in SOQL, you will need to write Apex to pull the data you need and marry it together.

Security

Security is another consideration when designing the data model. Who will have access to your data, is it accessible internally, or are external users accessing the data through Salesforce communities? By having an excessive number of objects with no relationships, you will need to define complex security rules requiring Apex. Also, are you solving one problem of making the Account object private so sales users can see their own accounts, but inadvertently encouraging the duplication of data?

Relationships

Aim to design your data model to have relationships between objects. We will discuss relationships in a later section, but having complex data models that are not well connected will lead to writing very complex queries that then require in-memory Apex operations to be joined and used.

If you determine that relationships will not be possible, for example, when bringing in external data, you can use external fields that allow for efficient SOQL queries and **Data Manipulation Language** (**DML**) operations.

Performance

Relationships are a great way to design a data model that will perform well, but the caveat is that as your data volume grows, you will start noticing a decline in performance. This is because more joins are needed in the database to query data. There are multiple techniques that can be used to handle that, for example, using skinny tables, creating indexes on certain fields (skinny tables and creating indexes can be achieved by contacting support), or using certain field types that automatically create indexes.

Scalability

As your business grows and evolves, you will need to extend the data model. Keeping scalability in mind when designing the data model will ensure that you don't run into issues when extending the data model. Whenever you are designing the data model, ask yourself this question – what will I need to do in order to extend this data model 5 years down the road?

Avoiding object proliferation

Think about the *why* when you want to create a new object. Ask yourself whether you can use an existing object that has similar functionality. Can you use record types perhaps on an existing object and extend it for the enhancement request? If an object is no longer required, consider archiving the data and deleting it from the system. For example, a custom application that is used to track quote requests for different divisions within the company has its own custom objects. This could have easily been avoided by having a single object with record types for each division. Let's look at record types and what they are in the next section.

Record types

In our recruitment application example that we used in *Chapter 1, Data Architect-Roles and Responsibilities*, we had the `Job` object, which had details about the job, description, grade, perhaps the hiring manager, and so on. The recruitment app is used by the two recruiting teams in the company based on the type of recruitment they do. One team is focused on hiring executives and jobs that are office-based, and the other team hires for union positions. The job requirements are different for each type of role; for example, union positions require mentioning the local union that the job is part of, hourly rate, ticket requirements, and so on. These are not applicable for jobs that the executive hiring department posts. This is a good use case to leverage record types that essentially delineate the object based on business usage. You could easily create one record type for Executive and another for Union and link them to different page layouts. That way, you can control the fields that the Executive hiring team will see versus those that the Union team will see. They also allow you to control picklist value fields.

Click versus code

One marketing strategy and one that works in practice is the easy way you can create and extend business applications to serve your customers using Salesforce. This is made possible because of Salesforce's click model, which encourages the use of UI tools to build your applications. The key to this being successful in your org is that your data model is simple, rational, and hangs together nicely. If you have objects that are related to each other with appropriate relationship types, then tools such as Workflow Rules, Lightning Process Builder, and Lightning Flows will work elegantly.

Conversely, if your data model is scattered with a lot of objects with no relationships, you will need to write a lot of code to even run queries on your data, let alone build your business functionality using clicks.

I am not saying that you should have few objects and that they must be related, but rather encouraging you to think hard and from multiple angles to ensure that you have a very good justification to have a very complex data model with few relationships.

Now that we have looked at the design principles and we've mentioned relationships a few times, let's dive into the different types of relationships we have in Salesforce and how we can leverage them during data modeling.

Reviewing object relationships

In a relational database, you would define primary and foreign keys to link up two tables; for example, in an Order Management application, you will have order and order line item tables in which the `Order Line` object will have a foreign key referencing the Order table. In Salesforce, because we don't get access to the underlying tables, we must establish relationships explicitly using the relationship types provided by Salesforce. In the following screenshot, three different types of relationship are shown:

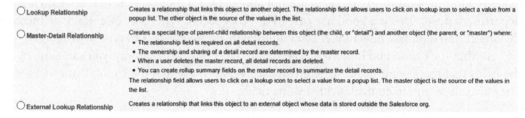

Figure 2.9 – Three common types of relationship in Salesforce

As can be seen in the preceding screenshot, a **Lookup Relationship** creates a loosely coupled relationship, a **Master-Detail Relationship** is useful for tightly linking the two objects together, whereas an **External Lookup Relationship** allows data from an external system to be linked up with data in Salesforce.

Lookup relationship

Like a **Parent-child** field, a **Lookup** field establishes a parent-child relationship, but it differs in many ways. The relationship is loosely coupled, so the record-level security is not inherited from the parent, but the child can have its own independent record-level access, which means a user accessing the parent cannot necessarily access the child record unless the configuration allows that. Unless enforced by configuration, you can have a **Lookup** field that's blank. This is a key difference between **Lookup** and **Parent-child** because in the latter, you don't have the option to leave the field blank.

A disadvantage of **Lookup** fields is that they don't allow roll-up **Summary** fields out of the box. You would need to write Apex to do roll-up-type operations or use AppExchange add-ons to achieve the functionality. There is no cascade delete with a lookup relationship. Instead, you have two options – allow the **Lookup** field to remain blank, or prevent the deletion of the parent record. Both settings are available via the UI:

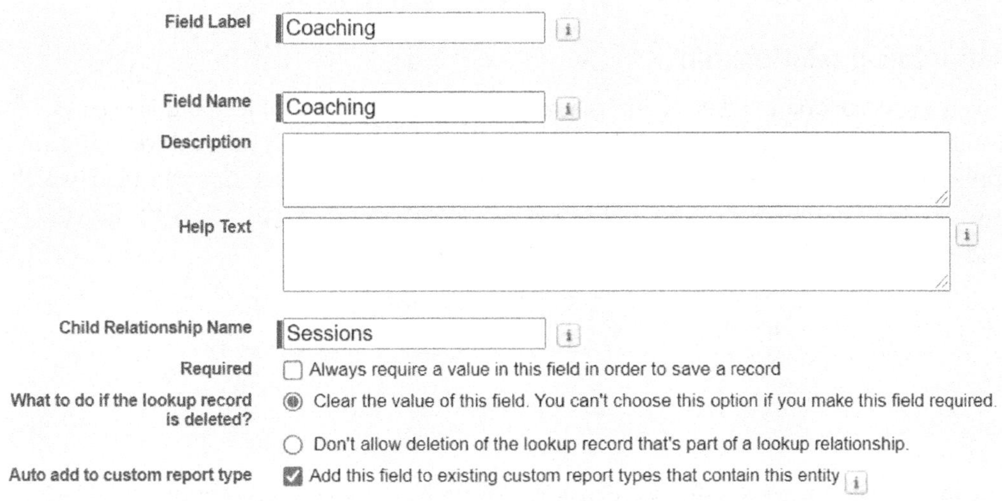

Field Label	Coaching
Field Name	Coaching
Description	
Help Text	
Child Relationship Name	Sessions
Required	☐ Always require a value in this field in order to save a record
What to do if the lookup record is deleted?	◉ Clear the value of this field. You can't choose this option if you make this field required. ○ Don't allow deletion of the lookup record that's part of a lookup relationship.
Auto add to custom report type	☑ Add this field to existing custom report types that contain this entity

Figure 2.10 – Creating a lookup relationship

Notice how, since a lookup creates a loosely coupled relationship, you can either make it required or leave it optional, in which case the field can be left blank. Optionally, you can specify the behavior if the lookup value is deleted.

Self-relationship

This is a type of lookup relationship, but rather than the parent-child being on different objects, the lookup relationship is on the same object. A good example of this is the Job object, which is used to store jobs that are posted in our recruitment app. If the recruitment team wanted to record similar jobs to the one being posted, they could create a **self-lookup** field that would allow them to record another similar job.

External lookup relationship

As the name implies, this type of relationship is used to relate to data that is outside of your organization and is another type of lookup but for external objects. Use this field when the lookup is an external object.

Indirect lookup relationship

This type of lookup relationship is used to link an external child object to a standard or custom parent object. You must specify the parent object field and the child object field that will match each other. Suppose a background check is performed for each candidate who has passed the first stages of the interview. Then, the external provider (child object) can be linked with the Candidate object using an indirect lookup field.

Hierarchical relationships

This is a special lookup relationship that is available for the User object and is used to associate a user with another user. It is handy when, for instance, you are developing an application that uses approvals, but they are not based on the direct manager field, which already exists on the User object, but rather a different user needs to be assigned as the approver. That is where you will use this type of field:

Figure 2.11 – Example of a hierarchical relationship

As can be seen in the preceding screenshot, this type of relationship is only available if you are linking up to the User object.

Master-detail/parent-child relationship

This type of relationship defines a closely coupled relationship between the parent and child object, which means, among other things, that this field must be populated, and you cannot leave it blank. This field is created on the child object and inherits record-level security from its parent. This means that a user accessing the parent record has access to the child record as well. You can also create **Roll-Up Summary** fields on the parent object, which is one of the big advantages of master-detail fields.

Roll-up summary fields allow you to have aggregate data from your child records; for example, if you want to know the total number of opportunities won on the account record, you can use a roll-up summary field and count the won opportunities. Similarly, if you were interested in remoting the total revenue generated from an account, you could create a summary field that sums up the amounts from all the won opportunities. Roll-up summary fields also have filters that let you limit the scope of data you are interested in.

By default, cascade delete is also set on the field, meaning that when the parent record is deleted, the child is automatically deleted as well. The **Organization-Wide Default** (**OWD**) on the child is set based on the parent and is non-editable:

Field Label	Session	ⓘ
Field Name	Sessions	ⓘ
Description		
Help Text		ⓘ
Child Relationship Name	Sessions	ⓘ
Sharing Setting	Select the minimum access level required on the Master record to create, edit, or delete related Detail records: ○ Read Only: Allows users with at least Read access to the Master record to create, edit, or delete related Detail records. ◉ Read/Write: Allows users with at least Read/Write access to the Master record to create, edit, or delete related Detail records.
Allow reparenting	☐ Child records can be reparented to other parent records after they are created
Auto add to custom report type	☑ Add this field to existing custom report types that contain this entity ⓘ

Figure 2.12 – Creating a master-detail relationship

We can define a master-detail relationship with different options as seen above by specifying what level of access to the master record is required in order to create, edit, or delete detail records.

Junction objects

Remember that parent-child and lookup relationships allow us to define one-to-many relationships, which means that there is one parent record and multiple child records, but what if we have a need to define a many-to-many relationship where we have many parent records associated with many child records. This is where a Junction object comes in.

A Junction object is a special type of object that lets us define a many-to-many relationship using two parent-child relationships on the object. In our recruitment app, we have a Job object and a Candidate object. The Job object is used to post new jobs, and the Candidate object is used to store information about candidates that are applying for a job. If we use a parent-child or lookup relationship, our candidate can apply for a single job at a time, which is not practical.

Our business requirement is that a candidate must be able to apply for multiple jobs at a time. For that, we will need another object, called **Applicant**, which will be a child to the Job and Candidate objects. The Applicant object will allow the candidate to apply for multiple jobs at a time. In other words, multiple jobs can be associated with multiple candidates and multiple candidates can be associated with multiple jobs via the Applicant object:

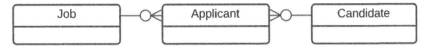

Figure 2.13 – Applicant is a Junction object. In the user interface (UI), you will notice on the Applicant record one field each to enter the Job and Candidate data

As can be seen from the preceding diagram, a candidate can apply for multiple jobs by creating an applicant record each time a job is applied for.

When defining a `Junction` object, it is important to think diligently about which object the first parent-child relationship will be created with. This is important because the look and feel of the `Junction` object are determined by the first parent object. Look and feel here refers to the color and icons of the detail and edit page of the `Junction` object.

The record ownership is also inherited from the first parent object as the `Junction` object doesn't have its own ownership. Another implication is that of record access. For either of the parent objects, you can define the sharing setting at the time of creating the field on the `Junction` object. The sharing setting can be either **Read Only** or **Read/ Write**. Both options allow full access to the child record. But if the OWD on either parent is **Public Read Only**, and the sharing setting on the `Junction` object is defined as **Read/ Write**, the user will not be able to access the record.

If either parent record is deleted, the child record is also deleted, but if both parent records are deleted, the child is permanently deleted. In the former scenario, the record can be restored from the **Recycle Bin**, but not when both parents have been deleted.

If, at a later stage, you decide to delete the primary parent relationship or convert it to a lookup, the second parent object becomes the primary. Based on all these implications, it is important to think hard in terms of which object will become the primary parent.

Now that we have reviewed the various types of relationships in Salesforce, let's look at some of the differences between SQL and SOQL in the next section.

Differences between SQL and SOQL

We have reviewed the different types of fields and the relationships that can be created in Salesforce. Often, you will need to pull in data using the Developer Console, Developer Workbench, or some other tool using SOQL. SOQL is a very easy language that can be used to easily query data from Salesforce. It is even easier if you have used SQL in the past. You will notice the striking similarity between SQL and SOQL, but they are fundamentally different. We will discuss the Salesforce platform architecture in the next section, but for now, just remember the following:

- Salesforce customers do not get access to the underlying tables of the Saleforce database.

- You can *indirectly* index your fields in SOQL, rather than doing so *directly*, as in SQL, using a DML statement.

- Some field types are automatically indexed for you, for example, external fields, and using SOQL, you cannot create new indexes.

- Triggers can also be written, just like you would on a database table, but Salesforce triggers are different in that you are basically sending instructions to the application layer to process your Apex code.

Some of the differences between SQL and SOQL are as follows:

- You cannot issue a `select * from SObject` (`Sobject referring to a Salesforce object`) in SOQL.

- SOQL is read-only and cannot be used to manipulate data, unlike SQL.

- When SOQL is used in Apex, it also protects you from inadvertent schema changes as SOQL cannot be used to change data types or field names on the fly. You can either do that through the UI or use specific metadata APIs to make changes to the underlying schema.

Now that we have reviewed the fundamentals of data modeling and denormalization, let's take a dive into the Salesforce architecture and understand how it operates beneath the hood.

Understanding Salesforce architecture

Since we are going to be talking about Salesforce, let's try to understand the Salesforce architecture as that will help us think in the correct context and understand why things are done the way they are in Salesforce.

Trust is the number one value at Salesforce and can be seen in the way the core architecture of Salesforce has been designed. Considering that there are billions of transactions happening on the platform, it is no small task to ensure that customer data is properly secured and protected from numerous attack vectors used by bad actors.

In this section, we will be familiarizing ourselves with the salient features of the Salesforce platform, such as multi-tenancy and major releases. Then we will review in more detail the major components of the platform that form the engine behind it. Let's start with multi-tenancy and dig deeper into what it is and how it benefits users.

Multi-tenancy

Salesforce works on a **SaaS (Software as a Service)** model, where customers pay a subscription fee for the services they use provided by Salesforce. If you have used email services such as Hotmail, behind the scenes there is no dedicated database server or an application server. Rather, Microsoft has designed the system such that hundreds of thousands of users can use the same hardware and software.

With SaaS, rather than having individual users, you will have multiple groups of users that access Salesforce. Think of these groups of users as individual companies that subscribe to Salesforce and what they are accessing at Salesforce is an org aptly named *organization*. The key aspect of SaaS is **multi-tenancy**, which means groups of users share resources. Behind the scenes, they use the same hardware and storage, but their data is kept separate by the software.

Another aspect of multi-tenancy is that since the resources are shared, no one tenant can be allowed to monopolize the system, jeopardizing the resources that could potentially impact performance or, worse, bring down entire instances. Salesforce employs governor limits and general good practices to encourage its users to write efficient queries and code. One of the things that I missed when I started to work on the platform was the use of the following SOQL query:

```
select * from TABLE_NAME
```

It never made sense to me why it wasn't allowed until I truly dived deep into how multi-tenancy works. In case you are wondering, the preceding query would return all columns along with all the rows in a typical relational database, but it won't run in Salesforce because it would like you to name the fields (columns) that you need and only return those along with a limit on the number of rows it will return.

Thousands of customers trust Salesforce with their business-critical data, and it is no small feat to ensure that *customer A* cannot access another customer's data. This is done by org ID, which is a unique ID that is assigned to every Salesforce customer's org. Whenever a database call is made to the platform to access data, the org ID is automatically included in it to prevent unauthorized access.

Salesforce customers also enjoy the benefit of being up to date with product release versions. There is always a single version of the platform running across all Salesforce orgs. This means that customers don't have to worry about upgrading or regression testing because all that heavy lifting is done by Salesforce.

The Salesforce platform architecture is complex, comprising many databases and application servers along with a multitude of services that perform different functions, such as searching, business logic execution, caching, and event management. We are not going to discuss these, but rather focus our attention on the data management aspect of the platform, which runs on a relational database.

Let's take a brief look at how the underlying architecture of this all works seamlessly in Salesforce.

Metadata-driven architecture

A multi-tenant platform such as Salesforce, which is cloud-based, has its own challenges in terms of scalability, reliability, and security that must be overcome. Most important of all, how do you make sure that a tenant's data cannot be accessed by other tenants. Also, since there is only one version of the software in production, applying updates without significant downtime to the platform is another challenge, especially when done three times a year. We talked about test classes and we will discuss how Salesforce runs the Hammer later in this chapter, but what happens when a tenant customizes an app that they built or customizes the out-of-the-box sales application to meet business requirements? Do their customizations get written when Salesforce updates the production instance? Does the tenant have to reapply their customizations? What happens when a customer stores large amounts of data on the platform? Does the system slow down for other customers? To answer these and other related questions, we will look at what the **metadata-driven architecture** is.

As can be seen in the following diagram, Salesforce uses an architecture that delineates between the system kernel – the main engine that does the virtualization, which we will talk about soon, the database, and the tenant application, which must be polymorphic in nature, in other words, dynamic, to meet the varying needs of different clients:

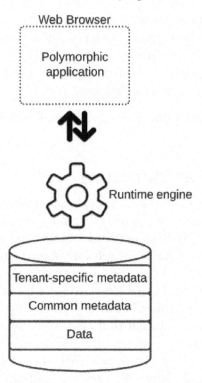

Figure 2.14 – Salesforce metadata-driven architecture

As can be seen in the preceding diagram, the runtime engine generates the application at runtime using metadata and data that belongs to the tenant.

Any updates applied to the kernel will not affect other layers of the architecture. Similarly, when a change is made to the common metadata, tenant-specific metadata is not affected, nor is the tenant's data. At runtime, the kernel or the runtime engine *constructs* the tenant's application using the common metadata, tenant-specific metadata, and data. In the following subsections, we will be looking at key components of the metadata-driven architecture. This is not an exhaustive discussion, but rather pointers for us to understand the key components to know about from a data architecture perspective.

> **Important note**
> I am using the term *customization* here in a general sense to mean any changes to the platform, whether done through clicks or code.

The kernel

The kernel, or the runtime engine, is the core of the platform that is made up of multiple services that work together to deliver services.

Since metadata is used as a key component to generate the client application at runtime, the platform uses a metadata cache to improve performance, otherwise, the system would not be able to scale with high loads. The metadata cache stores the frequently used metadata in memory, which reduces the need for performance-impacting expensive calls to the database.

The bulk data processing engine processes large amounts of data and works on performing data modifications in bulk. The engine has built-in fault tolerance that allows it to automatically retry bulk operations for records that can be processed successfully.

The platform also has a full-featured search engine service that optimizes access to full search capabilities. This service processes data updates asynchronously in the background. You may have noticed this when uploading large volumes of data and immediately afterward searching for the data. Because the engine runs asynchronously, you may have to wait up to 15 minutes before your search returns any results. This is different from a traditional database, where background processes run on the actual database tables and update indexes.

When you open a page or issue an API call to query data, in traditional databases, a query plan is created and the most optimal method to execute the query is determined by the optimizer and executed. This type of optimizer would not work with Salesforce because of its multi-tenant nature, in other words, physical tables in the database have data for tens of thousands of clients and the results from the query optimizer would not be accurate or efficient. This is where the multi-tenant query optimizer, which is a smart optimizer that *knows* the multi-tenant nature of Salesforce, comes into play. It determines the most efficient query paths by considering the user executing the query, and then uses the tenant-specific metadata maintained in the UDD, along with some other key tables, to execute optimized data operations on the database.

The Universal Data Dictionary (UDD)

The physical database at Salesforce looks very different from what you see when you look at an object's metadata in **Setup** or run a `decribeSObject` method from the backend. This is because Salesforce employs an abstraction layer in the application server, which, at runtime, reads data from the database and applies other logic resulting in the shape of your organization, in other words, objects, fields, relationships, list views, and so on. This layer, called the **Universal Data Dictionary**, or **UDD** for short, is declarative, meaning that object names, their attributes, and relationships are stored and not generated through code. What you see in the org is the result of the kernel acting on the UDD since the kernel acts as a mapping layer between the UDD and what you see in your org. The following is a diagram of the UDD and its components:

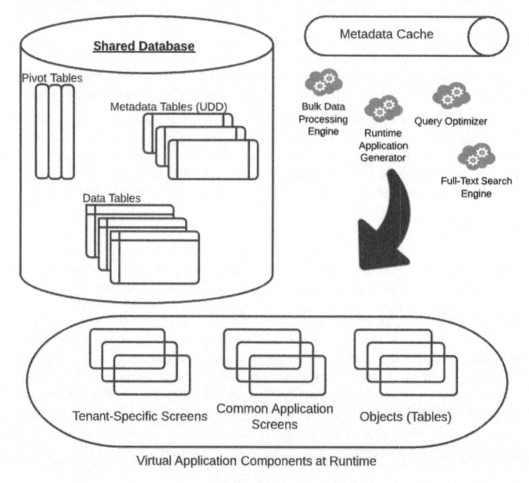

Figure 2.15 – The Universal Data Dictionary

As seen here, the UDD has multiple different components that come together to deliver the application at runtime.

When you create an object in Salesforce, you are not creating that object as a database table, with the object's attributes as columns, and the data that goes into the table as rows. If you have worked in a database, you use **Data Definition Language (DDL)** to create tables, add columns/rows, delete rows, and so on. This is not what happens when an object is created in Salesforce because you are interacting with the intermediary layer and not directly with the database. Of course, there is some object-related data stored in the database but, as mentioned before, a physical table with columns as fields for your object gets created. One of the reasons this is done is to scale the system and allow for this multi-tenancy model to operate efficiently. Another reason is to prevent the database locking of the table, which happens when a DDL is run for data integrity purposes. This is the reason you can't run a DDL directly on the database, such as `create table as APPLICANT`.

Because of this intermediary layer, you will not have indexes, foreign keys, or the ability to run query plans on your SOQL queries because it will not return actionable data as all of that is handled by the intermediary layer. Keep in mind that the UDD stores all the metadata defined by the tenant, be it through the UI or using APIs.

Since metadata is used as a key component to generate the client application at runtime, the platform uses a metadata cache to improve performance, otherwise, the system would not be able to scale with high loads. The metadata cache stores the frequently used metadata in memory, which reduces the need for performance-impacting expensive calls to the database.

All application data is stored in a few very large tables in the platform and the kernel materializes virtual tables at runtime. We will look at some of the key tables in the following sections, but the premise is that when the tenant creates, for example, custom objects in their org, the fields, any relationships between them, and other attributes are stored in the UDD. This metadata, along with data tables (tables that hold the tenant's transactional type data) and a few specialized pivot tables maintain the data in a denormalized format. This makes the architecture optimized and very functional for quickly presenting the *virtual* structure that we can then view from the UI. Some of the key tables are given here:

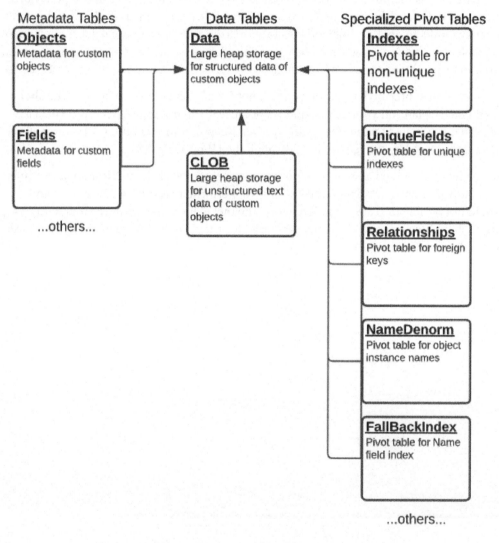

Figure 2.16 – Key tables in the UDD

As can be seen in the preceding diagram, all custom objects and custom fields are defined in tables and there are no physical database tables created. We next take a look at the key specialized tables that form this architecture.

Objects metadata table

This table stores the custom objects that have been defined in the org. The key attributes of this table are as follows:

- **ObjID**: Unique identifier of the object
- **OrgID**: Unique identifier of the organization
- **ObjName**: Name of the object

Fields metadata table

This table contains data pertaining to the custom fields that are defined for the custom object:

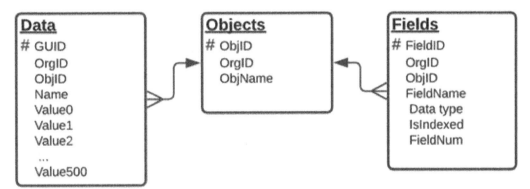

Figure 2.17 – Fields metadata table

All custom field metadata is stored in the preceding table. Also notice the presence of **OrgID** in all tables to ensure data partitioning and security for each tenant.

Key fields include the following:

- **FieldID**: Unique identifier of the custom field
- **ObjID**: Unique identifier of the object
- **OrgID**: Organization that owns the custom field
- **FieldName**: Name of the custom field

- **Data type** (for example, string, number): Data type of the custom field
- **IsIndexed**: Boolean value to indicate whether the field is indexed
- **FieldNum**: Position of the field in the object

Next, we will look at the data table.

Data table

As seen in *Figure 2.18*, this table contains data for all custom fields that are defined for custom objects:

GUID	OrgID	ObjID	...other columns...	Val0
a01...1	Org1	a01	...	Up
a01...2	Org1	a01	...	Flat
a02...1	Org1	a02	...	20201201
a02...2	Org1	a02	...	20210101
a03...1	Org1	a03	...	91.23012
a03...2	Org1	a03	...	-10.35

Figure 2.18 – Data table where custom field data resides

Notice that this table has a limit of 500 columns, which is also the limit for custom fields on a custom object.

Key fields include the following:

- **GUID**: Global unique identifier for each field
- **ObjID**: Unique identifier of the object
- **OrgID**: Organization that owns the custom field
- **Field name**: Natural name of the field

Another 300 fields are allowed from managed packages. These columns, called **flex columns,** can store data from multiple data types since, in the end, it all gets stored as a string data type. All fields in an object are stored in a different column and no two fields are stored in the same column. This table also has the four audit fields, which we will discuss later on in the chapter, and an **IsDeleted** column (not shown) to indicate when data has been deleted.

Character Long Objects (CLOBs) table

This is a CLOB table used to store fields that have been defined as long text fields of up to 32,000 characters. The platform also stores CLOBs outside the database for efficient searches.

Indexes pivot table

Relational databases use indexes to locate data when a search request is made. However, given that in the data table, different types of data types can be stored in a flex column, to get around this, the platform uses an independent table called **Indexes** that stores values for fields that have been identified to be indexed in the data table. It does this by synchronously copying field data marked for indexing to an appropriate column in the data table. The following diagram shows the Indexes table:

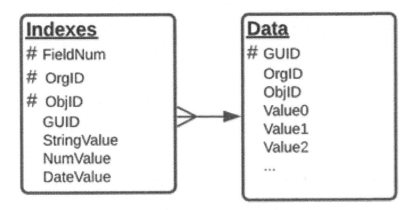

Figure 2.19 – Indexes table

As we can see, the Indexes table stores the indexes defined on objects. Some field types are automatically indexed, for example, external fields, and lookup or master-detail relationship fields.

Unique fields pivot table

For the same reason that indexes cannot be stored in the data table, this table is used to store unique fields defined in the object, so when you designate a field as unique in Salesforce, that field gets stored in this table. The metadata architecture at runtime checks this field and enforces uniqueness across data in the object.

Relationships pivot table

This table stores relationships that have been defined on an object. When a field is created with one of the relation types discussed in an earlier section, the platform maps the field to a value in the data table and uses this field to store the Obj ID of a related object. The relationships table is shown here:

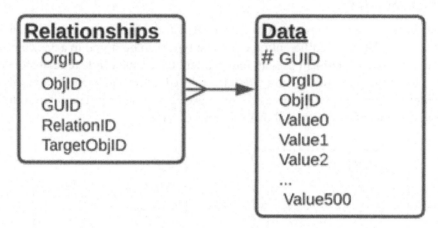

Figure 2.20 – Relationships table

In the preceding diagram, notice how relationship type fields are stored in this table that refer to the data table we looked at earlier.

FallbackIndex table

This is used if the external search engine fails to return a result. A fallback search is then performed. This is done by implementing a direct database query referencing the names of the target application objects. To enable this type of search, all object names are defined in this table, so the database has access to the most up-to-date information.

NameDenorm table

This table stores the Obj ID and name of each field in the data table. This is primarily used to provide hyperlinks to records for objects that are in a parent-child relationship.

HistoryTracking table

This table stores changes to fields that have been identified by the tenant for auditing. It stores the old and new values of the field along with when and who made the change.

Now that we have looked at the core architecture, let's briefly touch base on the innovation aspect of Salesforce and how it has been successful in releasing three releases per year.

New releases

Salesforce has been consistently ranked as one of the world's most innovative companies. One of the reasons for this is its extraordinary pace of innovation. One of the ways this has manifested itself is in the **three major releases a year** that Salesforce does. These releases include tens and sometimes hundreds of new features being introduced every year. The question then arises as to how Salesforce ensures that the configuration/customization of each of the thousands of customer orgs doesn't break with each new release.

This is where the **Hammer** comes in. The Hammer refers to the time period before every release when Salesforce implements an internal change freeze a few weeks prior to updating its sandboxes with the new release. The Hammer runs all unit tests that exist in customer orgs twice – once before the application of the release and after the release has been applied to a test environment. The results are then compared with the expectation that all tests that passed or failed prior to the release will still give the same result once the release has been applied.

Of course, things don't always go as planned in the software world and any discrepancies identified as regressions must be fixed quickly. An automated application analyzes the before and after results to ensure that the results have been scrubbed clean of any confidential data before being sent to the Salesforce team for taking action. This exercise is collectively referred to as the *Hammer* because of the massive effort it requires considering that it's not only Apex but Visualforce, and other metadata components as well. Now we can see why it's important to write test classes that actually test your code as they are also used by Salesforce prior to each release to run these millions of combined tests to ensure that the release is not going to break anything. This means that if in a new release your code was to break, Salesforce would detect that when running the Hammer and fix the code. But if test classes were poorly written, or with a view to merely passing the 75% test coverage requirement, then these may not get detected when the Salesforce team is running tests and you would then need to invest resources to fix your code.

With this introduction to Salesforce architecture, let's take a deep dive into Salesforce objects.

Introducing Salesforce objects

In this section, we will look at the foundational data structure in Salesforce – **objects**. This includes looking at what Salesforce objects are, their properties, and their usage. I will be suggesting best practices and principles to keep in mind when working with both standard and custom objects and other types of objects available on the platform. Applying these best practices when working with objects will help us keep our organizations scalable for that next enhancement or major project and deliver increased usability for our end users. The intent here is to briefly review the different objects and field types in Salesforce before we go into a detailed discussion of data modeling. This will make it easier to understand and grasp the data model concepts and provide a good foundation as regards when to use the different relationship types.

We will start with standard objects, which are the most commonly used and familiar to us, and then review other objects in Salesforce as well.

Standard objects

These are objects that come out of the box with Salesforce. Common ones include `Account`, `Contact`, `Opportunity`, and `Lead`, to name a few. Your license type and the version of Salesforce you are using will define which ones you can use in your organization.

Custom objects

These are objects created to support the business requirements of your company. Examples include the `Job`, `Applicant`, and `Candidate` objects that we looked at in our recruitment app in the last chapter. AppExchange applications will also have custom objects in them.

Big objects

This is a unique object because it can hold massive volumes of data from hundreds of millions of rows to billions of rows. They are well suited for archiving data or bringing in data from external sources. However, they are also limited compared to standard and custom objects. Some of the key features of big objects that differentiate them from regular objects are given here:

- They can only be created using metadata.
- They are prefixed with `__b`.
- They cannot have triggers, nor can they be reported on.

- They support limited numbers of data types, such as **Text**, **Number**, **Date Time**, **Lookup**, and **Text Area**.
- They cannot track record field history, nor can they be used to track activity.

> **Important note**
>
> Salesforce is making continuous updates to its big object functionality, so please refer to the latest release documents for up-to-date information.

External objects

These are objects that are used to bring external data into Salesforce. In our recruitment app, let's say we use an external service to do candidate background checks. Instead of bringing those results into Salesforce, we could simply use external objects and make them available to our users as required.

In the next section, we will look at some special field types in Salesforce and their use cases. Parent-child and lookup relationships will be dealt with in the next section in more detail, so we won't cover them here.

Fields in Salesforce

There are many different types of fields that are available in Salesforce. In this section, we will cover the special fields in Salesforce.

The Name field

This is the name of the record and is different from the record ID. This can be an auto-number or text field. This field is usually short and used by users to reference the record rather than using the long 15-character or 18-character (char) record ID. Most objects have this field except for the `Case` object, which doesn't have this. The `Case` object only has an auto-number field.

> **The Autonumber field**
>
> This is a special field that uses a system-generated unique number that is incremented every time a new record is created. You can define the format of the field along with a starting number, for example, for invoices, you could define the field to generate invoice numbers in the format INV-012345.
>
> This is also the field that shows up as a clickable option in list views, search results, and reports. Salesforce does allow this field to be text-based as well, which means that multiple records can exist with the same value since the system is not incrementing the number sequence anymore.

The ID field

This is the primary key (in relational database lingo) for the object and uniquely identifies a Salesforce record. This is an entirely unique field and no two records can have the same ID. The record ID can either be 15 or 18 characters long and the former is case sensitive; for example, if 003000000000BcA is changed to 003000000000bCa, Salesforce will throw an error. It is important that the 18-char ID is used in external applications because they may consider these two IDs the same, whereas Salesforce considers them distinct.

Audit fields

These audit fields are used for compliance, recording, and reporting on changes made to the data, as well as in Salesforce's process automation tools such as Workflow Rules, Lightning Process Builder, Flows, and Integrations. The most commonly used audit fields are as follows:

- `CreatedBy`
- `CreatedDate`
- `LastModifiedbyID`
- `LastModifiedDate`

There is another field called `SystemModStamp`, which is updated when an automated process updates a record. Automated process here refers to Salesforce internal code. Whenever a user, automation tools such as Workflow Rules, Lightning Flow, or Process Builder, an API, or a DML statement updates a record, both the `LastModifiedDate` and `SystemModStamp` dates will get updated. This means that these two dates can be different, and it is a best practice to not use the `SystemModStamp` date for integration purposes. Except for the `SystemModStamp` field, all four audit fields can be updated using Data Loader or a similar tool. The use of audit fields is helpful when migrating data so as not to lose important audit information and should be carefully used to protect data integrity.

Compound fields

These are complex data types that are created by grouping together multiple primitive data types. This is done to simplify the code that handles these fields. If you have used the `Account` object, the **Address** field is a compound field composed of fields such as **Street**, **StateCode**, **State**, **PostalCode**, **City**, **Country**, and a few other fields. Compound fields are read-only, and changes can only be made to the underlying individual field. The compound version of the fields is only accessible through the SOAP or REST APIs.

Another example of a compound field is **Geolocation**, which is a combination of the latitude and longitude fields. These are available by default on `Account`, `Contact`, `Quote`, and `User` objects and when an address is populated, Salesforce automatically populates the **Geolocation** field. In the following screenshot, you can see that the data type of the **Billing Address** field is **Address**:

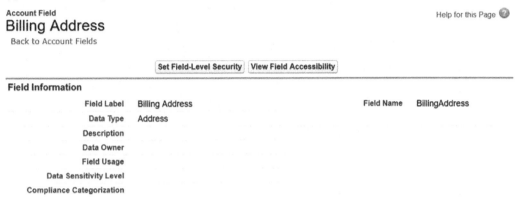

Figure 2.21 – Billing Address field

In the following screenshot, we have queried the same compound field using SOQL:

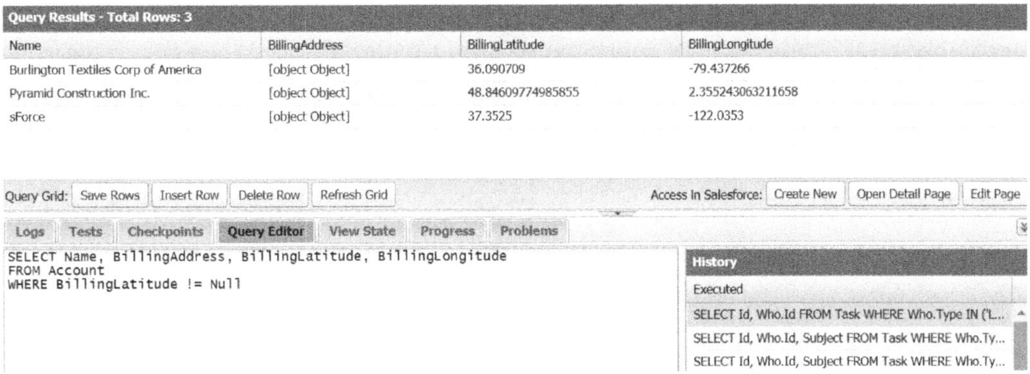

Figure 2.22 – Billing Address Compound field

The `BillingLatitude` and `BillingLongitude` fields form the `BillingAddress` compound field, which can also be queried. Note how it shows [**object Object**] under `BillingAddress`, which indicates that this is a complex data type.

AnyType fields

These are **polymorphic** fields that return string, `Boolean`, `date`, `number`, `URL`, `email`, or other data types. These are used when querying data through the APIs and are commonly used in history objects. A polymorphic field can be used to get information about related objects where these related objects can be of different types.

The `Owner`, `Who`, and `What` fields are examples of **AnyType fields**. The following example shows that `Who` can be of the Lead or Contact type:

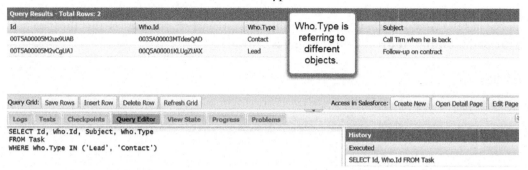

Figure 2.23 – The Who.Type field referring to multiple objects

Note how, in the preceding screenshot, `Who.Type` is referring to both `Contact` and `Lead` objects.

This can also be confirmed by checking the field properties via the Developer Workbench:

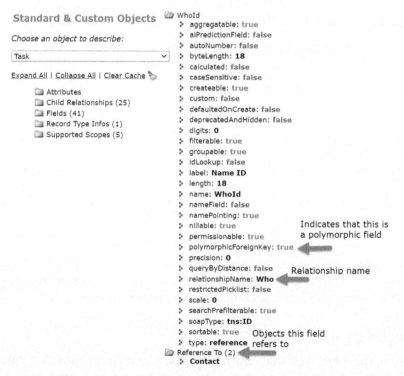

2.24 – Developer Workbench, Who.Id metadata referring to both Contact and Lead objects (In the diagram, Lead object is not shown in the Reference To field)

Notice how, when the metadata of the field on the `Task` object is viewed using the *Developer Workbench*, it has `polymorphicForeignKey` set to `true`.

Currency fields

These are used to store currency data, for example, the **Amount** field on the `Opportunity` object. When the multi-currency feature is turned on in an organization, another field called `CurrencyIsoCode` on the object determines the currency the field will be shown in. For example, if `CurrencyIsoCode` is GBP, then all currency fields will have values shown in GBP.

Salesforce has a multiple currencies feature that enables you to use currencies other than your organization's default currency. You can enable selected currencies that you do business in and the org's administrator can then maintain the conversion rates for those currencies. Another feature is advanced currency management, which allows you to manage dated currency rates in Salesforce. This feature stores historical currency rates allowing accurate reporting. Advanced currency management has some limitations and should be enabled after a careful review of its capabilities and your business requirements.

JunctionIDList fields

This field type is used to query and optionally use the returned results in Apex to modify a many-to-many relationship directly. This field type is enabled when **Shared Activities** is turned on through **Setup**.

Summary

In this chapter, we learned about the different types of objects in Salesforce and we looked at their usages and limitations. We then reviewed some specific field types and investigated details regarding their usage.

We explored database concepts including normalization and denormalization and what data modeling is. You also learned why Salesforce is different from other relational databases, at least from a tenant's perspective, and how it has been optimized for read operations. Next, we looked into some important design principles to consider when designing your data model.

We investigated the different relationships and their usages, limitations, and use cases. Next, we took a deep dive into Salesforce's multi-tenancy architecture, its different components, and how they come together to generate a virtual application at runtime that we, as users, interact with.

This chapter should have provided you with a solid foundation to be able to understand multi-tenancy architecture, and if you come from a relational database background, some things that didn't make sense earlier should now start to make a lot more sense. The data architectural principles learned in this chapter will help you design more scalable and efficient business applications, and understanding data modeling concepts and the different types will allow you to communicate effectively with different audiences. Understanding why having a cohesive data model that has objects linked with one another using relationships will help you adhere to the Salesforce click versus code methodology and allow you to frame conversations with different stakeholders in the right context.

In the next chapter, we will look at data management – what it is and its different facets. The knowledge acquired in this chapter will have set the stage to understand the upcoming topics with ease and clarity.

Questions

1. Precision Printers has an `Applicant` object that has many rows in it and users are reporting slow performance when running reports on this object. As the resident data architect, you have been asked to investigate this and suggest a solution. What can you suggest?

    a) View the filters used in the report and tweak them to use indexes on the report.

    b) Just create an index on the database table and use that in the report.

    c) Do nothing; it's probably just a temporary issue and will go away by itself.

2. Precision Printers has promoted a new integration to the production environment recently. It runs every 12 hours and transfers records from the `Account` object that have changed to an ERP system. The administrator is noticing that records are being transferred to the ERP even when there hasn't been an apparent change made on the record. What could be causing this problem?

    a) No action is needed; the integration will correct itself and the correct records will start to sync into the ERP.

    b) Take an inventory of the records in Salesforce that should have not been synched and then manually remove these records from the ERP.

    c) The criterion for determining records that have changed is based on `SystemModStamp`. Changing the criterion to `LastModifiedDate` will fix the issue.

    d) Delete all the records from the ERP and restart the integration.

3. A rookie admin has created multiple objects, including two objects for storing account and contact records for a custom app that is used to track incoming requests for quotes from potentially strategic prospects. The admin has been asked to create reports to show the prospects with the largest quotes, the products they are interested in, and the number of days the quote request has been in each stage. In addition, managers want to see on the `Account` object whether an open request exists for a quote. The admin is being told by the developer that a lot of code must be written to produce these reports. What could be the underlying cause of writing so much code for these reports? (Choose 2 answers)

   a) Appropriate relationships have not been defined between objects and that is causing Apex code to be written to query the data.

   b) The admin should open a ticket with Salesforce Support and get them to create these reports.

   c) The data model needs to be redesigned following architectural best practices and the application redone.

   d) Create a lookup relationship between the custom `Account` object and the quote request object and then write a trigger to aggregate the open quote requests and display them on the custom `Account` object.

Further reading

- Developer Force, *Multitenant Architecture*: `http://www.developerforce.com/media/ForcedotcomBookLibrary/Force.com_Multitenancy_WP_101508.pdf`

- *Normalization*, section 1.3.6, **DATA MANAGEMENT BODY OF KNOWLEDGE (DMBOK)**

3

Understanding Data Management

In this chapter, we will look at the importance of managing data and the risk and challenges related to data management. We will also discuss some principles of data management, the different types of data, the data life cycle, and the relationship between data management and data governance. This is going to provide you with a foundational understanding of why it is critical to manage data and some of the challenges that you will come across when managing your data. We will look at some strategies on how to overcome those challenges by applying some commonly used principles.

We will also review best practices related to data management, where we will discuss strategies related to managing data and metadata. Learning these best practices will allow you to use these in your organization to implement tools and processes that will enable optimal data management and efficient use of resources. We will also review backup and restore strategies, why they are critical to business, and how to go about implementing the tools that will help you manage your data. Given that Salesforce stopped providing data restore services in 2020, this section aims to equip you with the necessary knowledge to effectively implement backup and restore procedures right out of the gate. At the end, we will discuss some popular Salesforce tools and third-party tools that can be used to manage data, including backing up and restoring it.

The topics covered in this chapter include the following:

- What is data?
- What is data management?
- Aspects of data management
- Data backup and recovery
- Tools of the trade

What is data?

I have come across many projects where the terms *data* and *information* were used interchangeably, and this was fine in most cases, but in the same way that we established a common understanding of the term *architecture*, it would be prudent to do the same here.

Data is a representation of facts that are either stored digitally or on other media, such as physical photos or paper. It is important to acknowledge that not everything presented as data is factual, with *factual* here meaning that because it's the truth when seen in combination with other data elements, it will convey the full picture of the truth. Data shouldn't be reviewed without considering the context of the data, because data without context causes confusion and opens the door to misinterpretation. Consider how many ways there are in which dates can be presented. In fact, it is a common source of confusion when you see a date written like 12-09-2020. Are the first two characters representing the month or the day? When you have the context, perhaps on the paper form you are filling out, or the web form that instructs you to write the date in the MM-DD-YYYY format, that's when you know that the first two characters are representing the month. Therefore, presenting data in context is important, otherwise, it loses its value and effectiveness.

Data is sometimes referred to as the raw material for information and information as data within context. There is quite a bit of discussion ongoing regarding this that is beyond the scope of this book, but for our purposes, we will stick with the definition of data as mentioned earlier. In the next section, we will ask the question of whether data is really valuable and whether we should devote so much energy to managing it properly.

Is data valuable?

Data is and should be considered an organizational asset. This is now easy to understand given how social media users have had their data aggregated and sold to marketers in the past. Every organization, for-profit and not-for-profit alike, realizes the importance of data and tries to harvest it to gain valuable insights that can drive decision-making. For example, until a decade or so ago, very few mining companies had the knowledge or the expertise to understand fuel consumption and usage of their heavy-duty machinery, but today that data is sent through onboard sensors to centralized databases where it is aggregated and analyzed for fuel consumption. This helps the company to understand which machine is idling excessively versus those that may be using too much fuel, which could be an indication of an imminent breakdown. Proactively servicing the machine could save the company hundreds of thousands of dollars in downtime and maintenance costs.

Similarly, for a non-profit organization, understanding its donor base, their interests, and demographics are all vital for the organization's continued operations. Using data in its system, it can analyze the data to determine which channels to focus their ads on if they are targeting a specific demographic. Similarly, data can also be used to determine which areas need the most help traditionally so the organization can focus its energy on those areas.

As the science of AI matures and gains traction, data will continue to gain importance and form the backbone of many new businesses and existing businesses will continue to look for ways to adopt it. AI is the science of training systems that can simulate tasks based on data. These systems continue to self-learn and refine their decision-making capabilities as new data becomes available. For example, Tesla uses internal and external sensors on its cars that send data back to its data centers and can then be used to show the average increase in speed over certain patches of road, determining hazardous locations that are causing drivers to take sudden action. Tesla accords data collection and analysis a high level of importance, going as far as parsing its online forum for insights.

Now that we understand the value of data, we will look at what data management is and why it's important in the next section.

Introducing data management

Data management is the discipline of collecting, storing, and using data effectively and in a cost-effective manner. The key goal of data management is to put in measures to ensure that data remains viable and fit for its intended purpose and that when it has ceased to be useful, it is appropriately discarded or archived. Earlier, we established that data is a valuable resource and an asset to any company, but let's look at some of the benefits of data management.

Benefits of data management

Data is critical to businesses regardless of their size, revenue, or industry. From a small mom-and-pop donut shop that serves locally to very large businesses that serve millions of customers every day, proper data management practices, processes, and tools are essential. Of course, a small business will not need to implement a **Master Data Management (MDM)** solution to manage its data, but a large organization will not be able to operate efficiently without it.

Let's now review the benefits of data management more holistically:

- **Realizing cost efficiencies**: Think about how much time you have spent searching for the travel policy on the company portal, spending time looking for an expense reimbursement form, or simply looking up a non-standard abbreviation that's just used internally in the company. A 2011 survey by Gartner reports a 20% reduction in labor productivity due to data quality issues. However, organizations that have effective data management report spending less because of data being readily available.

- **Avoiding costly mistakes**: Mistakes happen, and they are part of any job function you are in. Whether you are a doctor, lawyer, architect, or cashier, everyone makes mistakes, but some mistakes can be costly. For example, if you were excited about your start-up, which was banking on footfall and certain demographics, but that data was incorrect, your start-up's existence could become questionable. In more extreme scenarios, consider a physician who just finished his 12-hour shift in ER and updates a patient's file with instructions and medication. The problem is that this patient has the same last name as another patient for whom these instructions are intended. Barring the fact that this is caused by a human error, nonetheless, the consequences could be life-threatening in this scenario.

- **Improving decision-making**: Effective data management leads to improved and effective decision-making with accurate, up-to-date data being available for decision-makers. For example, having access to reliable data helps organizations forecast their sales more accurately and proactively take measures in case forecasts show a downward trend in the market.

- **Creating more buy-in**: When decision-makers and other users of the data have access to reliable data that translates into more revenue, reduced costs, or both, people using the data feel more confident about it and are willing to learn and use the system more effectively, as well as to adopt new system enhancements. Conversely, when data is not managed properly, consumers of that data lose confidence in it and start to use other means to complete their tasks. For example, a quoting system was implemented at a large dealership with integration from the **Enterprise Resource Planning (ERP)** system feeding the quoting system, with prices for the products added onto the quote. A few weeks after going live, it was found that sales representatives from the trucking division were not using the system compared to their peers in other divisions because the prices pulled onto the quotes were not accurate. An emergency meeting was called with the IT support team and, after determining the root cause, a fix was introduced to rectify the problem.

- **Reduced security risks**: An effective data management policy ensures the security of your data. A 2020 *Cost of a Data Breach Report* (`https://www.ibm.com/ security/data-breach`) by IBM reported that the average cost of a data breach is 3.86 million US dollars and takes about 280 days to identify and contain. The 2019 *Global Risks Report* from the World Economic Forum rated cybersecurity as the top threat facing society. A key aspect of cybersecurity is protecting data so business operations can continue to run smoothly.

- **Reduced reputational risk**: Trust and reputation are key ingredients for any business to maintain and grow its customer base. Customers will trust organizations that will manage their data properly and do the right thing if their data does get mismanaged. The *Cambridge Analytica* scandal was the last straw for many Facebook users who quit the service after the scandal became public. Having a robust data management plan inspires confidence not only internally within the organization, but also with stakeholders because they know the organization has its bases covered if a situation like that was to happen.

- **Maintaining a competitive advantage**: If you are a company in the hi-tech industry and spend millions on R&D, having your intellectual property exposed to unscrupulous actors could be devastating and may lead to the demise of the company. In certain situations, it may be deemed a national security risk. This was the case with the Equifax breach in 2017 when roughly 147 million customers had their data stolen by alleged foreign actors. The fear was that the data could be mined and intelligence operatives who were in financial distress could be manipulated by foreign actors.

We have looked at the benefits of data management, so now let's look at the challenges associated with managing data.

Challenges of data management

Most organizations have volumes of data that keep on increasing, not only in size but also in terms of the sources of the data. Let's take the example of data from the Internet of Things (IoT) or social media. Neither of these was a source of data prior to this century, but nowadays they are probably among the top sources of data. These changes not only opened myriad opportunities for organizations to make the data meaningful and translate it into revenue but also brought challenges with it. Here are some of the challenges that organizations face today:

- **Putting data to good use**: Many organizations are collecting data and storing it, but just doing that is not good enough because data, by itself, doesn't provide any value unless something is done with it. Figuring out what to do with that data once it is collected is a time-consuming process and doesn't happen by itself. It requires dedicated resources and funds to make the data useful. With the advent of tools such as Salesforce's Einstein Analytics, organizations will be able to reduce the effort but nonetheless, the point is that data needs to be worked on in order to make it valuable.

- **Lack of executive sponsorship**: Data management should be weaved into the organizational culture, so everyone is made responsible for data and takes ownership in their respective areas. This requires executive buy-in, in other words, resources both in the form of human resources and funding that can be made available. This also requires that executives support and use data in their own decisions. However, this can be a challenge in more traditional types of organizations that have been operating successfully for a long time and don't see the need to invest resources and time in data management activities. With new industry disruptors such as Uber, Tesla, and Airbnb, it is not so farfetched that new data-driven technology can significantly uproot traditional business models and threaten their very existence. Many companies are realizing at the executive level that data is a key component to continued success and growth and have started to hire Chief Data Officers (CDOs), but this is still a relatively new phenomenon.

- **Compliance with regulations**: Regulations related to data management are complex and vary across jurisdictions; moreover, new regulations keep getting introduced while existing ones get updated. This is a challenge for organizations to keep pace with and to continue to be on the lookout for any non-compliance. Non-compliance penalties are not only hefty but pose a serious reputational risk to organizations.

- **Understanding what data is already there**: It used to be that organizations created data from several systems, analyzed and reported on that data, archived it, and eventually purged it when it was not needed. With smart devices, sensors, and social media becoming increasingly adopted and accepted in our societies, data continues to grow exponentially, quickly filling up databases. According to an estimate, every day, 2.5 quintillion (1 quintillion = 1,000,000,000,000,000,000) bytes of data are created. *IDC*, a reputable market intelligence firm, reports that worldwide shipments of smart devices alone are forecast to exceed 1.4 billion units by the year 2024 (`https://www.idc.com/getdoc.jsp?containerId=prUS47567221`). It can be a gigantic task to keep tabs on all this data and knowing what data is available. This also leads to a reactionary approach to data issues, which get addressed only when problems arise. Understanding the data also involves knowing which processes are data-driven and how critical data is for those processes to continue running.

- **Lack of effective communication**: Communication is very important and must happen if any meaningful change needs to happen within the organization. Strategic efforts, such as data management initiatives, cannot succeed without an effective communication strategy that helps stakeholders understand why data management is important and what is in it for them. Communication needs to be tailored for different functions in the organization to ensure that the message will get across and is appropriate for that function. Finance, for example, has different needs and requirements to HR as regards data.

- **Interoperability of data**: We have established that there are multiple sources of data and, when it ends up in organizational stores, it can end up in data lakes, data warehouses, or other databases. With these data stores having their own nomenclature and formats, data first needs to be transformed so that it can be easily consumed for analysis and reporting.

- **Lack of a holistic view of the data**: The ownership of data is sometimes fragmented, meaning data management may be the responsibility of a select few in a department or company. This is especially true in a decentralized operating model, which we will discuss in the *Data management operating models* section. This can lead to silos, resulting in the data being viewed at a department or function level rather than looking at it holistically from a company's perspective. This tunnel vision view leads to intra-office politics and slows down initiatives that are put in place to reap the benefits from this data.

- **Inadequate processes and systems**: Some organizations understand the importance of data but lack the processes and systems to derive benefits from this data. They may even have some processes to manage their data, but these may be insufficient in number or lacking in optimization, resulting in a lack of confidence in the output from that data. This can trigger a downward spiral effect where users are not confident in the data that they are receiving, resulting in a downward trajectory that can also result in key roles associated with managing the data losing motivation in terms of continuing to maintain their data.

In this section, we reviewed, what data management is, and understood the need for it and the challenges associated with having an effective data management strategy and its implementation. Now that we have looked at the benefits and challenges of data management, in the next section, we will review the data life cycle and other aspects of data management.

Introducing the data life cycle

In this section, we will look at the data life cycle and then look at an example within the context of Salesforce. The data life cycle provides a high-level overview of data from the time it is created to the time it is purged. Having clarity regarding how data gets created and moves throughout the life cycle helps in understanding where the activities that we perform daily fit, from an operational point of view, and how they are important. There are five stages a specific element of data will go through in its lifetime:

1. Data creation

2. Storage

3. Usage

4. Archival

5. Purge

We will now look at each of these in more detail.

Data creation

This is the first phase of the data life cycle. In this phase, data is created or acquired, which can happen in many ways. Consider the example of Dun & Bradstreet, which provides data enrichment capabilities for Salesforce. A more common example is the use of an IT application to create data; for example, creating a product catalog in an ERP. In other instances as well, companies may use devices to create data; for example, the use of scanners to scan multiple paper invoices and create the data directly in an invoice management system.

Storage

This is the second phase of the life cycle and pertains to safely storing the data that has been created. This is where database security, network security, and levels of security come into play to ensure that the data is adequately protected. A backup and recovery process is also implemented to ensure that the data can be recovered in case of issues.

Usage

This is the phase where data is actually put to use. It can be viewed, updated, moved to another data store, transformed, and have analytic processes run on it to generate insights from the data. Data can also be shared with outside organizations; for example, an organization submits quarterly tax reports to the federal tax agency.

Archival

Just like you may come across a job offer email from 3 years ago when searching for other emails and decide to archive it, data has a useful life of its own, after which time it needs to be archived. Archival is usually done when the organization determines that the data may not be very useful after a certain time frame, but is needed for regulatory or audit purposes. Occasionally, an organization may find a need to refer back to the archived data. For example, a large **Customer Relationship Management(CRM)** implementation project decided not to bring in all the data from the legacy system into Salesforce, but to ensure continued access to the data in case it was needed, it closed access to the legacy system for everyone except for the admin. This way, the company saved time and money by avoiding bringing in data that was not of very high value but also made sure that its business operations were not adversely impacted.

Purge

In the *Challenges of data management* section, we looked at how fast data grows, and it is not feasible nor useful to keep every bit of data forever. Depending on the industry of the organization, regulatory laws may dictate a data retention period, after which point it must be purged. Purging involves removing the data from your systems completely. This is especially important because laws such as the **General Data Protection Regulation (GDPR)** demand that when a subject whose information is being stored requests a *right to be forgotten*, their data must be completely and irreversibly removed from all the systems of the organization.

Now that we have looked at the data life cycle, let's briefly apply these to a Salesforce example.

Data life cycle – A Salesforce example

Let's walk through an example in the context of Salesforce to better understand how the data life cycle can be applied and the benefits of categorizing data like this. A hypothetical company, Magnum Health Services, based in the United States, is using the service cloud to capture its customers' health claims. Magnum has a large customer base of 60 million customers and growing. It receives about 10 million cases every year. The company is expecting 5% annual growth in its customer base and forecasts the caseload to increase to 11 million every year. Let's review how each phase of the data life cycle would apply in this scenario.

Data creation

Customers can create cases by calling the hotline or by email. Magnum's admins have also set up their system so that social media posts that mention the company on Facebook and Twitter are automatically created as cases in the service cloud. In a nutshell, Magnum has multiple channels of communication, which means that there are multiple sources from which data is being created.

Storage

All the cases that are created get stored in the Salesforce Platform and are protected by multiple layers of security, including IP restrictions, profiles, and other measures that Salesforce takes to protect its infrastructure, including databases, servers, and networks.

Usage

This data is available to internal as well as external users, in other words, customers. Internally, case owners can view, update, and delete cases; for example, a Facebook post that was automatically created as a case but doesn't need any response from the company. Managers and executives can run reports and view dashboards. Externally, customers can interact with their case by providing more details, uploading files, or simply marking the case as resolved through the Customer Community.

Archival

Because Magnum is dealing with customer health data, it needs to make sure that it is compliant. Salesforce is compliant with the **Health Insurance Portability and Accountability Act (HIPAA)**-compliant and provides the tool to ensure that its customers set up the platform to be compliant with health acts. Magnum has set up a **Field Audit Trail**, which is part of Salesforce Shield and automatically archives data as defined by law.

Purge

Magnum has developed custom processes that are run to delete data from archive objects once the required retention period has passed. This way, Magnum can meet its obligations to keep customer data safe and frees up Magnum resources to be used for the next set of records that can be archived.

Now that we have looked at the data life cycle, let's review the operating models of data management in detail and understand the pros and cons of each.

Data management operating models

You cannot have an effective data management strategy implemented if there is a lack of ownership, decision-making, and oversight. Having an effective operating model helps in establishing roles and responsibilities and accountability from the point data is created to the point it is purged in an organization. The most common operating models are the following:

- Centralized
- Decentralized
- Hybrid

We will review these models in the sub-sections below.

Definition

An **operating model** is a representation of how an organization operates. In the context of data management, it allows us to visually represent how an organization manages its data-related processes with appropriate checks and balances.

Centralized operating model

The **centralized operating model** is a formalized operating model that has a data management lead responsible for decision-making and providing vision and direction for the organization. Because there is a single individual accountable to lead the change, decision-making is swift and the role, due to it having proximity to the executive, yields significant influence and can lobby for resourcing and funding at the executive level.

The flip side is that this requires a significant shift in roles and new hires to form this type of data organization, resulting in longer times and increased costs. It can also result in excessive red tape because approvals must be sought for initiatives. This type of operating model can also have the data governance lead become overly influenced by enterprise-level targets, rather than also keeping the individual business units and the associated business process nuances in the decision-making process.

Decentralized operating model

The **decentralized operating model** is the opposite of the centralized model and decision-making is done by consent through committees. In this model, data management activities are the responsibility of individual business units or lines of businesses. Because each **Line Of Business (LOB)** understands its business very well, this model is relatively easy to implement because generally, data issues are very well understood, and because there is individual LOB ownership, they can be quickly addressed as well.

The challenge though is that it can be difficult to gain consensus in this model; for example, data management priorities for one LOB may not be the same for another LOB. Compared to the centralized model, it can be challenging to sustain this model over time because of a lack of clear accountability and ownership. One way to deal with this is to have ownership of data management initiatives rotate among the LOBs, but have a clear vision and guiding principles to guide the decision-making process.

Hybrid operating model

The **hybrid operating model** is a combination of centralized and decentralized operating models. In this model, a **Center of Excellence (COE)** operates under the direction and oversight of the steering committee, which comprises stakeholders that represent key business units in the organization. The COE guides in terms of tools and best practices and drives the vision of the organization. The steering committee has executive and senior-level managers that can drive decision-making and ensure that the vision is understood by the COE. The benefit of this model is that it grants autonomy to business units, but also has the oversight that's required to realize the data management vision. Business units also benefit from the expertise of dedicated resources that are part of the COE.

Although the hybrid model provides a good combination of benefits from the centralized and decentralized models, it does require additional **Full-Time Equivalents (FTEs)** to run the COE, which can increase the initial costs in setting this up. Sometimes, overly influential or outspoken executives that are part of the steering committee may drive the committee decisions that are not well thought through and may be perceived as self-serving. Another factor is that progress and meeting KPIs are dependent on self-reporting from business units, which can complicate oversight.

Now that we have looked at some of the common operating models in a data-driven organization, next we will review best practices for data management.

Learning data management best practices

In this section, we will be learning data management best practices within the context of Salesforce. You probably already realize that Salesforce is increasingly being used for more than just CRM, and companies are using it for critical business functions. Even if it was only used as a CRM, data would be very important and require continuous data management.

In my opinion, gone are the days when you could go to your production org and add or modify existing functionality because a user requested it. With more intra-dependencies between applications built on the platform and inter-dependencies between external systems and Salesforce, changes concerning **data** and **metadata**, in particular, must be thought through. I am not proposing spending hours and days analyzing what impact adding a new list view is going to have, but pragmatically approaching changes to your production environment based on the size of the change and how interlinked it is with other applications or integrations. For example, adding a new field to the object would not require as much analysis as changing the type of field from a multi-select picklist to a single-select picklist.

We must understand that data management is a marathon and not a sprint. It demands constant management by tweaking processes and tools and communication at all levels within the organization to remind users how important it is to the organization and for the user's own decision-making. Imagine a B2C business that sends out personalized *thank you* notes with special discounts to 50,000 top customers, but 5,000 of those didn't reach the intended recipients because the addresses were incorrect and the company hadn't provided easier ways for its customers to update their addresses when they moved. Not only did the company waste money by sending those brochures to incorrect addresses, but also lost potential revenue. In addition to that, the company also risked unhappy customers because when some or all of those 5,000 customers find out that they didn't get those notes along with the discounts, it will also undermine customers' trust in the company. It may cause them to think that they don't know – or worse – care about their customers.

The 1-10-100 data quality rule is another reason why data management is important. This rule states that problems caused by data issues will cost you $1 in prevention, $10 in remediation after an issue has materialized, and $100 after a failure. It must be remembered that the dollar amounts are relative numbers, but the principle still applies. Taking our earlier example, sending out 5,000 notes to the wrong address is in the failure section (see next figure), and will cost a lot more to fix. Let's say we knew about this problem and cleaned and validated our data by hiring some data entry clerks, then the cost would have been much less. The best scenario would have been to put tools and processes in place at the prevention stage, but companies either lack the will or consider it an expense to fund these tools and processes rather than an investment. In the following diagram, as we go down the pyramid, the cost of fixing a problem grows exponentially:

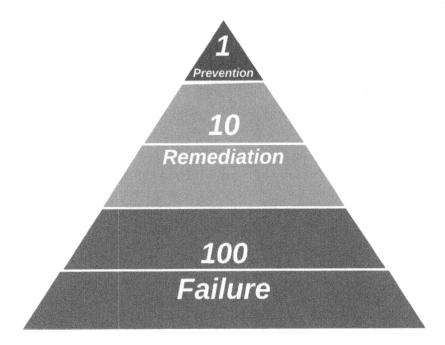

Figure 3.1 – Relative cost of prevention versus remediation and failure

The diagram demonstrates that resources spent preventing a problem from materializing cost much less than remediating them or rectifying them when a major failure happens.

In the following sections, we will look at some data management best practices related to both data and metadata.

Understanding data and metadata

Just as data is important for businesses, metadata is even more important because it forms the foundation of your organization. Think of metadata as the foundation and framework of a house, both of which cannot be seen once a house has been completed, but which form an integral part of the house. Another benefit of implementing data management best practices is that they facilitate development of metrics, which can be used to assess your organization against an objective criteria. Typically, when you ask someone how good the data management practices are, the answer is *pretty good*, *not great*, or something similar that is based more on a gut feeling rather than solid **Key Performance Indicators (KPIs)** that can be reported. If you are an employee working for a Salesforce customer, you can use these to continuously monitor your organization for metadata and data quality or, if you are a consultant, then use these as a basis to assess the state of the organization and to recommend steps to bring it to an optimal state with respect to both data and metadata. Knowing and adhering to these best practices will help maintain your organization and allow you to scale with ease while facilitating an optimal experience for users when they are working in your Salesforce org.

In the next section, we will do a deep dive into best practices related to metadata.

Metadata best practices

As mentioned earlier, metadata must be managed continuously as well. Think of unused fields and objects that have data and are no longer used because an AppExchange package has now replaced the functionality. These are just some examples. What follows below are guidelines and best practices that will ensure that your organization remains scalable and consequently, your data is valid and useful. I do want to mention that some of these, by themselves, may seem very innocuous, but combined they can seriously hinder velocity and slow down development. Remember, speed-to-value is a critical factor in the continued growth and success of any business in the global economy today. You will want to make sure that you have processes in place to respond quickly to changing market conditions so as to derive benefits from possible opportunities or reduce your exposure to risk, which can jeopardize your business' existence.

Required fields

Required fields are a great way to reduce data quality issues, but should be used prudently. An excessive number of required fields will slow down data entry for users and encourage behavior that is not congruent with a data-driven organization. For example, users would start entering random text in free-form text fields just to get through the form. My suggestion is to have no more than 5–7 required fields on a page layout.

Unless you are absolutely sure they are needed, try not to have the required fields at the object level. The reason is that any integrations that you put in will now need to populate the required fields as well. This may not work well for scenarios where the required field must be populated when a user is doing data entry but is not required when data is brought in via integration from another system.

Formulas and roll-up summary fields

This is another one where you don't want to be excessive with it, but also too few of these fields indicate that things may be being done in code. During assessments, I will look for key objects, such as `Account`, `Opportunity`, `Quote`, and, if it's a custom application, objects that are on the parent side in a parent-child relationship, as well as roll-up summary fields.

> **Limits**
>
> There is a limit on the number of parent-child or master-detail fields you can have on an object. There is a performance cost associated with these fields, and therefore, you want to be careful and use these only when it's absolutely needed. There are similar limits on roll-up summary fields, which out of the box only work with master-detail fields.

Similarly, look out for formulas on objects that are critical to the application and review the code to check whether there is logic in the code that could have been more suited to formulas.

Record types

Record types are one of the many powerful features that the platform provides, but being excessive may be detrimental. This is because record types control picklist values and, depending on how many picklist fields you have, it can quickly become cumbersome to maintain these for too many record types in particular. I recommend having no more than 5–7 record types per object. Having excessive record types in the org usually means there are as many page layouts for the object, which can be an administrative overhead to maintain.

Profiles

At the outset, the best practice is to control access via permission sets. It may be very tempting to create profiles to control access, but a large number of profiles can become an admin's nightmare. Consider an organization where you have 15 profiles and 100 fields on 10 objects. The initial setup alone for read-only access can involve a review of 15,000 checkboxes and another 15,000 for editing.

One good reason for creating profiles is for page layout assignments that can only be controlled through profiles and not permission sets. Even in this case, I suggest taking a good look at your design and seeing whether there are other ways in which you can achieve your business requirements.

Removing unused fields and objects

This is a straightforward one but, surprisingly, I have seen organizations where the admin created an object with a few fields in production to *try* out a *quick* **Proof of Concept (POC)** and never got to remove the object completely once they were done. You should make a habit of not doing these types of POCs or enhancements in production in any case, but if you have to for any reason, maintain a list of fields and objects you are creating so that you can remove them if they are not required.

The same guideline applies to fields as well. Unused fields are no fun and cause confusion for end users in reporting, and especially if they are on the page layout, cause integration problems and just generally lead to a cluttered organization. Remove them if they are not used. Aim for no unused objects and fewer than 15% unused fields, which you need to put on your backlog for removal.

Report proliferation

Try to establish a robust framework on how reports will be managed. The ease with which reports can be created in Salesforce is a double-edged sword. It is easy for end users to create their own reports in a matter of minutes, but without any guidelines and governance, this can lead to report duplication, a plethora of unused reports, and reports with no description so no one knows what they do.

Run the following query to assess when a report was last run. For example, have a rule that says if a report has not been run in the last 18 months, mark it for deletion after discussing it with the report owner. You can have any time period you want, but I recommend 18 months because that would cover the calendar year start and end dates and non-calendar fiscal year dates as well. This would cover your bases in cases where a report is specifically run at certain times of the year:

```
SELECT Id, Name, Description, LastRunDate, LastModifiedBy.Name
FROM Report
WHERE LastRunDate < 2019-06-01T00:00:00Z
ORDER BY LastRunDate DESC
LIMIT 50
```

Also question the value of reports created by users who are no longer active. Check whether the report is being used as a first step, and if it is, ask the person or the function running the report to create their own copy of it and then delete the report created by an inactive user.

Another thing to mention under reports is custom report types. Completely eliminate the fact that your existing custom report types cannot meet the reporting need before creating new report types. Large numbers of report types confuse end users when they are creating new reports and cause a maintenance nightmare because, for example, when a new field is added to the object, custom report types don't automatically get updated and require that you update the report type, field by field.

Create report folders and give access to your users through roles or other options that are available for sharing reports. If there is no folder structure, users will be creating reports in public folders, which makes it difficult to find the report a user needs to run. One approach for report management using folders is to create folders for each function, for example, marketing, sales, pre-sales, and finance. Another approach could be to create folders based on hierarchy, for example, an executive reports folder has all the files that executives need, with another one for directors, senior managers, managers, and so on.

Using multiple business logic tools for an object

Another metadata management practice to keep in mind is to avoid mixing a lot of tools on a single object. Take, for example, a workflow on a custom object, which already has two process builders, a flow and a trigger that has a `before update` trigger to validate data before it gets saved to the database. All of these can cause a real challenge in understanding the flow of data and cause unexpected errors. Depending on the use case, consolidate your business logic in a single trigger that can gracefully handle your business requirements. This is one of the few places where code should be used rather than clicks.

App proliferation

Pay attention to creating too many apps. Look for synergies between apps where possible and use permission sets to control access. For example, if there is a special price request, consider consolidating this with your sales app. Requiring users to switch between apps diminishes a great user experience and confuses them. In one organization, there were more than 20 apps for the sales team that were used in different parts during the sales process, but required additional training for users, not to mention the maintenance that was required for their upkeep. In rare situations, I found some apps had overlapping functionality, too, because they were developed over a period of time, and analysis to ascertain that a similar functionality didn't already exist wasn't undertaken.

Multiple triggers on single objects

This is not supposed to be a discussion of development best practices, but I feel this one item needs to be mentioned. Do not put multiple triggers on the same object. Instead, use trigger handlers or other frameworks to handle your logic. The reason I mention this point here is the sequence of when these triggers run cannot be controlled and it can lead to many data issues. For example, if you have a couple of developers independently working on multiple business requirements that are deemed to be best met via a trigger on the `Opportunity` object when a developer is done with their part, they promote their trigger to production and, after a few weeks, the second developer gets their trigger promoted to production. If the business logic depends on one trigger firing before the other, there is no way to control that. Sometimes, a trigger coded by the first developer may fire first and other times, the trigger coded by the second developer may fire. Another downside is that governor limits will be shared by both triggers, thereby raising the possibility of the code erroring out due to query or timeout limits.

External IDs

External IDs, if used properly, can be a very powerful tool for managing data. Use them when integrating Salesforce with external systems. They allow you to have a single version of the record between Salesforce and the external system. For example, when integrating products from SAP into Salesforce, the unique product ID in SAP can be stored in an external ID field in Salesforce. Any subsequent updates to the product in Salesforce can easily be made using that external ID. This avoids creating duplicates in Salesforce and makes pushing updates into Salesforce easy.

Naming conventions for metadata

Naming conventions are applicable to both data and metadata. If possible, have naming conventions and standards developed before implementing your Salesforce org. If this is not possible, try implementing naming conventions for configuration and development going forward, and, in the case of existing metadata, make a point to add this to your backlog and slowly work through it. Having standardization across this can reap many benefits and increases velocity. Consider, for example, a complex flow that has no description and the name is so ambiguous that it doesn't give any indication of what it does. Just to get the gist of what it does can take a significant amount of time. Similarly, if a class is named such that it doesn't give any indication of what it does, or worse, has no header comments that give the purpose of the class, you would need to look through the code just to get the gist of the class.

As mentioned, this can be very time-consuming, and note that any analysis or design work to fix the bug or enhance the flow or the class hasn't even started yet. Hereunder, I offer guidance on how best to name components in Salesforce. I will provide a general guideline, followed by an example of how not to name these components and then an example of how to name them. This is so it becomes crystal clear in terms of what to do compared with what not to do:

- **Lightning Flow (LF)** and **Process Builders (PB)**: Lightning flows and process builders should be prefixed with *LF* and *PB*, respectively. Then, proceed with the triggering object name and, in the case of an autorunning flow, use *Auto* and then give the process a descriptive name that's specific and conveys the gist of the process. As a rule of thumb, use verbs to describe the actions that your components are used for rather than nouns; for example, *set* field, *create* lead record, and so forth, rather than lead record creation, acceptance email, and so on.

  Do: *PB – Opportunity Set Custom Forecast Field, LF – Lead Update Lead Owner, LF – Auto Send Survey* – Clear names that denote whether the flow is a process builder or lightning flow, along with the functionality of the process.

  Avoid: *Update fields, Set forecast__c, Create child record v3* – Unclear names that don't reflect the intent of the application. It is unclear how the process is triggered.

- **Public groups**: Ensure group names are meaningful, complete, and specify the application name where applicable. Use the application name followed by the specific group of users or roles that the group contains.

  Do: *Data Governance – Midwest Data Stewards, Data Governance – Director and Above Approvers* – Denotes the application, along with the users or roles that are in the group.

Avoid: *Public Group 1, Role Groups* – It is unclear who the users are or what application the group is used with.

- **Email templates**: Email template names should be complete, meaningful, and have the application name they are used in referenced in the email template name. Use folders to group your templates for applications rather than storing them in the public folder. Start with the application name followed by the purpose of the template and the subject of the email template. If the email subject is very long, use a shortened version.

  Do: *Data Governance – New Account Request – Inform Data Steward* – Clearly identifies the application and the purpose of the email template, followed by its subject.

  Avoid: *Template 1, Send email, Inform record owner* – These are all examples where the intent and purpose of the email template are unclear.

- **Permission sets**: Where possible, permission sets should be used over profiles as a best practice. Given that permission sets are used to open access to objects, system permissions, or application permissions, the name should reflect that as well. For objects, it may not be possible to list all the objects in the name, in which case the permission set description should be used. Try to use a verb at the beginning and indicate the essence of the permission set. If it's an application-specific permission set, use the name of the application and the role of the user the permission set will be assigned to.

  Salesforce has recently released a new feature called permission set groups, which allow you to group permission sets for easier administration. Similar considerations should be applied when naming permission set groups that are applied for permission sets.

  Do: *View Setup, Read Only Sales App, Create Leads, Data Governance Stewards, Invoicing Administrator* – Different examples of naming permission sets providing the gist of the permission set.

  Avoid: *Permission Set Western Region, Quote Permission Set* – Use of the phrase *permission set* is not needed as we already know it is a permission set. It is unclear who the users are or what application the permission set applies to.

- **Report and dashboard folders**: Ensure that you have really good controls regarding report and dashboard naming conventions and general administration of these components because things can quickly spiral out of control with them. Train your users and encourage them to use report filters, rather than creating multiple copies of reports for each quarter, fiscal year, and so on.

Unless there is confidential data, encourage the use of report sharing between business functions. This way, users don't need to create new reports unless it's required and it increases collaboration between business functions. This can be done using folders. You can name them by business function or by usage. Another tip is to keep all reports that are used on a dashboard in a single folder for quick access, troubleshooting, and enhancements. Here are some guidelines for report folder naming conventions:

Do: *Data Governance – Records Management, Corporate Marketing Reports* – These represent clear names based on the application or the general purpose of the reports in the folder.

Avoid: *All Reports, General Reports, Europe Reports* – It is not very clear in terms of what reports are stored in the folder and who uses them.

- **Profiles**: Typically, profiles are named using the role that they would be assigned to. That makes it easier to get an idea of what the profile does just by looking at it. As mentioned earlier, use permission sets as much as possible in favor of profiles, unless they are absolutely required.

  Do: *Sales Operations, Service Supervisor* – Clear and ambiguous names that indicate what the profile does.

  Avoid: *Custom Profile for Users, New Profile* – Ambiguous names that don't convey any idea of what the profile is about. Also, there is no need to mention the term profile because we already know what the profile does.

- **Validation rules**: There is a limit to how many characters can be in the validation rule name, so you may want to abbreviate some of the terms but ensure not to do that at the expense of the name. The guideline for validation rules is to use the field name followed by a phrase to sum the purpose of the validation rule, followed, in turn, by the condition when the validation rule should be triggered in brackets.

  Do: *Loss Reason Required (Stage=Lost)* – Clearly indicates that the loss reason field is required when the stage is set to *Lost*.

  Avoid: *Validation Rule for Opportunity Record, VR for Account Object* – Unclear, repetitive, and ambiguous names that don't convey meaningful information.

- **Roles**: The key thing to remember as regards roles is that they don't need to reflect the business' HR hierarchy; rather, the role hierarchy controls data visibility and certain aspects of reporting, for example, the *My Team* hierarchy. Roles must never be named after a user's name.

Do:

- *Manager, BDR* – Clearly identifies that the role is for a manager in the **Business Developer Representatives (BDR)** team.

- *Sales Rep, Western Region* – Identifies the region that the sales rep is assigned to. It is meaningful and indicates that there are possibly other roles under this role reporting to it and that would assist in figuring out any data visibility issues.

Avoid:

- *Sales Rep 1* – Generic and doesn't convey any meaningful information.

- *Strategic Operations and Research VP* or *Business Applications Analyst* – An HR job title that should be avoided in roles.

- **Custom objects**: When naming custom objects, avoid the use of acronyms and abbreviations and, for application-specific objects, specify the application abbreviation or short name at the beginning.

Always avoid naming a custom object the same as an existing object because that can cause a lot of confusion during configuration and later use by end users as well. If you have to use a name that matches an existing standard or custom object, suffix the name with an asterisk (*) to indicate that it's a custom object. The system will not let you save a custom object API name if one already exists, but it won't do that for labels, so ensure that the labels are distinct as well. Also, make sure to populate a description every time and provide sufficient details on what the object's intent is. Also, keep in mind that the label is for the user and the API name is used by admins and developers, so they should be appropriately worded.

Do:

- *Quote** – Indicates that it's a duplicate version of another object, standard, or custom. For example, you may find that the standard `quote` object doesn't meet the needs of the business and a custom `quote` object is required.

- *DG Meeting Requests* – Indicates the abbreviation of the application, in other words, data governance and the object name.

Avoid:

- *Local* – Ambiguous and doesn't give any indication of what the object is for.

- *Svc Defs* – Meant to indicate that the object stores service definitions, but the name is ambiguous and unclear.

- **Custom fields**: These follow some of the same rules for custom objects. The API name can be long and descriptive and is preferred over using abbreviations and acronyms. Always use clear descriptions that provide sufficient detail of what the field is about. To provide guidance to users, fill in a value in the help text attribute of the field.

Do:

- *External ID* – A short name, but conveys the information that the field is an external ID field.

- *Platforms Used* – Provides clear information as to what the field is used for.

Avoid:

- *New Field* – A label that doesn't provide any meaningful information.

- *FTL* – Ambiguous and unclear as to what this means. If you must use abbreviations, then enter the expanded form in the help text attribute and the description attribute.

- **Workflow rules**: The name of the workflow should be defined as the object the workflow is on and the triggering event of the workflow. Avoid acronyms as much as possible and use whole words. Use the description field to elaborate on what the workflow rule is and the actions it performs. Avoid putting actions that the workflow performs in the workflow name field as those can change, which would require an update to the name rather than the **Description** field being used.

Do:

- *Opportunity – Stage Changed* – Notice how the name has the object that the workflow rule is on and the triggering event. Just by looking at it, you can tell that the workflow is triggered when the **Stage** field changes. If you have multiple fields triggering the workflow, it may not be possible to write all the field names, in which case use the field that is the most important in the process.

- *Sends an onboarding email to the customer when the Stage field value is set to "Won" and checks off the "Onboarding Completed" checkbox on the account record* – This is an example of a description that describes what the workflow actually does.

Avoid:

- *Send email and update record* – This is an example of the name of the workflow. It's very generic and doesn't provide sufficient meaningful information. Also, the workflow actions are described in the name.

- *Sends an email and updates the record* – This description is again generic and doesn't provide any specifics unless the workflow is explored further. It is very challenging to even get an idea of what it does.

- **Field update**: Since this is setting fields to new values, use the convention of *Set field name – new value of the field*. This allows the viewer to determine at a glance which field is being updated. Use whole words and, if required when space is limited, well-known abbreviations can be used. Always use the description field to provide details on what the field update does.

  Do:

  - *Onboarding Completed – True* – Describes the field and then the new value that is being set.

  - *Update the onboarding completed checkbox to true* – This example of the field update description provides sufficient details to the viewer at a glance.

  Avoid:

  - *Stage Set to Booked* – In this example, this is describing the triggering event, and not what the field update is actually doing.

  - *Stage is set to booked* – This description doesn't provide the details that the user can use to determine what this field update does and whether it is used anywhere else.

- **Approval process**: Similar to workflow rules, use the triggering event in the name rather than the actions. That way, you have flexibility in terms of updating the actions later on by adding further approval steps. Use the *Object – Triggering Event* convention for approval process names.

  Do: *Quote – Credit Terms Approval* – An example of an approval process name. Notice how it starts with the object that approval is on and the approval function. In this example, we are assuming that not all quotes need to be approved, but rather those that have credit terms requested on them.

  Avoid: *Approval and Rejection Email Process* – Contrary to our aforementioned example, this shows the actions the approval process will perform rather than providing an understanding of the intent of the approval process.

- **Approval step**: Use the convention similar to the approval process described previously, but in place of a triggering event, provide a description of what the approval step does.

Do:

- *Quote – Credit Terms - Sent to Finance* – Describes the object that the approval step is on and what action is being performed and why. In this case, it is being sent to the finance department because the quote has credit terms requested by the sales rep.

- *Opportunity – Royalty Deal – Sent to Sales Manager* – This is another good example because it clearly indicates that the approval is sent to the sales manager when the deal negotiated with the prospect is a royalty-type deal.

Avoid:

- *Approval Step 1* – Generic and doesn't provide any meaningful information.

- *Dollar threshold* – Provides some meaning that a dollar threshold is being exceeded, but insufficient details.

- **Apex**: Since Apex is used in many ways (triggers, classes, controllers, and web services) on the platform, I will cover some of the more common components here.

  - `QuoteAttribute` – Indicates a class name.

  - `QuoteAttributeSvc` – Use the suffix `Svc` to indicate a service class.

  - `AttributeTrigger` – The name of an individual trigger used on an object called `Attribute`. Use the suffix `Trigger` for a trigger.

  - `AttributeTriggerHandler` – Indicates that this is a trigger handler for the `Attribute` object. Use the suffix `TriggerHandler` at the end of the name.

  - `QuoteUtil` – Indicates that this is a utility-type class. Use the suffix `Util` for a utility class.

  - `QuoteWS` – Used to indicate that this is a web service class. Use the suffix `WS` for a SOAP web service class.

  - `QuoteREST` – Used to indicate that this is a REST service class. Use the suffix `REST` for a REST class.

  - `quoteAttributeCmp` – Indicates that this is a **Lightning Web Component (LWC)**. The `Cmp` suffixed at the end is used to show that this is an LWC component.

Now that we have looked at metadata and guidelines on naming commonly used metadata components, let's look at some practices regarding data.

Data best practices

It's no exaggeration if we say data is increasingly becoming one of the most important assets an organization has. We looked at an example earlier of how poor data can lead to time loss and cost companies significant amounts of unrealized revenue. There are processes and tools that you can use to ensure that your data stays as clean as possible and viable for continued use in your company. Keep in mind that these are best practices and should be considered within the context of your Salesforce organization, business needs, and drivers. In the following sub-sections, we will look at the guidance that you can use for data in your organization.

Leads and contacts

Ensure that leads and contacts have valid information in them. This can be done by running reports to check whether at the minimum either an email or phone number exists. Keep in mind that this a guideline only and for your company, it may be a set of criteria rather than one field. Do the same thing for contacts but apply more rigor to contacts than you did for leads. This is because, in most Salesforce implementations, **Accounts** and **Contacts** are mastered in Salesforce and you want to make sure that your data is reliable especially if it will be fed to downstream systems such as BI systems.

Inactive owners

Ensure that records are owned by active owners. Having records owned by inactive users can cause issues with data visibility, scheduled reports, and dashboards. Salesforce has tools to mass transfer records to a new record owner when the current owner needs to be deactivated. One tip is to freeze the user account, perform the transfer, and then completely deactivate the account. When doing record transfers, also ensure that any default owner fields are also updated. This will ensure that any processes running under the current owner don't error out and, by freezing the user account, it protects the system from unauthorized access by the user. Default owner fields are a *catch-all* that prevents records from falling through the cracks and allow processing to continue smoothly; for example, **Default Workflow User**, which is displayed when the user that triggered the rule is not active. Or, in the example of cases, a **Default Case Owner**, which Salesforce automatically assigns as the case owner when a case doesn't match any criteria defined in the Case Assignment Rule.

Orphaned contacts

Unless you are using personal accounts, there is no reason to have contacts that don't have a corresponding account. When this happens, Salesforce considers that contact as a private contact and allows access to the contact owner and administrators only. I suggest creating a dummy account, *Account for UNKNOWN Contacts*, and link any contact that doesn't have an account to this dummy account. That way, users will have visibility regarding these contacts and can work their way through either linking them to the correct account or deleting them from the system.

Contacts that move

Ensure that you have a well-documented plan on how to handle contacts that move companies. This can be a real source of pain for marketing and problematic for sales as well. Ensure that you have a good process in place and then enforce it. Options include using the **Contacts to Multiple Accounts** functionality, prefixing the contact with *MOVED COMPANY* or *NOT VALID*, or some indication that the contact is not valid. I don't recommend merely updating the contact's info, including the customer account information, because that can lead to all sorts of problems. When that's done, all the contact history, notes, events, and tasks get moved to the new account, which can be very confusing for someone who is referring to the contact later.

Record types

When you have existing records on an object and then you create a new record type, existing records will not be assigned the record type. Instead, going forward, new records will have the record type assigned depending on how many record types there are and the default record type. Make sure that you update existing records and assign the appropriate record type because otherwise, this can lead to a host of other problems with business logic tools, such as Process Builder and validation rules.

Naming conventions

Have a naming standard for your organization for key data elements. A very common example is *opportunity*, and there are numerous ways in which you can name an opportunity within the same organization but implement a consistent process, train your users, and remind them frequently. For a company that sells machines and focuses on categorizing its customers based on an industry such as mining, construction, and government, a good naming convention could be *MIN-ABC Inc-2020* to indicate that the customer is in the mining industry, the customer's name, and then the year when the opportunity was created.

If Salesforce is the master for accounts, consider having a standard to use for names; for example, using legal names where possible. This may not be possible at the beginning of the sales process when an account is created from lead conversion but, at the time of the quote, this can easily be enforced when you can ask the prospect to provide their exact legal entity name. Be careful though because data-enhancing services may not use the precise legal name, so do your analysis beforehand and understand what data they have and how it will impact your existing data. Another benefit of using proper account names is that it helps in duplication rules. For example, a sales rep created an account, *Harley Davidson*, and another one created an account called *Harley* or *Harleys*. Assuming that the duplicate rule is set to an exact match, it will not run and consequently lead to duplicates in your organization.

Don't underestimate the importance of naming conventions because they help in keeping the data organized, deliver consistency, and make it easier for admins to manage data. This can also help to keep your data accessible to others when a sales representative leaves the company. Consider a company where sales representatives don't enter full contact information, including names, but rather enter some random strings in the last name field to keep the contact information to themselves, so no one knows exactly who they are talking to. Now, if they leave the company, there may be unfinished business with the customer or, worse yet, they may take this customer's contact information to their next company, depriving the company they left of potential future revenue.

We have discussed metadata and data management quite extensively, but this discussion will not be complete without talking about backup and recovery strategies and some tools for doing that.

Introducing data backup and recovery

Backing up your data should be a critical part of your business continuity plan. In the Salesforce ecosystems, many organizations don't have consistent backup processes and tools implemented. The thinking usually goes that *Salesforce is backing up my data, so I don't have to*. This is a myth because Salesforce doesn't provide data backup and recovery services. I believe some people confuse Salesforce's near real-time data replication with providing backup services. Real-time replication is Salesforce's way of ensuring high availability for customers, and for maintenance and compliance purposes due to hardware failures or power outages.

When you log in to Salesforce, your instance is actively served from a location referred to as the active site. At the same time, any transactions that are happening are replicated to another instance in real time, but at a completely different physical location. This instance is referred to as *the ready site*. If the active site goes down, Salesforce seamlessly directs customers to the ready site. Because the data is replicated in near real time, the chances of customers losing data if the active site fails are very low. If a customer loses data due to human error or a flow deletes data, Salesforce will replicate that over to the ready site as well, so data replication should not be viewed as a data backup service.

Salesforce did have a data backup recovery service that was discontinued in July 2020. This was a costly service ($10,000 per incident) and took a lengthy amount of time (around 6–8 weeks) to provide the data. Even then, Salesforce couldn't guarantee the recovery of 100% of the data, which highlights the need to have your own fully implemented and tested data backup strategy. Salesforce provides tools that you can use to back up your data, but it is up to you to implement these tools and test your backups on a regular basis.

Although we have discussed data here to mean records in `Account` and `Contact` objects, and records in other standard and custom objects, backing up metadata is no less important. This is because admins and developers with the right level of permissions can inadvertently update configuration changes, such as fields, field types, page layouts, Apex code, and other developers' metadata. Salesforce doesn't track a lot of these metadata type changes and if you don't have a backup, you won't be able to restore to prior metadata.

Before we do a deep dive into data backup, we need to understand why it's important and the benefits of backing up your data.

Reasons to back up data

As mentioned earlier, some Salesforce users have misunderstood that Salesforce completely protects their data because it's in the cloud. No doubt, Salesforce has implemented robust processes and tools to back up and recover data in case of a catastrophic event, but it doesn't cover all the reasons why data could be lost in the first place. Ultimately, the customer is the custodian of their data, and not Salesforce, just as you would be responsible for the data if you had it in a data center.

This and other reasons below will elaborate on why it's important to back up your data and not rely solely on Salesforce.

Human errors

Most data loss errors happen because of **human errors**. This can result in the permanent deletion of your data without the person doing it even realizing what they have done. A few years ago, a Reddit post mentioned a user trying to update a few thousand records but they forgot to set the desired record type on those records. The platform automatically sets all the uploaded records to the default record type. When the person realized that the uploaded records had the incorrect record type, they proceeded to run a report for the default record type and subsequently deleted all of the records under the default record type.

The problem was that there were a large number of records with the default record type that also got deleted. The user then uploaded the initial load again with the correct record type. The mistake wasn't realized until the next day when it was discovered that a large number of records were missing. These and other scenarios like this can happen and can be very costly to the business.

Retired Salesforce data recovery service

As mentioned in an earlier section, if you were counting on having your data recovered by Salesforce, the data recovery service has not been available since July 2020. In this case, if you don't have a backup of your data and lose data, you will have to either rely on old backups (provided you have some) or rekey the data from other sources, for example, invoices and orders, but that may not be possible for leads or for data that is not in other systems. Even if the data recovery service was available, it was a less than optimal solution because Salesforce couldn't guarantee data recovery; it was just limited to transactional records, metadata was not included, and it would take 6–8 weeks to recover that data. The data was also in CSV format, not to mention that it would cost your organization $10,000 per incident.

The Recycle Bin

Salesforce does have the Recycle Bin, with which you can restore records in the event of adversity, but the Recycle Bin shouldn't be considered a backup solution because it can restore deleted records. If you have unintentionally updated records and want to restore those records, the Recycle Bin will not help you.

It's also worth pointing out that the Recycle Bin holds records for 15 days, after which point, they are deleted automatically. With the Salesforce data recovery service retired, once this happens, there is practically no way to restore that data.

Salesforce outages

Salesforce outages can lead to data loss, and this has happened in the past. In 2019, an unruly script gave view and modify all data permissions to instances that had integrated with Pardot. This incident came to be known as *Permageddon*, and caused admins to lose permissions in their orgs. The reason was Salesforce deleted all permissions that were affected to protect customers' data. It was a rude awakening for companies that didn't have metadata backups in place and admins had to manually recreate profiles and permission sets for their organization.

In another instance in 2016, a crash on one of the instances, NA14, caused a few hours of customers' data to be lost and it could not be restored. Salesforce has an excellent track record of protecting its customers' data but, despite the best of intentions, things can happen, and customers should be prepared for all scenarios.

Salesforce recommends backing up

In this help article (`https://help.salesforce.com/articleView?id=000334121&type=1&mode=1`), Salesforce recommends that customers develop a strategy as part of data management and back up their data regularly, and the platform has tools that can be used for this purpose. These tools are designed to execute data imports, updates, deletions, and so on, but there are lots of third-party tools that specialize in data backup and recovery and make the process simple and easy to implement.

Quick recovery from catastrophic events

When a catastrophic event happens, leading to potential data loss, your priority is to restore your business operations to provide an ongoing service to your customers. Having a data backup strategy that is well thought out and tested gives you the peace of mind that recovery will be quick.

Migrating data

When migrating data, having backups gives you the ability to restore data if the migration goes south. In certain situations, it can also provide you with the ability to retry your loads in a sandbox environment before executing the data migration in a production environment. For example, if you have large amounts of data for a new application that you want to load test before promoting to production, you would need to use the full sandbox, which can only be refreshed every 30 days. If you need to run your migration a few times after tweaking and refining it each time, you can use your backups to restore data in the full sandbox and conduct your testing.

Compliance and regulatory policies

Depending on the nature of the business, the jurisdiction, and its laws, there may be requirements to retain data for a certain period of time. You could take a backup of data and store it in an offsite or cloud location and reference it when needed. A company had more than a decade of invoicing data in its system and required 7 years' worth of data for compliance purposes. They still wanted to keep the rest of the data, but not on the platform, and used backups in CSV format to back up data that was older than 7 years and stored it in a cloud location. They then performed a few iterations of testing to ensure that their processes and the tools they were using if they needed to reference that data were meeting expectations and then proceeded to remove the data from the platform.

Threats becoming more sophisticated and malicious

As technology becomes more prevalent and AI becomes more common, data-related attacks will continue to evolve and become more sophisticated and malicious. In 2019, the *Global Risk Report* listed data theft and fraud in the top five global risks. Having a robust and well-tested backup strategy can help with these threats and ensure the continued operation of your business. An **Small to Medium-sized Business (SMB)** in 2014 got hit with a ransomware attack, where its previous estimates for the last 10 or so years that were on a senior estimator's computer were lost. There was no backup of the data and therefore no way to recover it, except to pay the ransom, which the company decided not to pay. Given that the company operated in an industry where there were a handful of very large multi-billion dollar customers, and it was critical to have estimates available from previously completed similar jobs, this was a significant hit to the company.

Reputational risk

There is a real cost associated with reputational risk, just as there is a monetary value linked with goodwill. It can be a bit challenging to put a direct cost on this, but studies show that customers start to move away from companies that they cannot trust. Imagine if, during Permageddon, Salesforce decided not to delete the affected permissions to protect customer data and users had access to unauthorized data, would that be a worse outcome or the fact that the admins had to rebuild permissions for their organization?

Data loss via integration

Consider a scenario where a company has been preparing for months to launch a product globally with multi-country advertising campaigns and then, just days before the launch date, an integration runs and corrupts some of the data that was to be used for the campaign. Not only would it lead to productivity loss to recover that data from backups (assuming they are there), but it would also delay the launch of the product, thereby impacting timelines and costing the company money and lost revenue.

Natural disasters

Although this is less likely to happen and something that Salesforce has thought of and is responsible for, natural disasters can, and do, happen. When a natural disaster strikes, you want to have your own peace of mind that your data is backed up and available for restoration.

Point-in-time recovery

One additional benefit of doing backups is that you can do data comparisons to understand what has changed. For example, field history tracking keeps data for up to 24 months, but if you need to compare data prior to that, that won't be available unless you are using Field Audit Trail, which retains historical data for up to 10 years.

Now that we have looked at the reasons why you should back up your data, we will dive into how you go about doing that.

Devising a strategy for data backup

A key item to determine as part of a backup strategy is to have a rough idea of how much it's going to cost if access to some or all of the data was lost, and the cost of replacing that data if it is lost permanently. This is where the **Recovery Point Objective** (**RPO**) and **Recovery Time Objective** (**RTO**) are important. The RPO defines the amount of data you can lose before a successful restore happens, whereas the RTO defines the amount of time a business can be without access to the data. The first one is a key driver in determining how frequently the backup should be running and the RTO is a key consideration for how much downtime you can afford when you don't have access to your data. It is important to note that the RTO and RPO mentioned here refer to the portion of the data and metadata that the customer is responsible for. Disasters that happen in the infrastructure for which Salesforce is responsible have very efficient RPOs and RTOs because their infrastructure is set up in a redundant configuration.

There are other factors that will influence your strategies, such as data security, scalability (think large data volumes), compliance, and regulatory policies. The backup strategy is also driven by the nature of the business. Consider, for example, the fact that RTOs and RPOs for a global e-commerce site will be very sensitive compared to those for a website for a small single-branch laundry business.

In this section, we will review some of the key considerations for a backup solution. This is intended to be used as a guideline and, depending on the industry of your organization, you may have some other considerations when selecting a backup solution. There are many backup solutions on the market and unless you have very specific requirements that cannot be met by these, chances are you will be implementing an off-the-shelf solution (the buy versus build principle). I have listed the considerations here, bearing this in mind.

Costs

This is usually the first aspect that comes to mind when looking for a backup solution. Although it's an important factor, you should really look at the cost from an investment point of view, in other words, what is it going to cost me to make an investment to protect my data? Some backup solutions require a simple setup, but others may require expertise that you may need to pay for, so take that into consideration. Another factor related to cost is understanding the technical and contractual limits of the solution. For example, are there any limits and associated costs for going over a certain storage limit? Do you need to purchase API calls from Salesforce in case you are using a Professional edition or if you reach limits with an API call? Also ascertain whether there are any infrastructure-type investments you need to make, for example, buying additional Amazon or Google storage to host your backups.

Security

This should be a top concern when choosing a backup solution because you want to ensure compliance with all federal, local, and any policies defined by regulatory bodies. Some other things to consider include whether the backup is encrypted at rest and whether you use your own encryption keys. The location of where the backup is stored is another important consideration. Usually, government agencies in Canada prefer not to have their data stored in the USA due to certain US laws that allow access to that data.

Another important factor is whether the data is stored on-premises or in the cloud. If you are using a third party recommended by Salesforce, does the said third party maintain its own data centers or procure services from another vendor. Physical access to the data is another factor, so you would want to consider who can access your data and what controls are in place to protect this data from unauthorized access.

Can you readily access audit logs, not just for internal controls, but also for when your systems are audited? What is the retention period for backups, and does it align with local laws and policies defined by your organization's privacy officer? What authentication mechanisms are in place to access the backup and do they align with your enterprise's security policies?

Service levels

You want to ensure that the solution is capable of taking backups in a reasonable amount of time. In large organizations with users spread across time zones, if the backup is taking too long and is not properly optimized, performance can be impacted and slow down operations for business users. What are the RPOs and RTOs defined for the service, and do they align with your disaster recovery plans?

Another consideration is support, whether you are using a third-party backup solution or hosting your backups in a data center. What are the SLAs around that and do they align with your organization's expectations? When using a third-party solution, what kind of monitoring is in place to ensure that backups are not failing due to, for example, infrastructure issues?

Ease of use

These are considerations related to the use of the solution. You want to understand how much manual intervention is required for the backup because ideally, you want to set it up once and then review your configuration and perform any necessary tweaks once every few months.

Another key consideration is the frequency of backups. Can you set up on-demand, hourly, daily, weekly, monthly, or annual backups, and how much involvement would this require from you? This can be useful when you back up your production environment before a Salesforce release is applied to it. Given that the dates for the next three releases are published in advance, you can easily set up your schedules to take place specifically before the release gets applied to your organization.

You also want to understand the architecture of how the backup solution you are planning to implement operates, because typically they require external fields on the objects you want to back up. Would you need to create these fields or does the solution create the fields for you? Although Salesforce makes allowance for a large number of external fields (25 at the time of writing) per object, you still want to confirm that there aren't any objects in the organization that have reached the limit or will exceed it if your selected solution is implemented.

The key users of your backup solution are Salesforce administrators, and you want to make sure that the solution is intuitive enough and not overly technical so that admins without in-depth technical knowledge can still use it. Another consideration is the availability of material to train new admins and understanding the ramp-up required to train new users.

One important factor is that the solution should be able to detect metadata changes on the Platform automatically or with minimal effort. For example, if new fields are added to an object, the solution should be able to add those fields for backup without requiring extensive intervention. This now brings us to versioning, which is a key factor when restoring data. For example, you made a change to a field from a text to a number and then to a phone type, and each time you took a backup before making the change. You now have a need to revert the field to text, along with the data that was there. This example demonstrates the need to have robust versioning available with the solution that you implement. Ask the solution vendor how they support versioning over multiple API versions, especially over releases.

Solution comprehensiveness

This is related to understanding how complete the solution is with respect to its offering. We will discuss in more detail the types of backup and restores in later sections, but things to consider here include whether the solution can back up data and metadata:

- **Data and metadata backups**: Some solutions only offer data backups, which then necessitates the need to get another solution or develop one internally for metadata backup. Similarly, can the solution perform both data and metadata restores, and how complete are they? Are big objects supported in the backup, and so on? One solution I reviewed in the past offered limited metadata restore capabilities, which meant that we had to implement processes for the metadata types that didn't back up for a comprehensive restore strategy.

- **Multi-orgs and Salesforce releases**: You will also want to consider how the solution works with multi-orgs if that is your requirement and how it works with Salesforce releases. Understanding the process your solution vendor takes to ensure its product will work with the next release is crucial as well. I have been in a situation where a vendor for a DevOps tool took more than 4 weeks following a major Salesforce release and during that time, automated processes for **Continuous Integration (CI)** stopped working. The chances of this happening are less with a backup solution due to API backward compatibility, but you should review this thoroughly with your backup solution provider.

- **Solution completeness**: Another very important consideration is the completeness of the solution in terms of backing up records and relationships. For example, can the solution back up accounts and associated objects that are, in turn, parents to other child objects. How many levels deep can you go for backup and restore? This is crucial if you have a complex custom application or if you are using Salesforce **CPQ (Configure, Price, Quote)**, which has many levels of nested relationships.

- **Data restore**: Understand any limitations in terms of the scope of objects that the solution can back up and restore. Do not assume that just because the solution can back up a certain item of data or metadata, it can also restore it. Document and validate any assumptions you make with the provider. Discuss with the vendor how the solution can be tested and perform different tests, such as backing up and restoring your production organization in a full sandbox organization. Attempt other tests, such as restoring a single record or data for a specific application. Again, discussing your requirements with the solution vendor will allow them to advise on what tests you should perform and the areas to focus on. When evaluating the solution, ensure that you are keeping your **Disaster Recovery (DR)** plan at the forefront because you want to align your solution with it. For example, does the RPO or RTO of the solution fall within the values specified by the DR plan?

- **Version comparison**: Another aspect that can be valuable is to understand whether the tool offers organization comparisons, both in terms of data and metadata. This can be very handy in synching organizations, but also in warning you in the event there are major differences in the metadata that would cause the backup to fail. Another consideration when choosing a backup tool is to check whether the tool allows you to seed sandboxes, which can alleviate the need to have another tool just for that purpose. Once a restore has been completed or a sandbox seeded, you also want to understand whether the tool has reports or logs allowing you to compare your data in the organization versus data that was in the backup.

Performance

This is a critical factor when choosing a solution and, as we mentioned earlier, you want to minimize any performance issues for your end users when they are actively using the organization. This can be a challenge in very large organizations that have users in multiple time zones because there is no real *downtime* when the organization is not being used at its peak and most users are offline. You could easily overlook data to be backed up in this case because users are still creating new records in the system.

For example, you started a backup at 09:00 GMT and a user in another region created an account and a contact. The contact record will have a missing account ID because when the backup starts for contacts, it won't find the relevant account for the contact. Your solution must be able to support the fine tweaking of the backup processes to prevent the adverse performance of the organization. This can include the ability to execute parallel backup processes, tweaking the degree of parallelization, the number of fields and records, and so on.

Most backup solutions these days use the Bulk API, which is optimized for large data volumes and can process millions of records per hour, but there are limits and you want to ensure that the solution can adequately support your backup and restore requirements. Another factor is whether the solution uses Bulk API 1.0 or 2.0. There are differences in limits between the two versions that could be material for your purposes.

The solution should also give you some measure of how many API calls will be used and you will want to ensure that it is within the range of calls you have available. Just because a solution uses the Bulk API doesn't mean that it is architected the same way, so you want to guarantee a solution that can adequately meet your needs, not just today, but also in the future, as data volumes scale.

In the next section, we will review the different types of backup.

Types of backup

In this section, we will look at the different types of backup and the use cases for them. There are three types of backup that can be performed:

- **Full backup**: The scope of this is all data, including metadata. This backup provides the peace of mind that all your data is backed up. The downside is that because it's a full database, restoring a subset of data can take a lot of time.

- **Incremental backup**: The scope of this type of backup is that any data that has not been backed up since the last full backup will be included in an incremental backup. In this type of backup, it is much quicker to retrieve data from a certain point in time. If this is restored, the system may not have all the related data and, in order to recreate that, a full backup restore would be required. Then, all the subsequent incremental backups would need to be applied to get to the point just prior to the data loss. This also depends on the frequency of data backups, as backup jobs are running 24/7, but rather are scheduled jobs. This approach would also be adopted when doing a major deployment to production and you want to mitigate risk by taking a backup of your data and metadata.

- **Partial backup**: This is a very specific type of backup that aims to back up a subset of data, for example, all open opportunities. This is ideal for archiving purposes, but the downside is that it may not have all the related data with it; for example, in the case of opportunities, products that were part of those opportunities may not be included.

Organizations usually use a combination of these backup methods, for example, schedule full backups on a weekly basis but incremental backups daily. To archive data and keep the operational part of Salesforce manageable, they may schedule a partial backup.

Now that we have looked at the different types of backup, let's review data restore, some considerations relating to it, and nuances when restoring data.

Restoring data

We have discussed the considerations and the types of backup, but without an effective recovery strategy, your data backup is of little use. There are different options when restoring data and you will need to determine which restore approach is the most appropriate for your use case. For example, if data on the Contact object became partially corrupted on a certain date, you don't need to do a full data restore for that. Instead, you could just do a partial restore from your backup of that date.

Let's first look at some use cases of when a data restore can be handy.

Missing data

This is the most obvious use case for data recovery. When your data gets corrupted and you need to restore it, data recovery will be handy. Some tools will allow you to go back in your backup versions, pick the date of the backup, and simply restore the data from that date. This can be really handy when data has been incorrectly updated or deleted.

Sandbox seeding

During projects when you have a need to seed your sandboxes, in particular, developer and developer pro-type sandboxes, you can simply restore data from your backup into your sandbox. Compared to using tools such as Data Loader and figuring out relationships and the order of insertion, this can save a lot of time and effort.

Citizen development

If you have citizen development at your company, most of the time, citizen developers will need a sandbox environment that has some data to start with. Having the ability to selectively restore data from a backup can be very effective and make the citizen development process efficient. Certain tools can back up and restore data with very complex relationships. For example, **Configure, Price, Quote (CPQ)** applications have complex data models that sometimes have circular references for certain objects and deep parent-child relationships. In one scenario, I was working with very capable business users who had previously worked with Salesforce and one was even certified, but our citizen development process was slowed down because we couldn't seed a sandbox with CPQ reference data that the business could work with.

We will discuss the different types of data restores, but let's understand what happens during the restore process.

Nuances of the restore process

One of the challenges of a restore process is that you will not have all your data restored like for like. This is because the Salesforce system is not a point-in-time static system, but a dynamic system and, by design, the data in your backup versus the data that gets restored will not be the same. For example, the values for the `CreatedDate` and `LastModifiedDate` fields will be different as data transformation will happen (Salesforce now allows a way to migrate exact values from the source system for these two fields). Let's look at some of the transformations that are possible:

- **Audit fields**: `CreatedBy` and `LastModifiedFields` are two fields that can change, but `SystemModStamp`, which is recommended to be used for integrations, will also change.

- **IDs**: Record IDs will also change, along with the user ID type fields. Therefore, `CreatedBy` and `LastModifidedBy`, assuming the restore is being done in a different environment, will also change. Any automation that is running off these fields will need to be updated if it has hardcoded values in it.

- **Autonumber fields**: If you have `Autonumber` fields on the object, when a restore is done, those numbers will change and could have an impact on downstream systems if these fields were referenced.

- **Automation**: Any automation you have in your organization, such as triggers, validation rules, and workflow rules, can make changes to your records. Some of these can cause the recovery process to fail, so it's important to take measures to ensure that the restore completes automatically.

The goal should be to minimize these transformations as much as possible so as to have a reliable data restore. The overall recovery process should be viewed as a multi-step process and at each step, certain things must get done to ensure an accurate and reliable data restore. Here, we go into each of these in more detail:

- **Establish your dataset**: This is the first step and an important one. You want to make sure you have a very clear idea of what you want to restore and what the end result should look like. What are the *from* and *to* dates for the data restore? From your selected dataset, are there any exceptions to the records that shouldn't be restored? For example, when restoring Opportunity records, you want to restore only those that are in the pricing negotiation stage.

- **Pre-processing**: This step involves adjusting any settings that could cause data transformation or cause the restore process to fail; for example, turning off triggers or deactivating validation rules. Some of the things that can be done in this step are as follows:

  - **Turning off validation rules**: Turn off validation rules on the objects that you are trying to restore data for. That will help to speed up the process and eliminate any chances of the restore process failing due to the hard stops when validation rules are triggered.

  - **Turning on audit fields**: These refer to the `CreatedDate`, `LastModifiedDate`, `CreatedBy`, and `LastModifiedBy` fields, which are used to reflect when a record was initially created and updated. The last two fields reflect who created the initial record and the user who updated it last. When restoring data, you want to ensure that the *Create Audit Fields* permission is turned on so that data gets restored with the correct audit field values. This is important if you have, let's say, workflow rules or process builders running off of the `CreatedDate` field. Loading data with the current `CreatedDate` field, which is the default behavior, can impact your business processes. Keep in mind that the audit fields cannot be updated once entered and are only available through the APIs.

  - **Synchronizing metadata**: Often, a restore would fail because the data and metadata do not align between the backup and the organization in which the restore is being done. For example, an opportunity stage value was deactivated in the environment recently, whereas in the restore, the data still exists for that stage. At the time of restore, it will try to restore that stage, but when it cannot locate it in the environment, it will throw an error.

  - **Turning off automation tools**: Make sure to turn off automation tools such as workflow rules, process builders, flows, and triggers that can cause significant transformation when data is being restored.

    - **Changing autonumber fields**: This is another area that can cause the restored data to be transformed. Make sure to change your **Autonumber** fields to the **Text** type before starting the restore as that will ensure that the data gets written the same way it is in the restore.

- **Data restore**: This is the execution step where data will be written back into the organization. Having the right tool to do the job at this stage can be of tremendous help. Imagine if you had to do a simple restore for Accounts, Contacts, and Opportunities and had half a million records in total. This can be done via Data Loader, but it can turn out to be a very cumbersome and painful process.

- **Post-processing**: This step involves reverting those settings that were made in the pre-processing step, specifically, settings such as activating validation rules, turning on triggers, process builders, and flows. You will also want to flip the **Autonumber** field back to **Auto**, making sure that you give it the correct format and a starting value. You will also want to ensure that the *Create Audit Fields* permission is removed from the profile or the permission set.

- **Verification**: This is the final step and involves verifying your data restore. Barring the items that we know would have changed, for example, formula fields, you will want to focus on whether the total number of records from the backup and the restored data matches. Then you can filter down on the restored dataset and compare a few other fields, such as **Stage** if it is opportunities, the **Status** field for cases, and so on. Again, having a tool that assists with verification activities can be a huge time saver, otherwise, be prepared to spend hours verifying the restore before it can be declared successful and operations can return to normal.

Let's look at some tools we can use to help us with data backups and restores in the next section.

Backup and recovery – tools of the trade

In this section, we will discuss some tools that are widely used for backing up and restoring data. As you will see, some of these are native and free from Salesforce, while others are third-party AppExchange applications. These are just a handful of tools and the list is not exhaustive by any means, nor is it an endorsement of any one tool. We have already discussed factors that may influence your decision-making, including costs, and those should be used as a guide to determine the most optimal tool for your organization. Note that I didn't say *best* or *cheapest*, but rather *optimal*, which means balancing the needs of your organization with practical constraints such as costs, the nature and size of your business, and data volumes.

Let's start with the native tools from Salesforce.

Data Export Service

This is a UI-based tool within **Setup** that allows you to either schedule or manually run backups of your data. It allows you to select the objects you want to back up and is limited to data only; metadata is not included in this. The on-demand export can be run every 7 days. Limitations include not being able to run an export from a sandbox environment and there is no restore mechanism, so you will need another tool to restore the generated .csv file to the org. Export files are held by Salesforce for 48 hours only (excluding weekends) and then they are deleted.

Data Loader

This is another free tool from Salesforce that can be used for both backups and restores. You can run this on-demand or schedule it using the command-line interface. Data Loader is a powerful tool that supports the Bulk API and can be used to export up to 5 million records. Beyond that, Salesforce recommends using an AppExchange partner for backups and restores. It is also limited to data only and metadata is not covered. Other limitations include an inability to export attachments, so you will need to use Data Export Service or another tool for that, and you cannot export compound fields with Data Loader. Remember that compound fields are fields that are a combination of other fields, for example, address or location fields. Data Loader can export individual fields that make up the address or location fields.

Odaseva

This is an AppExchange partner tool that was designed by a **Salesforce Certified Technical Architect (CTA)** and is a robust tool that can be scaled and used in small to very large Salesforce organizations. It provides both data and metadata backup and restore capabilities and supports the Bulk API along with other Salesforce APIs.

OwnBackup

This is another well-known backup tool that supports both data and metadata backups and restores. It also supports the Bulk API and other Salesforce APIs for backup and restores.

I have mentioned just a few here, but there are many other companies, including Skyvia and Spanning, that offer these services. Again, when evaluating these solutions, consider the factors we discussed earlier to ensure that your requirements will be adequately met.

Summary

In this chapter, we started off by defining data and information, understanding why data is valuable, and then the benefits of data management. We took a deep dive into understanding how increasingly valuable data is becoming for organizations with the advent of machine learning and AI. We looked at some of the challenges associated with data management. This should have given you an appreciation of why data is critical and managing it effectively is an essential element for the continued success of an organization.

Next, we reviewed the data life cycle and an example within the context of Salesforce and the various operating models that are in use today to facilitate data management. We also discussed best practices associated with managing data and metadata in the context of Salesforce and what steps we can take as data architects to make data management easier. Equipped with this knowledge, you can start to gradually implement best practices and avoid the pitfalls that materialize when data is not properly taken care of.

In the last couple of sections, we reviewed backup and recovery in Salesforce, why it's important to implement processes, and explained, barring certain scenarios that relate to infrastructure management, how protecting data is the responsibility of the customer. We discussed why we should implement a robust and well-tested backup and recovery strategy and then reviewed the key considerations when choosing a backup solution. The discussion around Salesforce discontinuing the data restore service and the other reasons we discussed will hopefully have provided you with a list of good reasons to implement robust backup and restore plans. Ensure that these plans have also been through several dry-runs to iron out any wrinkles in the process.

In the next chapter, we will look at MDM, which is becoming critical as companies grow and their data volumes grow with them, along with a plethora of different systems that are part of the system landscape in a reasonable-sized company.

Questions

1. **Precision Printing (PP)** has been using Salesforce for 15 years and has a very mature DevOps process. They developed a custom quoting solution on the Salesforce Platform that has served them well over the years, but it's showing signs of aging and requires significant maintenance efforts.

    PP's management has decided to implement the Salesforce CPQ solution. What options should the architect propose for the legacy solution when Salesforce CPQ is live in production?

    a) Remove all users' access and keep the legacy solution running. Users will just forget about it.

    b) When the Salesforce CPQ-managed package is installed, it will automatically remove the legacy application from the organization.

    c) Migrate or archive any data from the legacy solution. Then, proceed to remove all legacy objects, Apex code, Visualforce pages, and other metadata associated with the legacy solution.

    d) Run both solutions at the same time and give users the option to choose which one they want to use.

2. NewTech Inc. promoted their sales operations manager to a Salesforce admin position and asked them to implement Salesforce. The new admin excitedly watched a few admin videos on YouTube and completed some trails to ramp up their knowledge of Salesforce. They proceeded to implement the organization and successfully rolled it out to the sales team.

    A few months later, sales executives are complaining that reports do not show any meaningful data, except for long sentences entered by sales reps, while some critical decision-impacting fields are coming across as blank. What can the admin do to fix this problem (select two answers)?

    a) Do nothing as the complaints will just go away. As more data is entered into the system, the reports will start showing good data.

    b) Convert **Text Area (Long)** fields to a simple **Text** type field.

    c) Review the **Text Area (Long)** fields with the sales managers and identify opportunities to convert these into restricted picklist-type fields or multi-select fields.

    d) At the page layout level, mark the critical decision-impacting fields as required.

3. A new architect has joined XcelTek Solutions and has been tasked with improving adoption by the sales team at the company. XcelTek Solutions has most of its business running on Salesforce, including sales, sales operations, HR, recruitment, and legal.

    A preliminary analysis by the architect reveals that there are seven Salesforce applications for overlapping functionality that the sales team uses to complete 90% of their sales. What can the architect suggest to improve adoption?

    a) This is normal; you can have more than seven applications, too, if that's what it takes to do business.

    b) Complete an analysis of the functionality offered by each application and analyze whether the functionality can be merged between applications, thereby reducing the number of applications that the users have to be trained on and use.

    c) Move the functionality of these seven applications to Heroku and have a custom UI in Salesforce that pulls/pushes data from and to Heroku.

    d) Remove six applications and leave just one for users to use, thereby making it easier for them to learn and use the single application.

Section 2: Salesforce Data Governance and Master Data Management

This section will discuss master data management, the quest for the golden record, and how to align your MDM strategy with CRM. Later on, data governance, its multiple facets, and how GDPR compliance can be achieved with Salesforce will be considered. The latter parts of this section will discuss performance in Salesforce and how to use the query plan tool to understand how your data will perform on the platform.

We will cover the following chapters in this section:

- *Chapter 4, Making Sense of Master Data Management*
- *Chapter 5, Implementing Data Governance*
- *Chapter 6, Managing Performance*

4
Making Sense of Master Data Management

In the last chapter, we looked at data management, its importance, and the different aspects of data management. There are many types of data and not all of them are treated the same way. This is especially true now, given that sources of data have been increasing steadily over the last few years. Earlier data was mostly structured and easily manageable, but with social data, machine-generated **Internet of Things (IoT)** data, sound and video data, and much more, it is becoming increasingly important to ensure that the data that is core to your business is identified and managed properly. In this chapter, we will discuss **Master Data Management (MDM)**, different types of MDM data, its attributes, and why MDM is important.

We will also be discussing the Golden Record – the much sought-after record that accurately and comprehensively provides a single customer view. Next up will be the MDM and CRM strategy and the different ways that you can ensure that your **System of Record** and MDM can interface with each other. We will close the chapter by discussing Customer 360, the suite of products from Salesforce that tries to solve the MDM problem, along with other tools to deliver a complete and accurate picture of the customer.

The topics covered in this chapter include the following:

- Understanding master data
- The Golden Record
- MDM and CRM strategy
- Customer 360

By the end of this chapter, you will have a solid understanding of master data, its importance, and why the Golden Record is critical for data management and for organizations in understanding the customer's relationship with the organization. You will understand the correlation between the MDM and CRM strategy and the suite of tools that Salesforce provides to help achieve these business goals.

Understanding master data

In this section, we will first start with the definition of master data, the need to identify and manage master data, and the different types of master data. This is going to help us in our later discussion of the Golden Record and in the MDM and CRM strategy sections.

So, let's dive right in and define master data.

What is master data?

Master data can be defined as the data that describes the core entities of the business. This can include customers, suppliers, locations, leads, and so on. A good indication of whether a data element is master data is to review its use across multiple business functions, processes, or systems in the organization. For example, leads that funnel into the marketing team, once qualified, will flow down to the sales team. Once a deal has been won, the same lead, which is now a customer, will flow down to sales operations and in this instance, eventually into the ERP's contracts module as a customer. Sharing master data eliminates the need for each function to maintain its own list and facilitates uniformity across business areas.

We should note that master data is owned by the organization and not by a particular business function or department. This is important because master data requires stewardship, and this sets the context to communicate the right mindset in the organization, implying that everybody is responsible for master data. Otherwise, specific area or data specialists are left to clean up the data and ensure its accuracy, while users creating the data don't feel the same level of ownership and accountability.

The need for master data management

We established in earlier chapters that the volume of data has been growing and organizations are finding it challenging to keep pace with the volume as well as the sources of data. A typical organization will have dozens of different systems spread out and with their own proprietary data formats and ways to allow access to data. This is especially true for large organizations that are siloed and don't have effective master data management tools and processes in place. This can lead to the following challenges:

- **Data governance**: Mater data management and data governance go hand in hand. You cannot implement an effective data governance strategy unless you have identified and fixed any issues with master data. For example, a company has five **Customer Relationship Management (CRM)** systems across three regions as a result of acquisitions over the years. Some of the customers exist in multiple CRMs, with slight differences in addresses, phone numbers, and so on. Unless you can identify which is the most accurate and comprehensive record, enforcing data governance rules will not make a difference.

- **Reporting**: In the example stated in the previous point, how do we know who our high-value customers are if they have the same names, but with slight variations. For example, is *Precision Printers LLC* the same as *Precision Printers Inc* or *PP Inc*? Another example is if we have, say, five subsidiaries of a company but they are not identified as related to each other via an account hierarchy, and that knowledge sits in someone's head. Unless that person is around, we may be duplicating our marketing efforts and wasting time and money sending the same marketing brochure five times.

- **Integrations**: Integrations can become challenging when there is no consistent and accurately identified master data because, in a downstream system, which record are we going to send? For example, downstream call center software requires customer contact information. Based on the caller's phone number, the application matches it with the customer information sent by the upstream system and displays it to the call center agent, along with support levels and some other pertinent information. The customer contact information is held in CRM, but also manually entered in the ERP system. If we haven't defined which system is the source of truth and has the most accurate customer data, chances are we will be sending the incorrect customer contact to the call center system unless we incorporate additional logic in the interface that can send the correct information to the downstream system.

> **Downstream and upstream systems**
>
> In the context of integrations, downstream and upstream mean destination and source systems respectively. For example, if an ERP feeds product data into the Salesforce CRM and Salesforce has an integration with a call center system, then from the perspective of Salesforce, the ERP is regarded as an upstream system and the call center system is a downstream system.

- **Customer service**: In our call center example from the previous point, poor customer service could be a direct consequence of a lack of effective master data management. In this scenario, if the customer called in and the call center software matched it to the incorrect customer name or priority level, the customer experience with the call center would be less than optimal, resulting in a potentially disgruntled customer, if the SLA shown by the software is incorrect.

- **Realizing revenue targets**: Imagine going to a big-box store to purchase a laptop and you find the price tag at the store is different from the flyer you were mailed. Usually, the store will match the price on the flyer, but have you ever thought about why this happened in the first place? It could very well be a printing error, but could also be a master data problem. If the product pricing for the flyer was sourced from a different system than the one used by the store, a pricing discrepancy could arise. Now imagine if the price on the flyer was not intended to be 20% lower, the company just lost revenue, and for large volume stores, this can easily translate into hundreds of thousands of dollars, if not more.

- **Maintaining and growing customer trust**: A lack of effective master data and controls around it can lead to less customer trust. In one instance, due to a lack of effective master data management practices, branches were cannibalizing the company's own business by offering different prices for the same parts and repair services to reach their sales targets. Customers had less trust as a result and when they needed a repair, they would call three to five different branches to get the lowest possible quote. This happened because the manufacturer was continuously updating the pricing for parts and sending it over to the dealer. The dealer, in turn, was responsible for sending it to the branches, which then updated their rate sheets. Sometimes, the rate sheets were not updated for weeks, resulting in price discrepancies and, hence, revenue loss for the business.

- **Regulatory compliance**: Effective master data management can also lead to regulatory reporting and compliance issues. For example, how do you make sure that you have effectively removed all data for a specific person after receiving a *right to be forgotten* request if you don't have effective master data management processes in place to identify all possible instances of that person in the first place? Non-compliance with these regulations can be a costly business for organizations, not only in terms of bottom-line revenue but also reputation.

- **Data quality**: When data is stored in multiple systems with many different formats and these formats don't integrate, the usability of that data decreases. Having an effective master data management practice ensures that your data remains viable and trustworthy for users. Another aspect of data quality is duplication. Having master data in place ensures that you have taken care of the duplicates and that you are accessing the single most accurate record. For example, if a business function enters customers in the ERP after they have been vetted by the customer credit team, but the sale team is also entering the same customer in CRM, there are bound to be issues with that data. With master data management, you can rectify these types of issues and merge the records, leading to good data quality.

- **Communication**: Communication between departments can become challenging when there is a lack of consistency in identifying master data. This is pretty common in product-based businesses where one business department calls the product something else, while another function prefers to refer to it by yet another name.

Now that we have looked at the challenges when master data is not managed properly, let's look at the types of data that organizations have.

Categories of data

A lot of discussions are taking place regarding how many types of master data there are. Some say it's three, some five, but regardless, we have established that master data is critical for business operations and is typically found across the organization, meaning that one system may have all the customer contacts, whereas another one may have all the products that organization sells, while yet another system may have all the referential type data, including currencies and so on. Here are the five data types that a typical corporation will have:

- **Transactional data**: This is data generated by business activity such as sales orders, quotes, and invoices. This data is of importance to the company, either for historical reporting, analytics, legal, or regulatory compliance purposes.

- **Metadata**: This is data pertaining to data. In the case of Salesforce, this constitutes standard and custom fields, workflow rules, triggers, report definitions, single sign-on settings, and much more.

- **Hierarchical data**: This is data that stores relationships between data; for example, charts of accounts, and organizational hierarchies.

- **Reference data**: This is data that defines a collection of valid values and is referenced by other data, for example, a countries list, currencies, payment terms, and so on. This could also be data defined by international, regional, or industry standards and used in the organization.

- **Master data**: This is the core data that, within the enterprise, describes business entities around which business operations are conducted. This data is relatively static and not transactional in nature. Typically, the critical areas that master data encompasses are products, customers, locations, and a fourth area that consists of contracts and entitlements.

Understanding reference data and master data

Reference data is the data that is used to set the context for other data in the organization. For example, the **Stage** field on the opportunity object is used in conjunction with the transactional data (the opportunity itself) or different currencies that the opportunity can be in. Currencies, stages, statuses, and countries are all examples of reference data. Reference data not only provides context to the transactional data (stages on the opportunity object) but also to master data; by way of an example, on products, a picklist value that identifies whether the product is active or not or the **Salutation** field on the contact object.

A key difference between reference and master data is that in an ideal world, the former doesn't require record linkages, meaning that multiple instances of a similar record don't need to be resolved, unlike in maser data. In reality, there may be multiple sources of reference data; however, every effort should be made to identify a single source of truth to avoid confusion and the proliferation of bad data. For example, an account name (master data) may be coming in from three different systems and needs to be linked together to provide a clearer picture of the data. This is usually not needed for reference data, since it is more stable and changes less often. This doesn't mean that there are no challenges associated with reference data. Reference data can originate outside of the organization and therefore the consuming organization cannot exert any influence over it. For example, *Dun & Bradstreet (D&B)* provides data enrichment services.

It maintains up-to-date data, and once integrated, it can push automatic updates into Salesforce. For example, if an organization has the **Industry** field on the account object synced with D&B and the latter decides to make changes to a specific industry, that could potentially have a downstream impact within the organization.

Solving problems via master data management

Earlier, we reviewed challenges that organizations face when master data is not properly managed. In this section, we will review some examples to gain clarity in terms of where master data management adds a lot of value. Keep in mind that a small business with 50 customers that operates on repeat business will not require an extensive master data management solution. This is because, as you will see in the next section, they will not face the problems that comparatively larger organizations or businesses that have growing data face. However, this should not be misunderstood as smaller organizations not needing to manage their master data, rather that they may not need the extensive tools and processes that larger organizations need. In the examples coming up in the following sections, we will look specifically at customer data, but similar issues exist for other master data, such as products.

Duplicate data

This is a common problem and usually arises in a **Merger and Acquisitions (M and A)** scenario. When a company acquires another company, unless the acquired company is in another continent or in a different line of business, the majority of the time, customers between the companies will be shared. For example, an auto dealership acquired another dealer's three branches that are in the same territory. Both dealerships use the same CRM, but suddenly, the company now has to deal with redundant data and decide what to do with it. Implementing robust master data practices and tools can help alleviate these types of problems.

Source of truth record

This can easily happen in Salesforce when the sharing model has not been well thought out and is locked to such an extent that a sales representative cannot search for an account that may already exist within the database before creating a new account. As a result, you may see accounts created in CRM, such as IBM, IBM Ltd., IBM USA (Consulting), IBM USA (Health), and IBM Healthcare Management Solutions.

Data standardization

This is common in situations where there are multiple CRMs and, let's say, the **Industry** field has different values in each CRM, or the **Customer Priority** field on an `Account` object has `High`, `Normal`, or `Low` in one CRM, but `Platinum`, `Gold`, and `Silver` in another CRM.

Hierarchies

This is a problem when data has been entered in the CRM or multiple CRMs and adequate attention has not been given to defining a hierarchy for customer accounts. For example, a large global company can have hundreds of subsidiaries in different lines of business. How can an organization that is a major supplier to this global brand, including its subsidiaries, determine how much total revenue the account is generating? How much revenue is generated from a region, a line of business, or a sales territory? Unless there is some sort of hierarchy defined that properly links the subsidiaries with the parent company, it will require a lot of manual work to arrive at the numbers. Apart from this, hierarchies offer some further benefits, including the following:

- **Revenue opportunities**: In Salesforce, we know about the account hierarchy, but I want to drill down on the concept of hierarchies and why they are important. Earlier, we looked at how hierarchies can help us answer questions such as who our top customers are. Who are the top customers in a region or a territory? However, the benefits of hierarchies are not limited to this.

  When having a comprehensive view, we can look for opportunities as well as any credit risk that a customer and its subsidiaries may carry. For example, *Precision Printers*, a global provider of printers and photocopiers in 150+ countries, has 47 subsidiaries. You are in negotiations with the company to renew the contract for another 10 years and you notice that one of the subsidiaries has consistently ordered large quantities of photocopiers in the last few years. You recommend including in the contract a special deal for that subsidiary at a discounted price if they order a minimum number of photocopiers every year. This type of insight would not have been possible in the absence of account hierarchies.

- **Product insights**: Given that you can have many different types of hierarchies, including product, supplier, and location hierarchies, forming hierarchies for these entities can reap benefits for the business. For example, a product hierarchy could help identify insights that could not have been achieved by using the product itself. For example, for a dealer selling heavy-duty construction machines and providing parts and maintenance services, a bucket attachment for a machine is a product that rolls up into a wheel loader (another product), which then rolls up into the construction machines category. Immediately, you can see how the bucket is related to the loader and the construction machines category.

  This information can provide us with critical questions, such as should we be selling the bucket as part of the loader, or is there an opportunity for more revenue by selling it as a separate add-on? How does our loader compare to the loader from a competitor? Have they included the bucket in the base price of the machine?

- **Accurate reporting**: Another benefit is that hierarchies can provide a baseline for comparison between systems. For example, in the ERP, you may have the bucket attachment and the loader as two different products, but in the quoting system, you have them as one product, with the prices added up to come up with a list price. In your **Business Intelligence** (**BI**) tool, you add the prices of all machines sold in two territories minus the average national cost of the machine to come up with the final profit for each territory. What you didn't account for was the added surcharge that the manufacturer is adding to deliver the buckets to one of the territories that is in a remote location. This can give you skewed numbers, thereby impacting your sales and marketing efforts.

To be clear, this work of creating and maintaining hierarchies can also be done manually, and some companies do that, but it is tedious and error-prone. Consider, for example, your data team bringing in data from the ERP, CRM, and other systems, and then transforming the data so a valid comparison can be made. With MDM, the process, once it is set up, is automatic and the MDM tool does the heavy lifting that otherwise would be done by the data team. It is important to note though that having an MDM will not completely absolve the organization from any human intervention because there are going to be scenarios where a data steward will need to make a decision to confirm the matching and merging of records, but the overall process will be much more efficient.

In the next section, we will review the factors that can help us to identify whether a data element should be considered master data.

Deciding what data is master data

Companies should pay a lot of attention to identifying what master data truly is, as a loosely defined criterion can lead to managing data that is not that valuable and this can result in wasted effort and time. Some types of data can be clearly defined as master data, such as accounts and contacts, but other types of data may not be that clear. The criteria defined here would help in those situations and should be used as a guide in deciding what is and isn't master data within your organization:

- **Behavior data**: This is when a subset of data is analyzed to observe how it interacts with other data. For example, in transactional systems, master data interacts with transactional data. As an example, consider that a customer buys a product (master data), or a partner requests a new location (master data) to be added. The relationship between the master and transactional data can be viewed in a verb/noun construct where the transactional data constitutes a verb and a noun captures the master data. In our previous examples, the act of buying a product or tracking the partner's request to add a new location would constitute transactional data and the records associated with that would be transactional data. Master data would be the product being purchased or the location being added to the system.

- **Life cycle**: Master data can also be described by **CRUD (Create, Read, Update, Delete)** operations on it. For example, due to the need to ensure that master data is created accurately and completely, some companies will put in stringent processes to create customer accounts. Reviewing business processes that emphasize the creation of certain types of data can help in identifying master data.

- **Cardinality**: Cardinality is the number of elements in a set and if there are a few elements in a set, then the probability of the element being master data is low. For example, if an organization only has three customers, then in the context of needing an MDM solution, this would not be considered master data. This does not diminish the value of the customers, as they are essential in order for any business to survive, but it helps in deciding what data to consider as master data. In contrast, an organization with thousands of customers and multiple source systems could definitely make use of an MDM solution.

- **Lifetime**: Master data is more stable and less volatile compared to transactional data; for example, contracts are typically categorized as transactional data. An HVAC (**Heating, Ventilation, Air Conditioning**) company doing plumbing work for 2 weeks may just treat their contracts as transactional data, whereas when working with a large commercial client, they may decide to consider it master data. The company may decide to consider the 2-week long job as master data, too, just because it is easier to deal with it in the day-to-day business rather than separating it out. Similarly, work order estimates may be considered master data because they provide valuable historical intelligence when dealing with repeat customers.

- **Complexity**: This is another factor that helps to determine whether an element should be considered master data. The less complex an element, the less likely it is to be considered master data; for example, a manufacturer that makes one type of generic school bags and supplies large retailers such as Walmart or Target would be interested in knowing the count of the bags on hand rather than the type and other details. Because there is only one type and color, there is not much to manage in terms of master data.

- **Value**: This category is slightly subjective and leaves the consideration of a dataset to be recognized as master data to the entity owning it. For example, if the company considers all contracts regardless of duration and value as important and places high importance on all of them, then most likely, contracts will be managed as master data.

- **Reuse**: Reusability of data is usually a driver behind managing a set of elements as master data. A very common example of this is customer data since companies strive to have a consistent definition of customer data and make it available for widespread use within the organization.

Now that we have looked at some of the factors that can help us to identify whether a data element is master data, in the next section, we will review a common scenario that Salesforce data architects face, which is to design solutions to manage master and transactional data when there are multiple Salesforce orgs in an organization.

Multi-org scenario

A common scenario that is played out in organizations using Salesforce is the use of multiple Salesforce orgs, which can contribute to an incomplete view of the customer and other data. Multi-org scenarios can be the result of mergers and acquisitions, or with very large organizations that have many sales and marketing teams, and it makes sense to have distinct Salesforce orgs. This is not the place to discuss when a multi-org strategy makes sense, but the decision to go with multiple orgs shouldn't be taken lightly. Please refer to a blog post from Salesforce that goes into more detail on this topic: `https://developer.salesforce.com/blogs/developer-relations/2014/10/enterprise-architecture-multi-org-strategy.html`.

As seen earlier, not having optimal visibility of customer data results in missed opportunities, both in terms of sales and service. In terms of sales, it could be customer contact by different sales reps in the organization that are using the disconnected orgs and, similarly, when providing services, the disparate orgs don't facilitate a full view of the customer, oftentimes leading to the customer receiving conflicting information from service agents.

In an MDM scenario, multiple orgs can be piped into the MDM system, so it can handle the records from different systems, clean them, and push them back into the source systems if it's a co-existence-type MDM implementation, which we will look at later. It goes without saying that in the absence of MDM, processes and tools must still be implemented to ensure that data is not just moved from one org to the next, but it is ensured that it is clean data.

However, in cases where there is no MDM in the system landscape, the issues we discussed in this section materialize, and a solution is required for smooth business operations. In the next few sections, we will review some strategies on how this challenge stemming from a multi-org scenario can be managed while delivering consolidated data that's required for reporting and analytics. It must, however, be understood that although this discussion is taking place in the context of master data management, it must not be seen as tied to master data only. In a multi-org scenario, you would still want to ensure that not only your master data but also transactional data is properly managed.

The main reporting org

This approach requires designating a Salesforce org as the main reporting org, where data from source orgs is rolled up for analytical purposes. *Figure 4.1* depicts this approach diagrammatically:

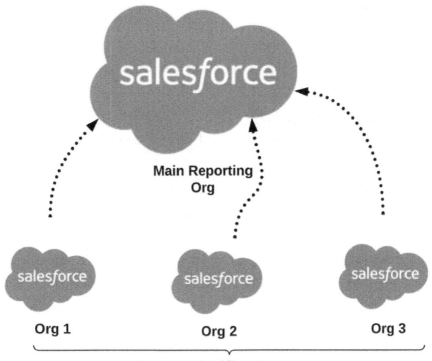

Figure 4.1 – Main reporting org

This master org doesn't send data back into the source orgs and reporting and is used to get that single customer record view. The benefits of this approach are as follows:

- It requires minimal changes to source orgs, as all the work is done in the master org.
- It results in an exclusive org that has clean and consolidated data for analytical purposes.

Some of the disadvantages of this approach are as follows:

- Manual and automated processes are still run from source orgs and do not benefit from the quality data that exists in the reporting org.
- Purchasing and maintaining another Salesforce org entails additional costs.
- The middleware that is needed to integrate the orgs entails additional costs.

As seen, this can be costly because of the need to maintain an additional org, but it has advantages over other models. Next, we will look at the parent org model.

The parent org

In this arrangement, an org is designated as the master org and is used for business processes and reporting. The child orgs report to the master org and data is synced between the orgs. The premise is that at any given time, data in all the orgs is synced. Some of the pros of this approach include the following:

- A single org for all business processing.
- Cleansed data exists in child orgs as well, leading to consistent data in MDM and source systems.

Some cons of this approach are as follows:

- This involves simple syncing, which can result in bad-quality data getting circulated in the systems.
- Additional costs in terms of integration processes and tools to keep the orgs in sync.
- It may require that multiple business processes are still maintained for each org.

As shown in the diagram, data is synced between parent and child orgs:

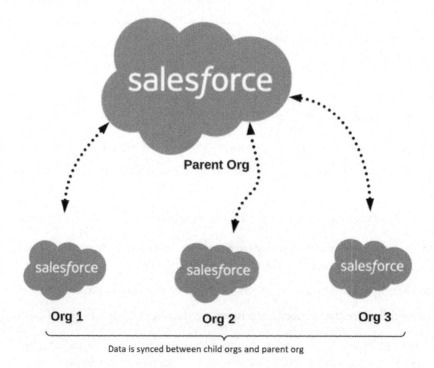

Figure 4.2 – Parent org model

The big benefit of this approach is the ability to keep all orgs in sync, but it requires fine-tuning and analysis to ensure that automation processes are run across the orgs.

The consolidation org

This approach requires that all Salesforce orgs except one are retired and data is consolidated into the main org. Some of the advantages of this include the following:

- Provides a single view of the customer
- Ease of maintenance
- Cost efficiencies via the consolidation of various orgs
- Effective central control of the main org

Some cons of this approach include the following:

- It could hit the org limits sooner.
- There is a potential for disruption to business users when they are moved to the consolidated org, especially given that Salesforce usernames are unique.
- It requires the recreation of business processes in the consolidated org.
- Massive volumes of data require multiple rounds of testing to ensure that data can be validated for accuracy and completeness.
- Consolidation-type projects are risky and costly in the short term.

As seen in *Figure 4.3*, one org is designated as the parent org and others are merged into it:

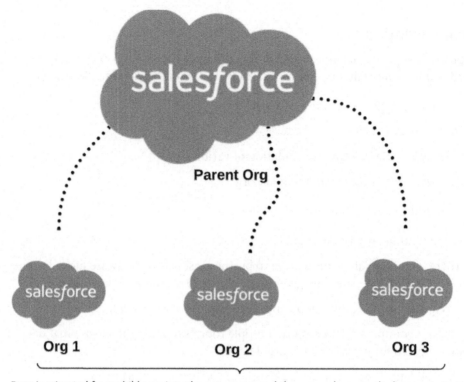

Data is migrated from child orgs into the parent org and they are subsequently decommissioned

Figure 4.3 – Child orgs are migrated into the parent org and then decommissioned

Whichever approach is chosen, make sure that you have considered the advantages and disadvantages of each approach within the context of your technical systems' landscape and business priorities. If reporting and analytics are key, then the main reporting org model may be more suitable, whereas if business processes are a priority, then the single consolidated org model could yield the most value.

Defining Master Data Management (MDM)

MDM is the technology, tools, and processes that ensure that master data is coordinated across the enterprise. It provides a consistent, accurate, and complete view of the data available to the organization and business partners.

In the next section, we will review basic concepts that can be helpful to communicate internally and externally when working on an MDM project. Having a clear understanding of these concepts will allow you to define your business requirements more precisely and provide a foundation that can be used to select the optimal solution for your organization.

Reviewing the basics of data quality

What comes to your mind when thinking about bad data? Is it that values in a **Phone** field are formatted the same way, or that a picklist is restricted so additional values cannot be entered? You may answer *yes* to all or most of these questions; these practices of ensuring that data is consistent and formatted properly are generally referred to as standardization and formatting. These form an integral part of a modern MDM system. An MDM system will allow you to define standards based on industry and business practices for each of your source systems. Let's review these practices in more detail:

- **Prevention**: The adage that prevention is better than cure applies to master data as well and we should be mindful of opportunities to prevent bad data entry in the first place. These are usually easier to implement and can be used to enforce certain data standards. For example, validation rules in Salesforce can be used to enforce good data entry practices, such as ensuring that a custom **Loss Reason** field is filled out if the opportunity is set to **Closed Lost**. In this example, if the loss reason is not entered and a sales representative tries to save the opportunity after setting it to **Closed Lost**, they will get an error. Similarly, a very common prevention method on the Salesforce Platform is the use of picklists. When you have checked the **Restrict picklist to the values defined in the value set** checkbox, users cannot add new values either through the **User Interface** (**UI**) or through the APIs. A third example of this is defaulting values in fields so that in the case where a user has not entered a value in the field, a default value exists.

- **Audit**: Another way in which data can be managed is by way of audits. Audits are often used to frequently assess and improve the quality of data and are an effective form of managing your master data. The downside is that audits are done after the data has already been saved in the database and may have been used elsewhere for reporting or integration purposes. However, this should not stop us from auditing our data frequently and there are out-of-the-box tools that can be used for this, or AppExchange apps to help with the audits. For example, after you have set up duplicate rules in Salesforce, you can run reports to detect any duplicates with your data and take appropriate action.

- **Correction**: Another approach commonly used during data entry is that of correction, but this is less used than prevention, mainly because of the rules that need to be defined and applied consistently. For example, a custom field on a lead object is used to capture the sales engineer working on the lead and, at the time of conversion, it gets read and entered into the **Opportunity Team Members** related list on the opportunity. A simple trigger, or preferably a Process Builder flow, can be used to accomplish this. Another example is updating the **Type** field from **Prospect** to **Customer** on the account object once an opportunity has been set to **Closed Won**. As you may notice, rules would need to be defined for each of these situations and at least in these examples, they are dependent on a value being present somewhere else before a correct value can be entered.

- **Deduplication**: This is a commonly faced business problem within organizations using Salesforce. This is because the nature of the CRM system is such that it has to have multiple data entry points into the system. Consider, for example, web-to-lead, marketing tools, and sales representatives uploading spreadsheets into the system, and the manual creation of records. All of these are distinct data channels into the system. Sometimes, even a single channel can cause duplication; for example, when a lead submits a web-to-lead form multiple times, this can create duplicate records in Salesforce. We mentioned earlier that if Salesforce record-level access security is not set up properly and the org is overly restricted, and a rep searches for an account and cannot find it in the system, they will create a new one, thereby establishing a duplicate. This is assuming that a record already exists in the system.

A key challenge with duplicated records is the numerous permutations that duplicate records could have, making it so much more difficult to correctly identify duplicates. For example, consider a contact record for *John Smith* with the address *123 Main St, Detroit MI*, a second record for *J Smith* with the address *Number 123 main street, Detroit Michigan*, and a third one for *John S* with the address *123 Main st, unit 7, Michigan*. Are these duplicates or different records? Reviewing the records carefully, we could safely conclude that these are duplicates, but how would you define rules so that when computer software reviews these records, it will correctly identify the duplicates? As this example shows, it can be quite challenging to correctly identify duplicate records, especially when the volume is in the hundreds of thousands of records.

One of the key functions of an MDM solution is to identify and resolve duplicate data as this is a critical step toward achieving a clean and trustworthy state for master records. This key function kicks in as soon as the data from different sources is consolidated in the MDM.

The first step in this process is to identify the duplicates, also referred to as matching. Typically, there are two ways in which this is done – a deterministic approach and a probabilistic approach:

a) **Deterministic approach**: In this approach, an exact match between data elements is sought and a score is assigned. This approach usually results in fewer matches. This is the ideal choice if unique values, such as Social Security number and social insurance number, are captured, but considering this is confidential data, customers are not willing to share them unless required. Therefore, the most commonly used fields include phone numbers, addresses, email addresses, and so on. This approach also introduces complexity as the number of data elements to match increases because that means requiring more matching rules. Excessive matching rules could result in performance degradation and a costly continuous cycle of maintenance.

b) **Probabilistic approach**: In this approach, matches are based on multiple criteria, such as phonetics, the likelihood of occurrence, and nuances. This approach uses weights to calculate the match score and employs thresholds to determine a match. This approach is more accurate in matching records. It is more suitable with a wider set of data elements that can be used for matching.

Once the record has been identified as a duplicate, the next step is to merge the duplicates to create the golden source, the single source of truth. The key challenge at this stage is which data elements from multiple records need to survive to form the Golden Record. This requires building some *intelligence* in the MDM tool to determine which elements should survive.

Key elements of an MDM program

It is crucial to understand that MDM is not a technological solution to a business problem. Although it will help, it won't solve all problems. This is a mindset that, if not recognized, can cause MDM projects to fail. The thinking that once we implement an MDM tool, all data problems will sort themselves out is just not realistic. A strong MDM program has key elements that must be implemented and adhered to, so the MDM investment of the organization continues to bear fruit and provide a high ROI.

The key elements of your MDM strategy should be the following:

- **Governance**: This is a set of directives that guide the organizational body, policies, principles, and qualities to promote access to accurate and consistent master data.

- **Measurement**: This involves setting **key performance indicators** (**KPIs**) to measure and continuously improve data.

- **Organization**: This defines the people and teams that will form data stewards, data owners, and those on governance committees.

- **Policy**: Requirements, policies, and procedures that the MDM program should adhere to.

- **Technology**: Selection, implementation, and management of the technology component of the MDM program.

Once an organization has defined what is considered master data, the next steps are to put an MDM program in place. The key steps in implementing an MDM program include the following:

- **Identifying sources of master data**: This step involves identifying all sources of master data. This is a critical step and should be thorough as, unsurprisingly, there may be multiple sources of master data, including in privately stored Excel spreadsheets, Word documents, and suchlike.

- **Identifying producers and consumers of master data**: This step involves understanding who produces the data and who its consumers are. Producers and consumers can be IT systems or humans.

- **Analyzing metadata regarding your data**: This step involves determining the attributes associated with the master data and what they mean. This can be an extensive step, especially if dispersed regions or business areas have different definitions of the data; for example, what defines a customer in the organization, or when does a new customer become an existing customer, because there could be processes associated with whether a customer is new or existing. Some of the attributes of master data that can be analyzed could include the following:

  - Attribute name

  - Data type

  - Allowed values

  - Constraints

  - Default values

  - Dependencies

  - Data owner

- **Appointing data stewards**: These are people who ideally have a well-grounded understanding of the data and can assist in maintaining master data going forward.

- **Implementing a data governance council**: This group has the authority to make decisions on how the master data is maintained, what it contains, how long it is kept for, and how changes are authorized.

- **Developing a master data model**: This includes deciding on what the master data looks like, including its attributes, size, and data type, what values are allowed, and so on; for example, in a large heavy equipment dealership, the parts department preferred to use the part number to look up parts, whereas technicians preferred to use the old part number because they had it memorized even when a new part number had been issued that superseded the old one.

- **Selecting the tool**: This is where you would select a tool for data cleansing, transforming, and merging data. The tools will have support for finding data quality issues, such as duplicates and missing or incomplete data. Typically, these tools will have a versioning mechanism, too, to track the history of the changes on the master data.

- **Creating and testing master data**: Once you have selected a tool, the next step is to create the master data and test it. You want to start with a small subset of data and ensure that your rules are properly configured and that the resulting master dataset is indeed what is desired. Once you have established that the rules are configured properly and generating the desired data, you can start loading in the rest of the data.

Creating master data

There are two basic steps involved in creating master data:

1. **Cleaning and standardizing data**: Before starting and cleansing data, you must understand the data model. You will have mapped each attribute from the master data to the source system. Some of the data cleansing functions include the following:

    - **Normalize data functions**: Make sure that fields have the same data and consistent formatting; for example, a phone number has numbers only and no text.

    - **Replace missing values**: Insert missing values, default values, and make use of services such as Dun & Bradstreet to fill in the gaps in your data.

    - **Standardize values**: Convert measurements to an agreed-upon system, convert prices to a common corporate currency, and so on.

    - **Map attributes**: Parse contact names into first and last names and move part # and part no to a **Part Number** field.

2. **Matching data**: In this step, you match the data records to eliminate duplicates. This step requires a lot of analysis and consideration since you can inadvertently lose data; for example, *John C King* and *John King*, entirely different contacts in a person account setup, are considered to be the same and important historical data is lost.

   The key is to match on more than one attribute and have an algorithm in place that calculates the likelihood of a record being the same as another record. When the match score is high and meets or exceeds the threshold, you can confidently say that the record is indeed a match.

In the next section, we will look at the different types of MDM implementation patterns, as well as their advantages and disadvantages.

Implementing MDM

In this section, we will look at how MDM can be implemented and the considerations for the different styles of MDM. Four implementation styles are used with MDM, mainly driven by whether the data is controlled from a central hub or the hub is synchronized from data sources. The reason this is important is that organizations need to have that single version of the truth. In an MDM implementation, the focus is on improving data quality, establishing data governance rules, and ensuring that data is easily managed and is available across businesses. The style you choose depends on the nature of your organization, business processes, and company goals:

- **The registry style**: This style assigns global unique identifiers to records in multiple systems that can then be used to define a single version of the truth. This system doesn't send data back to the source systems, so master data continues to be made through source systems. It matches and cleans the identifying cross-referenced data and relies on the source systems maintaining their own quality of the data. When a single version of the truth is needed, it uses a reference system to build a complete picture of the record. This style is useful when you have a large number of source systems and want to minimize disruption and significant changes in source systems. It is useful for situations where a read-only copy of the record is needed without the risk of overwriting any information in the source systems and avoids duplication of data in the MDM hub and source systems. It provides an efficient method to remove data duplicates and get a consistent view of your data.

Its low cost and relatively quick implementation, along with minimal changes to source systems, make it an attractive option. Here is a registry-style MDM depicted in a diagram:

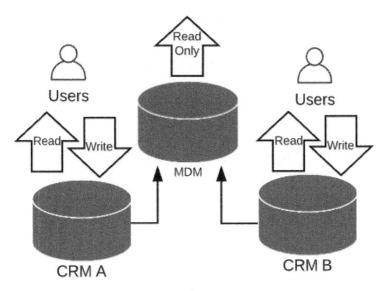

Figure 4.4 – Registry-style MDM implementation

Figure 4.4 shows data being read and written to each of the CRM by the users. The narrow arrows from the MDM into the CRMs depict the read operations that the MDM has to perform when a query is received.

The biggest benefit of this style is that minimal changes are required in source systems and therefore, it can be implemented in a relatively short timeframe.

- **The consolidation style**: In this style, data is consolidated from multiple systems into the central MDM hub. It is then transformed, cleansed, and matched, resulting in the single source of truth (Golden Record) that is then made available to downstream systems for use by other systems. This style is typically used for reporting and analytics. Here is what a consolidation-style implementation looks like:

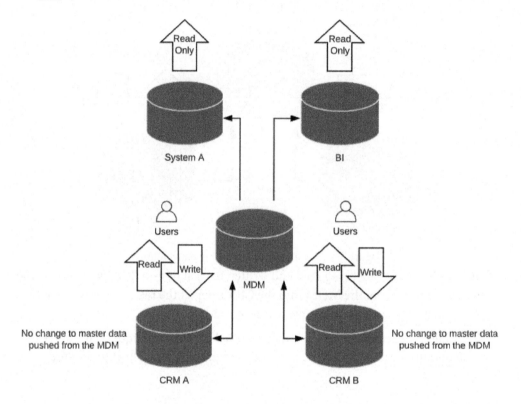

Figure 4.5 – Consolidation-style model

As seen in *Figure 4.5*, the MDM hub becomes the single source of truth for downstream systems. Any updates to the golden record are also written back to the source systems. However, source systems are not to manipulate that master data.

As the name suggests, this is a very involved process and requires data transformation, cleansing, and matching that requires extensive testing.

- **The coexistence style**: This implementation style is very similar to the consolidation style, but source systems are permitted to make changes to the master data. This means sending back the Golden Record to each source system, thereby enabling real-time synchronization between the MDM and source systems. The coexistence style is depicted in the following diagram:

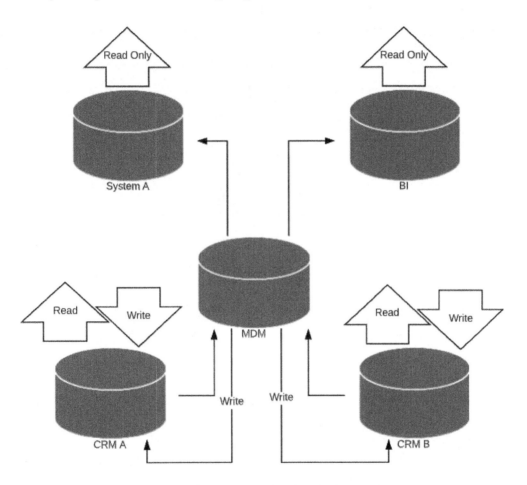

Figure 4.6 – Coexistence-style MDM implementation

As per *Figure 4.6*, this style is very similar to the consolidation-style implementation but this style allows the flexibility of making changes directly in the source systems.

In this style, the source systems are also updated alongside the MDM hub, which makes for consistent data across the systems. The downside is that any data errors will also get propagated throughout the system.

- **The transactional/centralized hub implementation style:** This is where the master data hub becomes the single source of truth and system of record and any system that needs access to the data must subscribe to the hub for up-to-date data. Systems other than the hub are not allowed to create or modify data. Rather, they get their up-to-date data from a single source, which is the hub. Implementing this style requires resources and time in order to be implemented because removing functionality so master data cannot be created in source systems can be costly and requires extensive testing:

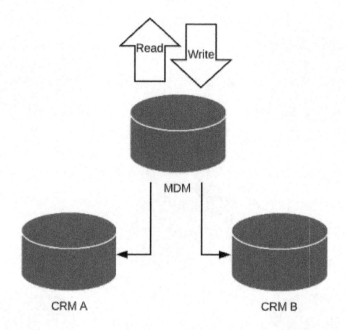

Figure 4.7 – Centralized hub-style MDM implementation

This type of style provides more control and cleaner data since there is only one point of data entry, but it is costly to implement and reduces the benefits from other systems that could have been realized if data was directly entered into the respective system.

Whichever MDM implementation you choose, one of the most important things you can do is to thoroughly understand and define the business challenges you wish to solve with an MDM implementation. It's important to have a clear understanding of the end goal of where you want to be with MDM, as implementing the wrong style and backing out can be expensive and a frustrating experience.

Now that we have reviewed the different MDM implementation styles along with the advantages and disadvantages of each style, next, we will look at the considerations for selecting an MDM solution.

Considerations for selecting an MDM solution

There are so many MDM tools out there and selecting the best fit for your organization can seem like a daunting task. One of the key steps that I recommend is to spend the time and define in reasonable detail what the objectives are that you wish to achieve by implementing an MDM solution. A common problem is that companies will jump right into selecting an MDM solution while not truly understanding what business problem(s) they are trying to solve, how it fits with the organization's short- and long-term vision, and what the other projects on the roadmap are that could have a significant impact on the implementation of your MDM solution.

Make sure that you have your business requirements defined and prioritized, which will help you to evaluate a solution later on. This can really help you cut through the fluff of vendor demos and sales pitches and prevent what I call the *bells and whistles pitfall*, in which the solution selection committee gets sold on the nice-to-haves rather than the core functionality that will add real value to the business.

This pitfall is easily avoided by having a solution selection scorecard that has scores for each of the key functionalities required based on the prioritized business requirements. For example, an important criterion in the scorecard should be ease of maintenance, as well as supportability. You don't want a solution that takes extensive effort and a specialized skill set for seemingly small problems and, at the same time, consider the type of support that the vendor provides for the solution.

Here are some key functional and technical capabilities that I recommend when choosing an MDM solution:

- **Integration connectors**: It is very important that the solution supports out-of-the-box connectors to interface with different applications, including Salesforce, otherwise you may find yourself spending time building MDM interfaces. For example, does the solution have a connector to use with SAP using, in Salesforce terms, clicks, or does it require one to be coded from scratch?

- **Deployment options**: Some MDM solutions offer on-premises or cloud-based solutions only. Look for a vendor that can support both and that has them integrated. The reason is because of the nature of master data, companies are still reluctant to move their master data completely into the cloud and a hybrid approach may work well.

- **Multiple domains**: The solution should support multiple domains rather than just one or a few domains; for example, ascertain that the solution can support products, customers, locations, and other domains that have been identified as master data.

- **Scalable solution**: Understand how well the solution can scale both horizontally, meaning in terms of the nature of master data that can be supported, and vertically, and the volumes of data that the solution can support.

- **Total Cost of Ownership (TCO)**: Drill down on what it would take to implement a select few use cases and then incrementally build the solution over time. Your objective should be to prove the value of MDM, which will help create buy-in and willingness on the part of stakeholders to see more use cases implemented. What sort of skills would be required to enhance the MDM implementation? Are these skills easy to find, or are they highly specialized and therefore costly?

- **Licensing model**: I cannot stress enough that this should be very well understood because some vendors charge more as your data grows, so ensure that you go through a sizing exercise before selecting a solution to understand what type of storage requirements you have. As your MDM footprint grows, how will your licensing be impacted, and are there any technical or contractual limitations that you need to be aware of?

- **Technology roadmap**: Understand the roadmap of the solution and where it is going in the next few years. Ensure that it aligns with your MDM strategy and your existing and future-state system landscape.

- **Architectural model**: As seen earlier, there are multiple topologies (co-existence, consolidation, registry, and so on) in which an MDM solution can be implemented. You want to ensure that your chosen solution can support different topologies rather than locking you into a specific topology. This gives your more maneuvering room to properly assess and select the topology that makes the most sense for your business. It also gives you the ability to leverage the tool in a new acquisition that may have similar complexity to your system's landscape.

- **Supportability**: Understand how the vendor supports its product. Given that MDMs form the backbone of business due to the critical services they provide, ask questions about **Service-Level Agreements (SLAs)** and details on past planned and unplanned downtimes for maintenance and patching. Check references from existing customers if possible and ask questions about what works and what's not working for them.

Now that we have looked at some of the criteria for choosing an MDM solution, in the next section, we will look at the Golden Record, why it's important, and some of its use cases.

The Golden Record

The Golden Record, sometimes referred to as the single customer view, is defined as that single data point that captures all the necessary information that we need to know regarding a data element. It is the most accurate source of truth that the organization has. For example, a customer record for Acme Inc. (a hypothetical company) may exist in multiple databases, and having that one record that is *the* most accurate and complete is what is sought after and desired in MDM.

A matching methodology based on business rules determines which record to keep and which ones to discard. Usually, three types of determining methods are used:

- **Most recent**: In this method, the record with the most recent date stamp is considered the most accurate and considered the Golden Record.

- **Most frequent**: This method defines that if the same information exists in more than one record, then that can be considered eligible as the survivor record.

- **Most complete**: This method considers field completeness as a criterion for the most viable record.

The problem with using these survivorship methodologies is that they are more reliant on superficial attributes of data rather than a solid understanding of the data.

For example, you could have two similar customer contact records and one is more recent than the other, but it has an invalid phone number. In this case, going with the most recent record will cause the Golden Record to have an invalid data element.

Another example is when, let's say, three customer contacts exist for the same contact and two are considered the most frequent because they have the same data elements. Assuming both have invalid phone numbers and the third record, which is considered infrequent but has a valid phone number, will cause the Golden Record to have an invalid phone number. These examples illustrate the importance of also using trusted, third-party data sources to validate and enrich your data.

Why is the Golden Record important?

Although we have looked at some examples earlier in the context of master data management, I want to look at another example here so we can understand the importance of the Golden Record. Suppose a customer, *Tony Alex*, went into an electronic store and purchased a gaming console. When paying for the device, they provided their name as *T Alex*, along with their address. Upon reaching home, they create an account on the store's website and register with their full name to receive updates and special offers from the store. Later, the store decides to mail a special holiday offer to Tony and because the store doesn't have the Golden Record, Tony receives two special holiday offers, one addressed to *T Alex* and the other to *Tony Alex*. Tony can only use one because the store policy requires the ID to be presented and only vouchers with names matching with the ID are accepted.

This is a simple example with only two input points that resulted in this discrepancy. What if Tony had also visited the website to access gated content and provided *Tony A* as their name? Then there would be three records in different databases, and what would we use to get to the single version of the truth? In this simplified example, we have a one-person record, but in a real-world scenario, we could be dealing with hundreds of thousands or millions of records. In this example, the business lost time and valuable resources that could have been put to good use somewhere else simply because the master data was not reliable.

So far, we have talked about the value of the Golden Record from a revenue perspective, but achieving that state and maintaining it where you have the single source of truth record is also important from a regulatory point of view. Policies such as the **General Data Protection Regulation (GDPR)** and **California Consumer Privacy Act (CCPA)** have some aspect of consumer access requests – it is the right of a consumer to request and receive full disclosure of all the data that the organization has pertaining to the consumer. This is simply not possible without having good master data management practices that lead to the Golden Record. Non-compliance with these regulations can result in heavy fines and penalties, thereby impacting the company's bottom line.

Detractors of the Golden Record

Although the Golden Record philosophy is widely accepted and implemented, the discussion around it wouldn't be complete if we didn't talk about an opposing view, which is that the pursuit of the Golden Record is not needed and that it's a flawed concept that needs to be revised. This is a theoretical discussion, but nonetheless valuable for consideration purposes. The premise of this argument is based on the foundation that there are closed and open **Information Systems (ISes)**. Closed ISes are systems that organizations develop themselves or are responsible for maintaining, whereas open ISes are systems that are developed and maintained by independent vendors. Organizations today are moving from using closed systems to open systems, which means that data federation becomes challenging because the format, structure, and other characteristics of data are different. In addition to that, additional sources of unstructured data are emerging, such as digital sensors, social media, and IoT devices.

In a closed IS, the organization knows the data precisely, including the meaning of data entities, attributes, and their dependencies between different systems. Integrations are relatively easy to build because so much is known via the data model of each system. In other words, data can easily be interfaced and federated by leveraging the data model of integrating systems. **Data federation** refers to bringing data from diverse and distributed systems to a single data store while implementing a common data model.

Many organizations today rely on a combination of on-premises and cloud systems and have various types of master data, such as that pertaining to customers, vendors, and products, in various systems, leading to fragmented data stores. Of course, MDM tries to solve this problem by combining all this data in one place, de-duplicating, and removing any inconsistencies, but the issue of the growing number of systems that may be partially **Systems of Record (SORs)** also complicates these efforts. Furthermore, data federation also becomes challenging due to synchronous and asynchronous systems in the mix, or automated processes that run at different times, and may have an impact on data federation processes.

The other flaw pointed out with the Golden Record approach is that it assumes a single version of the truth for the record and leaves out the contextual information or the metadata of the record. This is because getting to the Golden Record involves matching and merging data records that may be essential to retaining the context of that data.

The argument is that the context is important and applicable for the business areas where the data was produced, but in an attempt to get to the Golden Record, which can then be used organization-wide, we are sacrificing that important context that was useful to those business silos in the organization. The other assumption of the Golden Record is that even though various systems may have different data models, it is possible to develop a single data model for sharing data. This idea of harmonizing data forms the backbone of the Golden Record philosophy.

The contrary view claims that the meaning of data is contextual and subject to changes over time. For example, a Golden Record for a customer in the MDM system exists, but does a customer refer to the person who made the purchase, the user of the product where the delivery was made, or who paid the bill? Because these could be three different persons. This context would exist in CRM and the **Accounts Receivable (AR)** system.

If the person who made the purchase and had it delivered to their address is the same, but the product user is different, in MDM you will see two records – one for the person who made the purchase or had it delivered to their address, because they would get matched and merged, and the other perhaps for the person who is the user but without any context in MDM.

Another example to clarify this is the use of medical data for patient diagnosis. Suppose patient data, including prescriptions, hospitalization records, vaccinations, allergies, and other self-reported data, such as physical exercise and temperature, is stored in a data store. It is then federated using the Golden Record philosophy to a downstream diagnostic assistance system that is used by medical providers to view past data and assist with diagnoses.

We can see that this could lead to a seriously flawed diagnosis because the doctor may see an average number for temperature readings without knowing what time the reading was taken, the condition of the patient when the reading was taken, and any activity performed before taking the reading, while other relevant contextual details may also be missing.

An important reality to always keep in mind is that customer interactions usually involve more than one domain. For example, when a business sells a product and signs a contract, the customer master data, along with the product as well as contracts (if considered master data) will be impacted. If it's a commission-based sale, employee (also master data) will be impacted as well because commissions need to be paid.

According to the detractors of the Golden Record, organizations have been attempting, with varying degrees of success, to implement MDM and get to the Golden Record and have had mixed success. This may be because of the desire to get to that one organizational view of the record rather than leverage data while keeping it within the context.

Fixing the flaws

The detractors of the Golden Record philosophy recommend considering all master data of a process or activity, rather than just the single domain, as in the customer record in the example in the *Detractors of the Golden Record* section. The proponents of this new framework advocate understanding the various meanings and links between data attributes. As a result, multiple interpretations/contexts of data are allowed and considered part of the *global master data*.

In this model, each system has its own master data registry, which preserves the context of the data within the application. A central MDM system has interoperable attributes with their corresponding metadata descriptions and when a change is detected in the master data of any federated system, the MDM populates the data using the known metadata and attributes.

Keep in mind that the foundation for this approach is still rooted in MDM, but improves on the current Golden Record philosophy that is in widespread use today. Its claim that data may have several different contextually dependent meanings rather than one metadata description at any given time (which is what the Golden Record is based on) has weight and can open up doors to view and report on data through various contexts. Here is a depiction of what this would look like in a practical setting:

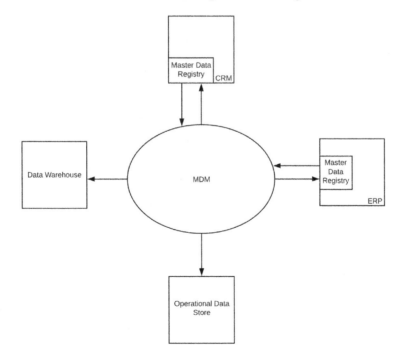

Figure 4.8 – Fixing the flaws in traditional MDM architecture

In the next section, we will look at the linkage between MDM and CRM, the challenges with CRMs, and how some of these challenges can be mitigated using MDM. We will also briefly touch on the challenges that organizations face when implementing MDM solutions in the cloud.

MDM and CRM strategy

The MDM and CRM strategy should be considered hand in hand because CRM is typically the entry point for customer data. Large companies also have multiple CRMs and there is usually an overlap of customer data within these systems. There is also the need to manage customer hierarchies and typical CRMs are not optimized to manage hierarchies.

Some of the specific challenges include the following:

- Multiple versions of the truth with no rules for matching and merging. As mentioned, CRMs are not optimized for hierarchy management and multiple records for a customer in a CRM system with no standardized hierarchies makes reporting a challenge.

- With **mergers and acquisitions (M&A)**, multiple copies of customer records can exist in many CRMs, resulting in multiple versions of the truth with no rules for matching and merging, nor a clear identification of the source of specific data elements.

- Multiple systems of record also result in the duplication of data without identifying the correct version, and when this data flows down to downstream systems, it can impact business decision making, customer engagement, and retention.

- Incorrect data also results in non-standardized data where a customer may be identified with an industry, let's say manufacturing, in one system, and because a small portion of their business is retail, retail in another system.

Having an MDM implemented can address some of these deficiencies in CRM by providing consolidated and trusted customer data, the much sought-after Golden Record. It can improve the overall data quality and provide an easy mechanism to manage customer hierarchies.

We should acknowledge that due to the nature of master data and how it forms the backbone of a business, some organizations are reluctant to implement cloud-based MDM solutions due to data privacy concerns, the perceived lack of control of data, and concerns regarding the security of cloud-based solutions. Salesforce Customer 360 addresses some of these concerns, which we will review in the next section.

Customer 360

You may have noticed that the organizational structure of enterprises is often reflected in the way digital transformation is talked about and implemented. Everyone realizes the need to keep pace with the changing business and regulatory environment and transform their business to stay competitive. However, at the time of implementation, for example, a division selling large mining trucks will implement its own quoting solution when there was already a solution that was used by the construction division. The rationale may be that the construction business is so different from the mining business that it requires its own quoting solution. With more and more organizations realizing the importance of business and enterprise architecture, we may see fewer of these types of scenarios playing out, but nonetheless, they remain a reality and present good examples of how silos are formed and ultimately reflected in digital products that a company creates.

This siloing of IT systems leads to multiple databases and applications and the disparate use of technologies, which makes it challenging to get a single most accurate view of the customer. You may ask why this is important, especially when companies have been generating profits operating like this for so many decades. The answer is that as the marketplace becomes more competitive, it's not enough to merely sell a product/service and deliver it. Customers are demanding more, and they expect more, and world-class companies are delivering on these expectations. Customers are looking for an experience along with the product/service they are to receive. That customer experience cannot be fully provided unless companies understand the customer's journey, and the multiple touchpoints with their digital or physical assets. In summary, not having a complete view of the customer will hinder this goal.

How can this view be achieved? It requires connecting your sales, service, marketing, supply chain, commerce, and other systems, but that is easier said than done because these systems sometimes use propriety data models, which makes them hard to integrate, or use technology that is old and doesn't facilitate easy integration. The goal of building that single view of the customer has been around for a long time but has not been easy to achieve due to the reasons we discussed previously in this section. Salesforce's Customer 360 promises to achieve that goal by implementing the **Cloud Information Model (CIM)**, but more on the model later. First, let's understand what makes up Customer 360. It is a set of tools and services that enables customers to deliver intelligent and highly personalized customer service.

Customer 360 consists of four elements:

- **Customer 360 Data Manager**: This is the key component that allows companies to connect and provide a single source of truth of customer records across Salesforce and other enterprise systems. It does this by creating a single universal Salesforce ID that is used to represent a customer. This allows companies to provide a personalized experience to the customer and, internally, allows companies to get that unique insight into customer behavior through Salesforce Einstein.

- **Salesforce Identity for Customers**: This component allows companies to provide a uniform, consistent login experience to their customers. Rather than customers requiring multiple passwords to log in and access different company assets, such as mobile apps, websites, and e-commerce sites, customers can use one login with multi-factor authentication enabled and securely access these resources.

- **Customer 360 Audiences**: This creates multiple customer profiles across website visits, first-party IDs, emails, and suchlike, and allows companies to create customer journeys and gain AI-driven insights. **First-party IDs** are IDs associated with first-party cookies. First-party cookies are cookies (small text files) that are placed on a user's device when they visit the site. First-party cookies are different to third-party cookies in that first-party cookies can only be placed by the website host you are visiting. For example, if you visit `google.com`, it can place cookies on your device but `youtube.com` cannot. First-party cookies are generally considered more privacy-safe.

- **Salesforce Privacy and Data Governance**: This allows companies to collect and enforce their systems' customer privacy preferences. Part of this is also the data classification label that can now be applied to fields in Salesforce. This helps companies to ensure that they are compliant with privacy laws.

Common Information Model (CIM)

CIM is an open source data model that standardizes data interoperability between systems. It is a data model that allows data sources with different formats and structures to be connected. It forms the backbone on which Customer 360 is architected. When data sources are connected to Customer 360, data, in essence, is mapped from those sources to a canonical data model.

Canonical Data Model (CDM): This is a data model that can contain all the data from different data models that source systems may have; for example, let's say we have MS Dynamics, SAP, and Salesforce in our systems landscape. All three will have their own way of storing data and in a CDM, we will be able to bring this data, translate it, store it, and easily map it back to the source systems. Therefore, in our preceding example, we will be able to bring in the data from MS Dynamics, SAP, and Salesforce, making it available for other systems to consume that data easily without having to do their own transformation or translation.

Data lakes

Typically, when you are storing data in a data store, you have to structure it in a certain format. Data lakes are data stores that don't require data to be stored in any strict format and allow users to store structure as well as unstructured data.

In Salesforce, the CIM is exposed to the platform so you can run SOQL queries against it, build triggers, or create **Lightning Web Components** (**LWCs**). The strength of Customer 360 lies in the fact that there is no need to move massive amounts of data into a data lake; rather, the use of a unique reference back to the source allows the data to remain in place. This also means that there is no need to make a change to the source systems to accommodate integrations.

Summary

We started off with the basics and reviewed master data and its importance in any organization, whether small or large. We reviewed the different types of data, especially comparing master data and reference data in the context of Salesforce. When most people talk about master data, they are usually referring to both these categories under the master data umbrella. We discussed at length what data is master data and the business problems that it helps us to solve. This should have provided you with an appreciation of why adequate resources and time should be spent in identifying master data with a solid plan to manage it properly for smooth and ongoing business operations.

We discussed **Master Data Management** (**MDM**), starting with its definition to establish a baseline understanding of the term, and then briefly discussed how an MDM program can be implemented. The discussion around different styles of implementing MDM provided a good understanding of which style would be appropriate for your organization, followed by a discussion of the criteria when choosing an MDM solution. We also discussed the Golden Record, its importance, and what the detractors of the Golden Record philosophy argue. This should have provided a balanced approach to the Golden Record when discussing it, keeping in mind its benefits and the perceived disadvantages that you can mitigate when implementing an MDM solution.

Lastly, we discussed the new offering from Salesforce called Customer 360 and its components. Customer 360 is Salesforce's attempt to provide a solution to master data issues that organizations face today, but it doesn't stop there. It takes it a step further and brings the customer into the conversation, too, by attempting to provide a unified login experience to the customer via Salesforce Identity for Customers and ensuring that customer data is properly governed and that requests from customers regarding their data that the organization possesses can be properly addressed via the Salesforce Privacy and Data Governance component of Customer 360.

In the next chapter, we will discuss data governance for enterprises and privacy acts such as the GDPR and the CCPA, along with discussing ways in which to assess our current state from a data governance perspective.

Questions

1. **Precision Printers** (**PP**) has multiple CRMs in each region and has decided to implement an MDM system to consolidate records and arrive at the Golden Record. The project team has decided to use survivorship rules for selecting the record that would need to be kept during the merge operation. What do the data architect and the project team need to consider in this scenario?

   a) The team must define multiple survivorship rules, one for each system, to arrive at the Golden Record.

   b) Survivorship rules cannot be used for this scenario because they are not intended for duplicate management.

   c) The project team needs to define the specific criteria that can be used to arrive at the Golden Record.

   d) The project team needs to set up probabilistic rules to determine the Golden Record.

2. Alpha Big Box Inc. has multiple systems, each of which has been determined to be the system of record, having a portion of the master data related to accounts and contacts, in other words, data is entered or updated, and for those specific data points, the system where these data points are updated is considered as the system of record. A CRM is being transitioned to Salesforce that is defined as the source of truth for accounts and contacts going forward. An MDM has also been recently implemented that is now pulling data from Salesforce.

   Users are finding that some records in the MDM have blank or incorrect values, such as *Test Contact*. What could be the root cause of the problem? (Choose two answers):

   a) Test data generated during **User Acceptance Testing (UAT)** in Salesforce still exists and has not been removed.

   b) The project team should turn off the MDM interfaces immediately, remove all the data from the MDM, and restart the integrations all over again.

   c) All the data has not yet been migrated to Salesforce and it has been prematurely defined as the system of record for accounts and contacts, causing the MDM to pull in those specific fields for some records.

   d) Only one system should always be the system of record; this configuration is invalid and the source of this problem.

3. Koolio Box Inc. is a consumer goods retailer that operates on a B2C model. It has 20 million person account records in Salesforce and the number is growing by 5% each year. Koolio's management is concerned that these are not unique records and, due to a number of data entry channels, such as web-to-case, web-to-lead, and outbound marketing efforts, the situation is going to get worse if nothing is done on a priority basis. They have hired a data architect to recommend a solution. What should the data architect recommend?

   a) Hire several interns and have them manually sift through the records in Excel and determine duplicate records. Delete those records from the system.

   b) Develop a custom solution that uses APIs and **Lightning Web Components (LWCs)** to assist in determining potential duplicates based on a limited number of criteria, for example, email and phone number.

   c) Use an AppExchange package to clean up the existing data and leverage it to ensure data quality on an ongoing basis.

   d) Use **Dun & Bradstreet (D&B)** services to clean up the data.

5
Implementing Data Governance

In this chapter, we will do a detailed review of data governance: the need for it and the risks associated with improper data governance. You will learn the differences between data governance and management. You will also learn the key principles for a successful data governance program and some key steps that you can take to ensure your initiative is successful. We will then get more specific and discuss what we can do to govern data in Salesforce.

We will learn about doing a current state assessment so next time you are tasked with one, you can easily assess the current state and make recommendations to rectify any problems or improve the current state. You will also learn about relevant metrics that can be put in place to ensure that you are tracking progress.

Data privacy is a topic that's gaining more and more visibility as regulatory bodies around the world enact laws to protect personal data. There is a slew of regulatory laws depending on the jurisdictions an organization operates in but we will look at two of them – **General Data Protection Regulation (GDPR)** and the **California Consumer Privacy Act (CCPA)**. You will learn the key definitions of these laws and the principles behind them, which can then be applied in the context of the Salesforce Platform.

The key topics of this chapter include the following:

- Enterprise data governance
- Assessing the current state of data governance
- GDPR compliance and CCPA
- Putting it all together

So, let's dive right into enterprise data governance.

Enterprise data governance

Every organization, whether small or large, collects data, usually from multiple sources, and is responsible for ensuring that processes are in place to handle data in a consistent manner. It must do that in such a way that is compliant with data-related regulations and laws that the organization is subject to.

Organizations also make decisions about data, for example, where to store data, who can access it, and how long to keep it, but some organizations consciously put in the effort and formalize this decision-making process while others may not do so. Those that do this in a formal manner realize more value over a period of time while also minimizing their exposure to the risk caused by informal data governance processes.

In the next few sections, we will start by defining data governance, clearly articulating the business drivers behind it, the benefits of formal data governance, and other related aspects of data governance.

What is data governance?

You would find a multitude of definitions if you did a simple search for the phrase `data governance`. This is an indication that there is no one agreed-upon definition and this complicates matters when communicating with stakeholders. The definition I prefer is that data governance can be defined as a collection of principles and practices that govern data from its inception to its archival/purge, that is, throughout the data life cycle.

Data governance is an overarching discipline that permeates almost every aspect of businesses today because data is now considered an asset. This is due to the heightened awareness among businesses that data can be used as a competitive differentiator in an increasingly dynamic and competing market. For example, before the advent of machine learning and artificial intelligence and myriad other advanced tools available now, gaining insights from, say, sales data was very challenging. This was because it required manual number crunching, which was a time-consuming and error-prone process. It also cost a company hard dollars to undertake these types of activities and, typically, only small sets of data were ever collected for analysis. These days, it's almost become the norm to receive a survey in your inbox once your ticket has been resolved by a call center agent. This allows proactive organizations to act on your feedback before it's too late and customers start to take their business to competitors. Simply put, data governance enables organizations to create value with their data.

It's important to also understand that data governance and **Information Technology (IT)** governance are not the same. IT governance is focused on making decisions on the software, the hardware assets of the organization, and the technical architecture of those assets. Data governance is focused on governing data assets with the focus being on data. Having said that, there will be crossover during decision making; for example, data governance policies in a health insurance organization could dictate at the field level who should have access to sensitive fields. As this would require the ability to manage field-level security in the application, at the time of solution selection, this will be an important consideration and impact the decision-making process.

Understanding the need for data governance

We have discussed the value of data throughout previous chapters and that data is now a critical asset for organizations. Perhaps, in the future, we might start to measure data quality, governance processes, and other attributes just like we measure business goodwill today. Businesses are realizing the value of digital transformation and adapting to it; especially with the COVID-19 pandemic, some businesses have moved their operations completely digital and others are pragmatically assessing the functions that they can digitize. This means that more data will be created that will need to be properly governed. Let's discuss some of the key drivers for data governance:

- **Revenue growth via process improvement**: Every business function in the organization is interconnected and will reap the benefits of data governance in its own way. For example, top management can reliably use analytics to explore opportunities for revenue growth; finance can accurately report on the financial health of the company; sales and marketing can derive valuable insights about customer behaviors and preferences; the supply chain can focus on areas for cost reduction and introducing operational efficiencies. All in all, having well-governed data inspires confidence in data-driven decision making and creates trust within the organization and with external stakeholders. When you have robust data governance practices, you can confidently let your customers know how their data is stored, processed, and discarded, which can lead to increased customer trust translating into more revenue.

- **Regulatory compliance**: This is probably the most common driver for data governance programs, especially for heavily regulated industries such as banking and healthcare. This also applies to countries or regions like the **European Union (EU)** that may have their own set of rules that businesses operating in those jurisdictions will need to comply with. Non-compliance with these regulations can result in heavy penalties and, more importantly, reduce trust in the organization's brand.

- **Data quality**: It is critical to have accurate and complete data. Organizations need to ensure data quality so the data can be trusted throughout the organization and can be used to make critical decisions. Without this trust in data, organizations find it challenging to leverage data to make decisions leading to missed opportunities, inefficiencies, and ultimately a loss of revenue.

- **Data standardization**: Nowadays, organizations often have tens if not hundreds of systems in use. Each of these systems come with their own data formats and standards. This may seem trivial but it often leads to inconsistencies and the misintrepretation of data resulting in sub-optimal decision making and potential loss of revenue.

- **Data security**: One of the top priorities for organizations today is data protection and ensuring policies and tools are in place to protect the data from unauthorized access. This also includes how, when, and what data is going to be distributed internally or to external stakeholders.

Now that we have looked at the drivers of data governance, let's briefly touch on the benefits of data governance.

Benefits of data governance

A good data governance program will reap many benefits over a period of time, some of which we will discuss in this section. However, it must be remembered that data governance is not a project with a defined start and end date; rather, it is a continuous process where the output, that is, quality data that is usable for operational and analytical purposes, feeds into further refining the inputs just like a feedback loop. As companies start to see the results of data governance processes and policies, they can further tweak them to ensure that the desired data output is achieved. Here are some of the benefits of data governance:

- **Data discovery**: Proper data governance leads to the easy discovery of data within the organization and increases the adoptability of data across the organization. Data governance practices drive consistency and adherence to agreed-upon standards, leading to data being more readily discoverable. This also means that data is understood and can be easily accessed by authorized parties when needed.

- **Data security**: Cybersecurity-related threats are a major cause of concern for a lot of organizations. When governance processes are implemented with clearly defined roles and responsibilities, it reduces the risk of data getting lost, stolen, or accessed by unauthorized parties. Data governance practices drive the identification of critical assets and the controls that are needed to protect those assets.

- **Brand trust**: Implementing data governance processes will improve your data governance maturity level over time, which increases trust not only within the organization but also with your external stakeholders. Customers are more willing to do business with organizations that can clearly demonstrate they have adequate processes to maintain and protect consumer data.

- **Integrations**: It is becoming the norm to have multiple business applications and systems running in organizations today. For example, a marketing system would need to integrate with the **Customer Relationship Management (CRM)** system to send over marketing qualified leads, whereas a CRM may need to integrate with an **Enterprise Resource Planning (ERP)** system for order fulfillment once a quote has been approved in the CRM. Not having properly governed data can lead to the proliferation of bad data in downstream applications, making the job of maintaining a certain level of data quality that much more difficult. Imagine a data warehouse having inaccurate data that is then used in data marts. How would that impact decision making? Or say the CRM sends the wrong address into the order fulfillment system, which then ships the order to this incorrect address. How will that impact your relationship with the customer and ultimately your revenue goals?

- **Efficient use of resources**: Not all data is useful, and you don't want to be collecting data that will not provide value to your organization; you'd rather put your resources to better use. Having data governance provides the ability to closely analyze and collect data that will actually provide value. Remember, it's always easier to prevent unwanted data from getting into your organization rather than bringing it in and then removing it after having determined that it is of no value to you.

- **Handling complexity**: The number of sources that data can be gathered from is increasing along with the volume. Good data governance will provide the ability to manage these data sources and volumes of data, making it easy to respond to internal and external requests for data and comply with privacy regulations.

- **Analytics**: More companies are using data science, machine learning, and artificial intelligence to drive insights for optimal decision making and identifying risk. Sound data governance practices and a foundation are imperative if any of these disciplines are to yield useful results that are reliable and trustworthy.

Understanding the difference between data governance and data management

Many people confuse data governance and data management practices. Although they are linked, understanding the distinction is important. Data management practices are IT practices to ensure data accessibility, reliability, and security at the tactical level, whereas data governance is more of a business strategy that is used to securely leverage data to create value and reduce the risk to the organization.

IT teams focus on data management aspects when they implement processes and tools to collect, store, organize, and process data to maintain data quality and trust in data, whereas data governance focuses on identifying data and the associated data assets so the company can reap the benefits of data. This is not to say that data governance doesn't use any tools to achieve its purpose, but what it means is that the tools used for data governance serve a broader purpose. For example, a Salesforce admin decides to implement Dun & Bradstreet's Optimizer tool for continuous data cleansing and data enrichment. This is an example of data management. But if a business decided to implement a data catalog of business entities or define roles and responsibilities associated with managing data in the organization, such as data stewards and approvers, that would be an example of data governance in action.

Another way to look at this is the way auditors define and implement policies and procedures and financial management execute these policies, the same way data governance pertains to defining the process in relation to data and the people who will interact in some way with that data. In the construction industry, the blueprint of how a building should be erected is analogous to data governance, and the construction of that building is analogous to data management. Data governance also includes the technology to achieve the goals of governance, for example, data governance tools that help users build a business data catalog, including defining business terms, any synonyms for those terms, and related business attributes. Some tools have capabilities to score and evaluate data quality while others may have capabilities related to data access policies and the ability to connect with different systems to consistently apply your data governance policies.

Part of data governance is also defining the metrics to measure the performance of governance policies and procedures. Some metrics that typically get measured in the beginning include the completeness of data, accuracy, and the percentage of duplicate data records. Having even some preliminary metrics is important to measure the effectiveness of your policies and how well they are being adhered to. Keep in mind that these metrics are not merely technical but have an impact on business metrics as well.

For example, **Days Sales Outstanding (DSO)** is a metric used to measure the financial health and cash flow of the company. If the DSO will be high due to incorrect or incomplete customer addresses, external stakeholders such as an analyst may see this as a sign of weakness and downgrade the company's outlook. This can result in increased costs for the company to borrow capital to run operations.

This example is a good way to demonstrate the linkage between data governance metrics and business metrics. This is another difference between data management and data governance – since data management is the execution side of data, it may not have its own data-related metrics but will need to meet the metrics defined by data governance.

> **DSO**
>
> DSO is the average number of days it takes a company to receive payment once a sale has been made.

In the next section, we will understand metadata management – an essential component of data governance.

Metadata management

Metadata is *data about data*, meaning it provides the necessary context for data. For example, you have a **Formula** field called **Days between Stage** defined in Salesforce to calculate the number of days between each stage on the Opportunity object. The value in the field is the data that needs to be managed but the fact that this field is of the type **Formula** with a return type of **Number** and the actual formula definition to calculate the result are all examples of metadata.

This is the technical aspect of metadata, but metadata encompasses the business definition as well. In a comprehensive metadata document, you will notice that it answers the *five Ws and the How* question. Let's use our example from the previous section and see how we would drill deeper to understand the metadata of this field in more detail:

- **Why?**: This is related to understanding the rationale of why we are storing this data. This is the most important question to ask. For our example, the reason why we are storing this data is so we can report on the number of days it takes to move between stages.

- **What?**: Another question we need to ask is the purpose of the field and the drivers behind using it. This pertains to the business definition of the data and the business rules applicable to it. For our example, the business definition could be *calculate the number of days between the current stage and the previous stage for an Opportunity record*. Another question answered is what are the business rules for this data? For example, when the Opportunity record is in the Initial Discovery stage (the very first stage in the Stage picklist), the value of this field will be blank.

    Another aspect of this question is to ask what the acronyms or abbreviations for this field are. For us, it could be **NoD (Stage)** referring to **Number of Days** for the **Stage** field or **NDS** referring to **Number of Days** for the **Stage** field. The database field name is also mentioned here, which in our example is `Number_of_Days_Stage__c`, where **Field Type** is **Formula** with the return type as **Number** and 0 decimal places.

Typically, security-related questions will also be answered here, such as what the privacy level of this field is. Salesforce provides a number of fields related to data privacy, such as **Compliance Categorization** and **Data Sensitivity Level**, which can be used to properly classify data. **Number of Days (Stage)** is an internal-use field only so we will select **Internal** for it. Other options are **Public, Confidential, Restricted**, and **Mission Critical**.

Referring to the *what*? question, we can now say that the purpose is to report on the average sales cycle period for comparison with industry and peer averages. The business driver is to identify the bottlenecks and remove those, so the average sales cycle time periods become consistent and comparable with the company's operating industry and peer metrics.

- **When?**: This answers the question of when the data is created and updated and when it can be archived or purged from the system. In our example, the **Number of Days (Stage)** field is populated initially when the opportunity is created and updated when the **Stage** field on the Opportunity record is changed. The field is copied to a data warehouse on a nightly basis along with other data and removed from Salesforce after 3 years from when the data in the Opportunity record was set to **Closed/Won** or **Closed/Lost**.

- **How?**: This answers the question of how many places this data is stored in and how long it should be stored. In our example, the field is stored in Salesforce but also in a data warehouse for analytical reporting. It is archived from Salesforce after 3 years and deleted from the warehouse after 7 years. Since we use a third-party AppExchange app for backing up data, it is also stored in their data centers. In this case, the data is stored in three different places.

- **Who?**: This answers the questions who created this data, who the user of the data is, who the owner of the data is, who can modify the data, who the data steward is, and who can impact this data either internally or externally? For our example, sales **representatives (reps)** are the users of this data and the data is automatically created by the system based on the sales reps' actions. It can be indirectly modified by the sales reps as well as their direct managers and the sales operations team when they update the Stage and save the record. The data can be influenced by internal executive-level staff or externally by an investment firm that partially owns the company by demanding that the sales cycle be shortened to increase cash flow and revenue.

- **Where?**: This pertains to where the data is stored, where the data is used and shared, and where the data backup is. In our example, our data is stored primarily in Salesforce but also in the data warehouse. It is used in Salesforce reports and dashboards but also shared with partners via Salesforce communities. The data is backed up by Salesforce in its data centers but the company also backs up the data using a third-party AppExchange tool, which should be considered in terms of whether it's compliant with regulations such as **GDPR** or **CCPA**.

Metadata management is an important aspect of data management and using this technique, you can easily define your metadata in a comprehensive manner.

In the next section, we will review core guiding principles that can be applied for a successful data governance program.

Guiding principles for data governance programs

Everyone understands the value of data, especially now that we have so many examples of data being used in innovative and creative ways. The problem is we also need some signposts along the way to keep us on track on our data governance journey. Data governance principles are these signposts that help us in making decisions and ensure that although the paths to get to a quality data state may be different, the result will be the same. Here are some key guiding principles for a successful data governance program.

Data is everyone's business

Most data that organizations have today is shareable across the enterprise. Depending on the type of data, multiple business functions are usually interested in it and, nonetheless, if an organization has matured analytical and data science practices, the data scientists will be interested in that data. For data to become valuable across the organization, it needs to be understood by its users. This requires that the data is consistently defined with unambiguous and agreed-upon definitions.

Wider access to data leads to a more efficient, data-driven organization, making it easier to provide great customer service whether it's internal or external customers. In most cases, it is more cost-effective to have a single source of data that can provide the information in a timely manner rather than multiple sources that need to then be integrated and translations performed to standardize it for consistent use across the organization. Data must also be protected from unauthorized access and policies and procedures implemented to prevent data-related incidents. All of these things require that everyone in the organization considers and feels the responsibility to treat data as an asset just like organizations treat physical assets. This is no different than when managing a company's financials: it's not only the **Chief Financial Officer's (CFO's)** responsibility to manage them but the onus is also on every employee to use the organization's resources effectively.

Having siloed data and implementing your own divisional system not only costs more at the organization level but also leads to problems trying to integrate that data, such as determining where fields are mastered in a scenario where multiple systems are updating data records. Not having proper policies and procedures in place to protect data can, for example, lead to treating data with a casual mindset, exposing the organization to serious reputational and financial repercussions.

Another aspect of data governance is that it should not be seen as an IT initiative – because it is not. Data governance is rather a partnership between IT and business. This is important because, traditionally, many businesses see the IT function as the owner and custodian of data and it can lead to data quality issues and the inability to see the value of data and how it can add value to the business.

Data must be appropriately managed

This pertains to consciously implementing the management of the data life cycle from the point of its inception to the point it's archived or purged. It is always easier and cheaper to implement measures for good data quality rather than in downstream processes and systems. This was the idea behind manufacturing techniques such as 5S and Kanban that realized fixing a defect early in the process is much cheaper than fixing it once the product has been shipped.

Let's have a look at a simple example to demonstrate this. If a web-to-lead form has the **Country** field that doesn't match with the country picklist values enabled in Salesforce and a prospect fills out the form and enters a country that's not on the list, the lead will not get inserted into Salesforce. Rather, an email to the system administrator will be sent with the lead information and they can then enter the lead manually in Salesforce. They can opt not to do anything in this case and wait until the next time a lead with the same country value is entered and the process is repeated, or they can add it and ensure that the correct country exists matching the values on the website. It's obvious that the latter approach is more appropriate than having to manually add the leads, notwithstanding the fact that if the email is missed or, for some reason, not delivered to the admin, the lead could get completely missed, costing the company potential revenue.

Managing data also encompasses having data quality standards that are well defined so data can be appropriately measured and reported on for its quality. Data stewards should help define data definition standards and what constitutes quality data for their domain. Accountability for data quality, standard definitions, security, privacy, and standardization must be owned by designated roles in the organization. These roles must ensure that the data is used consistently with the internal policies of the organization and also complies with any external regulations.

Data must be recognized as a strategic asset

Data must be recognized as an enterprise asset by all levels of the organization starting with executive buy-in. It must be communicated that data is a shared resource that is critical to the foundation of data-driven decision making. This needs to be done frequently so the strategic value of data doesn't get forgotten as time passes or as new employees join the company. When an organization's culture starts to value data as an asset, it prompts discussions and the need to treat it just like physical assets are treated. For example, does the data comply with regulatory requirements, how can it be tied to achieving organizational goals, and how reliable, timely, accurate, and complete is it?

Another benefit of treating data as a strategic asset is that it changes the conversation from "my" data to "our" data as teams become more willing to share their domain data and assist in managing the data. For example, sometimes there are perceived or genuine concerns on how another division will use the data if it's shared with them. Would they start marketing to my existing customers when I am also marketing to the same customers or start cold calling them? These types of doubts and suspicions can slow down the sharing of data but having a clear objective of what you want to get out of that data and how it's going to be done can put these concerns to rest.

Single source of truth

IT landscapes today comprise multiple systems and databases all playing their role in the smooth operation of the business, but this leads to complexity by having multiple copies of the same data. With data-driven decision making taking the front seat, it has never been more important to have reliable and trustworthy data. Sometimes business functions within organizations debate and defend the data that their function produces, all of which leads to confusion and doubt about data. Data governance initiatives must strive to always have a single version of the truth that is reliable and trusted by everyone in the organization.

Data governance is a marathon, not a sprint

Some may not consider this to be a principle, arguing that it's too soft and intangible, but my argument is that the majority of the employee population is used to working on projects with a defined start and end date and expect the same with data governance initiatives. Although data governance will have projects as part of it with a start and end date and KPIs, it is an ongoing initiative. This mindset enables you to properly plan, allocate funding, and provide the necessary exposure and buy-in for data governance programs.

In the next section, we will look at some key things to keep in mind to ensure a successful data governance program.

The keys to the kingdom – making your data governance program successful

Data governance can seem like a daunting task given the volumes of data that organizations have and the number of sources this data originates from. The best approach is to use the crawl, walk, and run methodology. Here are some key things you can do to ensure a successful data governance program in your organization:

- **Crawl, walk, and run**: This is probably the most important thing you can do to ensure success with your data governance program. Many companies fail with their initiatives because they take on more than they can handle. The opportunities that await once you have mature data governance programs are exciting and can lead to setting unrealistic targets. Do yourself a favor and focus on those things in data governance first that are low-hanging fruit and can result in quick wins. This will be beneficial in a couple of ways:

  - Firstly, as people start seeing results of data governance initiatives, it will motivate the teams that were working on them.

- Secondly, it will give you data for your business case for the next data governance initiative. As a result, your business end users who use that data will start demanding more, making your job even easier to get that next business case approved.

- **Metrics**: Before embarking on any data governance initiative, ensure you define metrics that can be used to measure the success of your work. In the beginning, this doesn't have to be very elaborate, but simple things such as defining the business data catalog for three domains or defining a quality standard for x number of domains. This gives you not only something tangible and objective to measure progress but also the ability to communicate the value that your data governance initiative is creating for the organization.

- **Metadata management and data stewardship**: Since metadata provides a framework to ensure data is aligned with business objectives and data standards and policies are adhered to, the importance of metadata management must not be underestimated for a successful data governance program. Metadata management and data governance go hand in hand because metadata management provides that linkage between the business objectives and data. This implies that effective metadata management is a key responsibility of the data steward. The data steward ensures that the metadata gets created and that it delivers the value that the business wants to realize from its data.

- **Iterative approach**: I mentioned earlier in this section to take baby steps, and one way to do that is to have a planned iterative approach. This means having a few weeks to a cycle when reasonable, otherwise, they might need to be longer, and deliver something at the end of the period. This could be something as simple as a catalog of business terms defined, standardized, and approved by all functions of the business or designating and appointing key roles such as identifying and training data stewards for your selected domains.

In the next section, we will look at some of the key elements to administer data quality.

Data quality

Since we have been discussing keys to successful data governance, it is prudent to briefly discuss the key aspects of ensuring data quality as well. These can be used by the business to comprehensively cover all aspects of data quality, which is a key concern for data governance. The reason I discuss this here is that I want to make sure that we don't forget the connection between data governance and data management. The following aspects of data management provide a tangible connection and clarity when you are planning your governance initiative:

- **Data profiling**: This is the process of reviewing source data and understanding its structure, content, and relationships between data. In a nutshell, it's really about understanding your data. For example, in Salesforce, this would be a list of data sources and the fields where the data is stored. It also involves identifying issues with your data, such as duplicate fields on different objects that allow entry in both fields rather than using a relationship between objects to pull the data from one object and populate it into the other using an automation tool. A good example of this is, say, a legal address field is created on the account and another field on the quote, and both allow edit permissions. This means that these fields could be out of sync very easily. An optimal way would have been to make one set of fields read-only and populate them using an automation tool such as Process Builder or a trigger.

- **Cleansing**: This involves fixing the anomalies identified in the profiling stage, for example, ensuring that the fields we used as an example in the profiling stage have the same values. Other examples include cleaning up any legacy fields that are not used or fixing typos in the data or errors that have been introduced during imports. The last one usually happens with the Opportunity stages when you do an import of records from another system. If the stages are not matched properly, the values from the other system will automatically get inserted in Salesforce. You will then need to fix them using the **Replace** function for picklists.

- **Standardize**: This step includes the standardization of data so that the matches between data are performed optimally. The scope for this could be structured or unstructured data. For example, a sales rep may have entered the street address as `457 S Gate St`; when standardized using established business rules, this may get updated to `457 South Gate Street`. The use of single or multi-select picklists is another example of standardization and is commonly used throughout the platform. For example, when an opportunity is lost, sales managers want to know why it was lost, so rather than providing a freeform text field, you can provide the values in a picklist that the sales rep can choose from. As a bonus, you can make a freeform text field available should they wish to provide additional details.

> **Caution with multi-select picklists**
>
> Multi-select picklists are a great way to standardize data in your environment but you must also be aware of the downsides of using them. Reporting can be really tedious and limited, with multi-select picklists requiring the use of `CONTAINS`, `INCLUDES`, or `EXCLUDES` operators, which can severely impact performance for large datasets. The grouping of data can also be very challenging with multi-select picklists. For example, if you have selected Edmonton, Calgary, and Toronto in one record, Edmonton and Toronto in a second record, and just Toronto in the third record, you will not be able to group the records to show those that have just Toronto in them as the chosen value.
>
> A major limitation is also that you cannot track changes on these types of fields, for example. Unlike most other field types that show you the old and new values, multi-select picklists only show that the field has changed – not exactly what changed. They also work with a very limited number of functions in a formula. Refer to this Salesforce Help article to review the complete list: `https://help.salesforce.com/articleView?id=sf.tips_for_using_picklist_formula_fields.htm&type=5.`

- **Match and merge**: In this stage, you would apply the different techniques available (probabilistic or deterministic) to determine matches and merge the records. You apply data survivorship rules to arrive at that single record that is the most accurate and complete.

- **Monitor**: Once you have gone through the previous steps, you now need to monitor the health of your data using various processes and tools that are available. This is especially when data governance processes and the data steward role become very important. The data steward can use reports and dashboards to monitor the state of data along with third-party or customer tools that can help make their job easier.

There are many tools that can be used to ensure data quality, some of which are free. RingLead's Field Trip app is one that has very good reviews and is well-liked by the admin community. Salesforce also offers an app called Data.com Assessment App v3.2, which is privately listed on AppExchange (`https://appexchange.salesforce.com/listingDetail?listingId=a0N30000000puBxEAI`). Another offering from Salesforce is their accelerators. These are sessions with a Salesforce expert that would guide you on your specific use cases for data quality and governance. I would suggest contacting your account executive to get help on which ones you should start with. If you are a Premium Support customer, these are included free of charge with your subscription.

In this section, we reviewed the key items to implement a successful data governance program. In the next section, we will discuss key elements of a Salesforce data governance program.

Successfully governing Salesforce

So far, we have discussed what data governance is, its benefits, and principles to keep in mind when implementing data governance. In this section, I want to delve deeper into governance in general from a Salesforce perspective because merely having data governance policies and procedures laid out will not help; rather, all of the five components discussed in this section need to come together to produce results that a world-class organization would hope to realize.

Many customers somehow form the notion that because Salesforce is in the cloud, changes can be made directly in production or do not have sufficient input and involvement from IT. In other cases, customers may have worked with traditional on-premises systems and desire a platform that can keep pace with the changes that the business requires and view Salesforce as a platform that requires little or no governance. Salesforce, just like other platforms, whether on-premises or in the cloud, requires governance for the continuous optimal operation of the platform.

The five components we will discuss in the following subsections are not meant for an academic discussion but rather positioned as practical steps that you can take to govern your Salesforce implementation effectively.

Vision

You may have worked on those projects where the project team painstakingly worked to deliver a great solution only for it to be rejected by the business in the end because it didn't meet the expectations. This is the *why* (the goals) of the initiative or project. It attempts to answer the rationale of the initiative, the strategy to realize those goals, and the benefits that the company hopes to realize from the initiative. Vision also provides clear and objective KPIs to measure whether the benefits have been achieved by the company or how closely the company is tracking those objectives. Keep in mind that every Salesforce initiative should align with a business goal that is going to be achieved. For example, if major releases require extensive testing and the architect is requesting funding approval for an automated test tool, there must be a business benefit that should be achieved from this. In this example, it could be that business resources have to have been involved in testing for major releases requiring them to be pulled from their daily jobs or other projects. Therefore, we will eliminate the need to pull in five resources for a week for user acceptance testing at the time of every major release.

There are multiple benefits of documenting the vision. A major benefit is that it facilitates decision making because stakeholders have agreed on the vision and the strategy. Therefore, high-priority items that align with the vision can be delivered first. Sometimes, despite following project management methodologies and practices, there is still a communication gap and stakeholders are not aligned. In such cases, having a documented vision and strategy benefits you by removing that ambiguity and giving everyone the opportunity to align themselves and their expectations with the vision.

By defining well-thought-out KPIs upfront, project leaders can evaluate the success of ongoing and delivered initiatives and, of course, correct them if needed. It eliminates the mistake that many companies make where a project is launched with a vague understanding of business goals that the company wishes to realize. In some cases, the goals are such that they cannot be measured objectively. And once the delivery is complete, there is no measure of whether the business objectives are being achieved or not.

Another benefit is that it creates alignment between business and IT and gives the business a sense of ownership, increasing the chances of the solution getting adapted by the business, driving the success of the project. Let's look at the steps in creating a vision document.

Creating a vision document

There are a few steps in creating a vision document:

- **Identify stakeholders and business goals**: This step involves identifying all of your internal and external stakeholders that will be impacted by the initiative. Part of identification is also doing a stakeholder analysis, which is to understand each stakeholder.

> **Stakeholder analysis**
>
> A key component of stakeholder management, stakeholder analysis is the process of identifying internal and external stakeholders that have an interest in the project and can influence it. It helps in understanding the needs of the different stakeholders and allows the project team to balance competing priorities and a way to address stakeholder interests. It also includes stakeholders' preference for mode of communication and how frequently they would like to be informed of the project progress.

Once the stakeholders have been identified, you will want to collaborate with them and identify the business goals and the strategies that have been defined to achieve those goals. You may find that some stakeholders may not have a clear idea of how to achieve their vision, in which case, they may also need to define their strategies.

- **Identify operating principles**: Consider principles as a set of rules that will be used in the decision-making process. For example, it is important to identify whether the project will be run using the Agile methodology or the company is expanding rapidly via acquisitions and scalability for painless operations in the future. Another one could be that customer experience is a top priority to expand the service part of the business and that will an important factor in decision making.

- **KPIs**: Ensure that you have discussed and agreed upon a set of KPIs that will be used to measure progress and benefit what was initially proposed. Ensure that you have two to three KPIs at most and make sure they can be objectively measured. In fact, I recommend defining the method by which these KPIs will be measured in the document as well. That way, there is no ambiguity on how the KPIs should be measured.

Once you have the vision document defined, the next thing you will want to define is to have a solid communication strategy.

Communicating with stakeholders

The **communication** strategy creates the alignment between stakeholders, especially from a user's perspective as they understand the need for the new tool, how they will be impacted, and the benefits that the system will bring to them. You should consider forming personas for communication that will help you tailor your communication and these could be based on the roles that constitute your stakeholders; for example, a persona could be built for executives, senior managers, and analysts. Having communication profiles created is immensely helpful because it lets you tailor your communication and provide just the right level of detail to each stakeholder profile.

A good communication strategy will proactively address questions that could be asked by executives down to the end user and ensure that your stakeholders can provide candid feedback without any fear of repercussions. If this is not possible, encourage them to contact you directly and ensure you take action and provide updates back to the stakeholder. Expect some resistance if your project is truly transformational in nature, but it's better to hear objections and concerns at this point than hearing it when the solution is developed and ready for production deployment.

A communication strategy document also helps cut through the noise given the volume of information that everyone is bombarded with but having a well-articulated strategy that is understood by all levels will greatly increase the success of your implementation.

Creating a communication strategy

A communication strategy involves answering the five Ws and the How question:

- **Why?**: Give the details of why the initiative is being undertaken. Explain the business value to the organization and try to link it with departmental, team, and personal goals, if applicable. This is a good way to motivate and create buy-in for your project.

- **What?**: What is being done and what will be done differently going forward. This question also addresses the channels that will be used to communicate with stakeholders, for example, email, group chat messages, and meetings.

- **When?**: This is about communicating when the change will impact them. This should be well understood and communicated. For instance, sales teams usually dislike system changes at the end of a quarter or a major change being introduced close to the year end.

- **Where?**: This addresses the question of where stakeholders can go for more information, concerns, questions, or feedback.

- **Who?**: This is about who is being impacted: the business functions, regions, or divisions? This can also define the roles and responsibilities of the teams that are part of the project, which can help communicate exactly the resources that have been allocated to the project and identify any stakeholders that may have been missed.

- **How?**: This addresses the frequency of the communication, that is, is it daily, weekly, monthly, or some other frequency that suits the recipients.

Do not underestimate the importance of communication as that can be a deal-breaker to the success of your initiative regardless of how well the solution is built.

Data architecture and governance

As we have been discussing in previous chapters, data is an asset that must be managed just like physical assets that organizations have. This requires understanding and documenting how data is architected and flows through systems in the organization.

An important aspect in defining data architecture is to keep the business architecture at the forefront because the latter reveals the structure of an organization in terms of its processes, capabilities, and information. Since information forms a key component of business architecture, you need to make sure you are aligned with the goals of business architecture when developing your data architecture.

Once the business architecture is understood and the data architecture is defined, you move on to the ongoing treatment of data, that is, how new data will be brought and cleansed and how existing data will remain in good quality. A very important component of this is data backup and archiving.

Data architecture and governance make it easy to maintain the reliability of your data over the long term and provides a clear understanding and guidance, since the physical state of data is also defined and available, on how to treat data anomalies or scenarios where there are large volumes of data. Having the data architecture drives easier integrations with other systems, prevents technical debt in the organization, and improves the user experience because there are clear guidelines on treating data as it passes through the data life cycle. For example, archiving opportunities once 3 years have passed from the time of the **Close Date** field on the Opportunity object will run reports quickly or the list views will load in a timely manner.

Let's discuss the practical steps in creating the artifacts to define and understand data architecture in the context of data governance.

Creating data architecture and governance

The result of doing this exercise could be a combination of artifacts but what's more important is spending the time and thoroughly going through these steps to understand the business intent. Then we can translate it into a workable solution that will facilitate the needs of the business rather than slowing them down:

- **Business architecture and roadmap**: It is imperative that the business architecture and the roadmap are defined and considered. It ensures viability from a cost perspective and scalability to accommodate future needs of the business when the data architecture is defined.

- **Physical data architecture**: This is the detailed database-level architecture that should be defined keeping the business architecture in view. The physical data architecture is what makes it easy to integrate systems and quickly conduct impact analysis when changes to existing data architecture are required. Not having this leads to spending hours and hours deciphering and making fundamental mistakes when defining the physical data model.

- **Data governance**: This defines what data will be managed and identifies the processes, policies, and roles that are needed to ensure data quality and the protection of data. With so many sources of data and huge volumes of data generated every day, it is imperative to have clear policies, roles, and responsibilities on how to treat data during its life cycle. It also defines when access to data should be provided, to whom, and for how long.

- **Data backup and archiving**: This defines the policies, procedures, and tools needed for data backup and archiving. From a Salesforce Platform perspective, this is probably the most overlooked area because until problems start to happen with data, no one will even notice it.

In the next section, we will review technical change control.

Technical change control

This pertains to applying software engineering processes and industry best practices when developing and maintaining software solutions. This involves processes and policies around the development of the solution, environment management. It also involves details about where different types of tests will be conducted; for example, full testing of the solution should be done on a full copy sandbox. Having an effective technical change control mechanism will assist in the goal of maintaining metadata management effectively. This is because technical changes will go through a known process and get communicated and documented on their way to the production environment.

Another aspect of technical change control is technical governance. For instance, how the solution is built, whether it follows best practices, whether it respects governor limits, whether it's scalable for future expansion, and how paintable the solution is. This would also include the release cadence for releases. A critical break-fix type release needs to be put into production on the same day versus a new initiative that is ready for production; promotion may need to follow the usual bi-weekly or monthly cadence. All of these details should be laid out clearly to avoid confusion and prevent any mistakes from happening that could adversely impact the production environment.

In the beginning, it may seem like a lot of work, but it makes IT more responsive to change requests from the business. Remember, businesses have to change at a rapid pace today to remain competitive and if IT cannot keep pace, the business will abandon the use of the solution or, worse yet, turn to other siloed solutions that may not be aligned with the business goals and architecture of the organization. It also minimizes the impact on end users since they are aware when changes are promoted to production, and an additional benefit is that it establishes trust with IT because they are following a controlled process for changes.

Implementing technical change control

Effective technical change control will increase velocity, reduce risk, and prevent resources from getting overwhelmed with the amount of change that they have to deal with. Start with the following steps to implement a technical change control process:

1. **Document current state**: This step pertains to documenting your process of solution design, the principles used to make decisions in design, tools and methodologies used for development, development standards, and best practices. Documenting this allows you to communicate with other stakeholders and to compare your practices with Salesforce recommended practices.

2. **Gap analysis and future state**: This involves doing a gap analysis of where you are with respect to industry and Salesforce best practices. For example, in an organization that's heavy on developers, most things are done through code rather than doing an analysis of whether the same could be achieved with configuration.

3. Once you are done with the gap analysis, the next step is to determine the optimal future state. Notice I didn't say *ideal* but rather optimal because this is a continuous improvement process and as Salesforce evolves, you will need to evolve your organization and, therefore, there is no constant ideal state.

4. **Plan and move to an optimal future state**: This involves planning and moving from the current state to your optimal future state. A key ingredient for success here is to ensure that you are taking small steps rather than making a big jump towards your future state.

5. **Monitor and tweak**: No plan is perfect and this will not be perfect either so once you have moved to the new state, monitor how things are panning out and seek feedback internally, but also check what others are doing in similar industries. Then make incremental changes to improve your current process and remember this is a journey, so continue to do so as you gain more insight into what's working and what's not working.

Let's review the last foundational piece of the puzzle, that is, the business backlog.

Business backlog

The **business backlog** is dependent on the business roadmap. A roadmap should be created taking into account all current and anticipated projects with each project mapped to a business objective. This roadmap is reviewed regularly based on changes in organization priorities, re-organizations, or after a major Salesforce release.

The backlog is created from the roadmap in partnership with IT based on the business priorities that will return the most **Return on Investment** (**ROI**) and that align with the vision and strategy of the organization. Having a business backlog provides a path for alignment between different business units and transparency as everyone involved understands the importance of the prioritized items in the backlog and how they contribute to the organization's strategic goals.

A business backlog will also allow the business to optimize its investment and realize optimal ROI. By clearly mapping the backlog items with business objectives, it introduces objectivity in the process, thereby reducing or eliminating altogether any chances of internal politics to influence decision making.

Creating a business backlog

Before you can start creating a business backlog, ensure you have a roadmap created. This is done by understanding the business vision and strategy and communicating with the executive stakeholders to understand what's on their minds. Then you create a roadmap of the initiatives identifying any dependencies between projects so they can be acted upon appropriately. The following are the points to consider while creating a business backlog:

- **Understand Salesforce's capability roadmap**: This involves understanding the capability roadmap of Salesforce for the initiatives identified in the roadmap. This is important for the backlog because you may be planning to implement something in the next 2–3 months, but Salesforce may be releasing the same functionality in its next major release. Knowing what's upcoming in the next releases will help you guide the prioritization for the roadmap, thereby optimizing the organization's investment.

- **Developer backlog**: Once you have the roadmap defined and understand the Salesforce roadmap, the next step is to meet and discuss with the stakeholders to start identifying the top priority items for the backlog. Once again, this priority should be based on the vision and strategy document and it should clearly identify the value that the business wishes to realize from the initiative.

- **Refine backlog**: Once you have the first pass completed, develop the backlog, review it with the business stakeholders again, and refine it. Usually, at this time, new items that got missed last time around pop up.

- **Communicate**: Ensure you inform the stakeholders once the backlog is complete. Ensure that you are reviewing the roadmap and the backlog on a regular basis and especially as major changes happen within the company, such as re-organizations, acquisitions, and switches to a multi-org strategy. As updates are made to the roadmap, ensure that the backlog is aligned with it as well.

We have discussed in this section governance in Salesforce holistically, including data governance. This should have provided a foundation that you can use to implement this learning at your organization. The key learning is to start small and focus on the low-hanging fruit. This helps showcase the benefits achieved and builds momentum that can then be used toward larger, more complex data governance initiatives.

In the next section, we will discuss assessing the current state of data governance and the tools available to assist in the process.

Assessing the current state of data governance

We have discussed data governance and how it's different from data management and the ways to implement data governance policies with respect to Salesforce. But before we start to implement data governance policies and tools, it's recommended to do a current state assessment. The reason is that every organization has some form of data governance in place and there is no need to scrap these practices. Rather, we need to understand what these are and identify the gaps. After we validate and realize that the existing policies are adequate, we can turn our attention to these gaps and ensure they are taken care of.

In the following sections, we will discuss what a data governance assessment is, some of the challenges that we may face in an assessment, and high-level steps on how to go about doing it.

Assessing the current landscape

The goal behind a data governance assessment is to document the knowledge, skills, and attitude about data governance. The following are some questions that will help you understand the data managing environment:

- How much awareness is there within the organization with regard to clean data and its importance?

- Does everyone interacting with data understand the impact of their actions?

- Does the organization take measures to ingest accurate and clean data right at the source or does it wait until it gets the data and then reactively validate the data?

- Is there a clear understanding of which fields are updated by the marketing tool versus which are mastered in Salesforce, or are the account records updated by multiple departments leading to inadvertent data loss and accuracy issues?

These are all examples of what a current state assessment would help to flush out and get documented.

Challenges with data governance assessments

There are some challenges with doing assessments attributable to a few factors. These are related to the depth of assessments, the type of organization being assessed, and, in general, the lack of a robust set of standards when it comes to assessing the organization, which introduces the risk of subjectivity.

A common issue with assessments is that they are done as a result of a knee-jerk reaction. This is usually when a significant data-related incident happens, and the focus turns to data. These are usually short-lived and don't create the necessary buy-in that is required for data governance initiatives. The sequence of events unfolds such that the assessment is done in the heat of the moment and then there is no meaningful action taken. That is why it is important to recognize data as a strategic asset so long-term investments can be made in data governance-type initiatives and the organization can fully reap data-related benefits.

When doing an assessment, you would want to evaluate against defined metrics but when there are no metrics available, then that makes it challenging for an objective assessment. I would recommend exploring the organization's industry and determining what other companies in the same industry are doing. Industry-focused associations can also provide data that can be used as a basis for metrics, such as the **National Automobile Dealers Association (NADA)**, which represents new car and truck dealerships, or the National Association of Realtors in the **United States (US)**. These types of associations collect data from their members for improving their services, advocacy, and other reasons and since data is becoming such a critical asset, they may also have data that can be used as a metric.

Another challenge worth mentioning is performing an assessment using internal resources. This is not to cast a doubt on the skills and experience of internal teams, but blind spots are mostly discovered when an external party does an assessment. Another benefit of having an external assessor is that they'll presumably have the experience and the skills necessary to perform such an assessment after having done it for multiple other clients and industries.

Let's look at the steps to go about doing an assessment.

Conducting an assessment

In this sub-section, we will discuss the high-level steps on how to conduct an assessment. Keep in mind that you may need to tailor these to suit your needs and the type of organization you are doing the assessment for:

- **Stakeholder analysis**: Complete a stakeholder analysis by asking the key contact(s) at the organization about the team members and their roles who will be part of the assessment. Try to gather as much detail as possible about these team members, including their areas of expertise, skills, and experience in the organization. This will help you put things into context when you are reviewing the documentation. Since data governance is a business and IT partnership, ensure you have good representation from each area.

- **Review documentation**: Review existing documentation to understand the current practices and tools that are in use today. Make sure that you start with reviewing the organization's strategic objectives and short-term goals as they will help form the context for current state documentation.

- **Business requirements**: Once you have reviewed the current state documentation, it is time to start interviewing the key members that were identified earlier. Ask questions to clarify your understanding of their current state and identify their requirements and pain points.

  When you are interviewing your users, your users will also share scenarios of data quality issues. It is best to document them in a data quality issue log to pass on to the relevant stakeholders so they can take remediating actions.

- **Assessment report**: Create your assessment report highlighting existing practices, business requirements, pain points, and the gaps that you identified. Make recommendations on how to fill in the gaps and alleviate the pain points that the stakeholders shared with you. Use the metrics that the business already has, identify metrics that the business should be targeting, or use the metrics that are suggested in the next section. The recommendations should be in the light of our discussion in the *Successfully governing Salesforce* section.

Common data governance metrics

In this section, we will discuss some of the common metrics that can be used to measure the maturity of your data governance initiatives. These are grouped into categories to provide a more holistic approach to measuring success rather than just having metrics that focus on one aspect of data governance, that is, data quality:

- **Data quality**: Perhaps the most common data governance metric, the following are the key attributes of data quality:

  a) **Completeness**: This relates to how comprehensive the data is. Suppose that you ask a customer for their cell phone, home phone, and work phone numbers and the customer provides their cell phone number only, but from a practical standpoint, the data is complete. Metrics for this include the percentage of data fields that include the needed information.

  b) **Accuracy**: This data attribute reflects how much the data reflects reality. For example, if the CRM has the contact's email but the contact has changed companies and has a new email, that record would not be considered accurate. This would also include typos that make their way into the system during data entry. Metrics for this include measuring the ratio of data to errors, so a high ratio would mean that the data is clean whereas a smaller number would signify problems with the data.

  c) **Auditability**: This pertains to ensuring that changes made to data are auditable and can be traced back to where, what, and who made the change. Some example metrics include the percentage of untraceable data with respect to changes and the percentage of data that has been altered.

  d) **Timeliness**: Data is available in a timely manner when needed. If you make a request to your sales operations team for a copy of a contract for a specific customer so that you can negotiate an up-sell opportunity better, you will expect to receive the data in a timely manner. The metric for this attribute is the timely availability of data, which measures how quickly the data is available after a request is made. The request could be manual or automatic but regardless of the medium, care must be taken to set reasonable expectations around this metric. One executive may be fine getting the data in a 3–4 hour window after a request has been made whereas another executive may expect the results to arrive within minutes of submitting a request.

e) **Validity**: This measures whether the data is actually valid. For example, the data may be available in a timely manner and is auditable, accurate, and complete but if it's not in the correct format, it may be useless. Consider the example of date fields and whether a date of birth is entered in the field; does 02/03/1999 mean March 2, 1999, or February 3, 1999? Metrics for this attribute include the percentage of fields that follow the defined standard.

f) **Uniqueness**: This attribute is concerned with how many copies exist for the data. Having two duplicate contacts, for example, can be very confusing because you don't know which one is the **real** one that the sales team is working with. Metrics for this attribute include measuring the percentage of duplicate data in the objects. The higher the percentage, the more duplicate records there are in the system.

g) **Consistency**: This relates to how much consistency there is with respect to data across the organization. For example, if the CRM has *Peter Simpson* as a contact with a free email account but there is a contact in the ERP by the name *Peter Simpson* with an official work email, are these two records referring to the same person or different people? A metric for this includes measuring the consistency of records between systems and applications.

Let's continue reviewing the other metrics for data governance.

- **Data controls**: This measures compliance with the controls that the company has put in place with respect to data. Metrics in this category can include the percentage of completed metadata (such as description fields populated for objects, fields, Process Builder, and the like), frequency of data backups, and the number of data security-related issues rectified.

- **Organization**: This measures the skills, training, and overall organization's maturity in terms of data governance. Metrics for this include the percentage of employees trained in data governance practices and the number of business owners identified and assigned to each business domain (such as sales, finance, and supply chain).

- **Infrastructure**: This is related to measuring progress on the physical infrastructure supporting data-related activities. Metrics for this include the number of systems using MDM and the consolidation of systems resulting in a percentage decrease in the total cost of ownership.

We discussed in this section the benefits of current state assessments, the challenges, and how to go about doing an assessment. I also presented some metrics that can be used as a starting point for your data governance initiatives. It should be noted that there are other metrics that can be used as well such as data security, data accessibility, data encryption, and others. It's up to the organization to decide what is important to track and measure but always start with a select few metrics and work your way upwards as data governance practices mature in the organization.

I want to end the section by briefly discussing the importance of maturity models, which can provide a good foundation for objectively assessing your data governance practices. I will not go into the details of each model because that is outside the scope of this book, but I provide a few pointers in the next section so that you can do your own research and determine whether they're something you would like to use.

Need for data governance maturity models

We have looked at how managing data can be challenging due to various factors such as increasing sources of data, the volume of data, decentralized operating models, and others. There are also organizational and cultural barriers and conflicting agendas that can make data governance programs challenging to implement. Another challenge is that funding is limited and because the fruits of data governance efforts take time to bear, it is not straightforward to prove the ROI. Especially, funding models in organizations lean toward project-based work whereas data governance is a program requiring continuous effort with appropriate resources and funding to realize the true value of data.

Capability maturity models provide a framework through which assessing the current state of data is made easier along with deriving objects that the organization can use to work toward higher capability. These models were traditionally applied to software development processes but have been applied to processes governing data as well. These models also provide a framework to determine what level of data maturity is required by an organization and what would be required to move to the next level.

Here are a few other reasons why organizations might decide to invest in a data maturity model:

- **Strategy**: Implementing a data governance program may seem like a daunting task with a lot of areas to address. A data governance maturity model can be the bridge between feeling lost and where to start implementing governance to a blueprint that can be used to start implementing data governance processes.

- **Benchmarking**: Businesses are interested in intelligence related to their competitors or just generally their industry. This can be a good way to justify the business case for data governance initiatives especially when you are not performing as well as your competitors or the industry that you operate in.

    Another reason why benchmarking can be important is to assess the performance of regional or country-wide units for the same business. Keep in mind that even in the same company, practices related to data governance will be different, especially in a decentralized operating model.

- **Acquisitions and mergers**: Maturity models also provide a tool to have objectivity in assessing another business that you may be acquiring or merging with. Data issues are a significant source of issues that, if very significant, can prevent companies from proceeding with mergers or acquisitions. When making these transactions, you can use the maturity models to not only assess but also get a high-level understanding of what you would need to do to integrate the two companies if that fits with your **Mergers and Acquisitions (M&A)** strategy.

- **Regulatory compliance**: Depending on the nature of the business, there might be certain regulatory constraints that the organization must comply with in terms of data governance and management. Maturity models provide a framework for regulatory bodies to assess organizations and require them to meet certain requirements in order to qualify or maintain compliance. They may not necessarily say that you need to be at a certain level. Suppose that the business must be at level 4 but provide guidance that makes the organization achieve that level.

- **Progress tracking**: A framework is also a way to report progress and communicate the roadmap to achieving mature data governance practices. Most maturity models have a numbering system that represents levels within the model and indicates the level of maturity, therefore making it easier to communicate the current state and vision for data governance.

There are many capability maturity models, such as Oracle's data governance maturity model, Garter, and then there are others from educational institutes such as Stanford University and Open Universiteit Nederland. You can read about these on the internet. There are many considerations and nuances to consider when choosing a maturity model and my recommendation is to consult with a data governance specialist who can guide you through this process.

In the next section, we will discuss privacy regulations and the tools in Salesforce to stay compliant with privacy laws.

Data privacy and privacy laws

There is a growing trend in the business community to collect data and then use it for trends, reporting, forecasts, and various other things. But with the growing data collection, consumers have also become wary of how their data is stored and used and for how long. A growing number of well-established companies have also been hit by bad actors that have hacked into systems and stolen millions of consumer records, putting them at risk, including the Yahoo data breach a few years ago, which resulted in a whopping 3 billion user accounts being compromised.

Governments around the world have been enacting legislation and enforcing them to ensure consumer data is protected with an expectation for the transparency of this data. These regulations significantly impact how businesses can collect, store, and handle consumers' personal information. This legislation is intended to provide transparency of how consumer data is used but also legal recourse for consumers in situations when there is non-compliance.

This means that organizations that are not proactively assessing and implementing measures to comply with these regulations may be exposing themselves to hefty fines and penalties from regulatory bodies. Not only that, but it also exposes these organizations to massive reputational risk if they are the subject of a cyber-attack. In the last few years, many well-known businesses have been targeted and their users' data exposed, eventually forcing them to pay millions of dollars in penalties and rebuild a tarnished brand. For example, British Airways was fined around $30 million following a data breach that resulted in exposing the personal and credit card data of 400,000 users in 2018.

Over the years, governments have proactively, and other times reactively, enacted regulations to protect the personal information of consumers. While it is out of the scope of this book to discuss all of these, I will mention a few to provide context and then delve into more detail about regulations, specifically **GDPR** and **CCPA**:

- **GDPR**: At the moment, GDPR is probably the most comprehensive and toughest privacy legislation enacted to protect consumers. It was developed by the **European Union** (**EU**) for citizens of the EU and companies that deal with data for individuals living in the EU.

- **CCPA**: This was enacted and came into effect in 2020. Its main purpose is to protect the data of California residents and enable residents to decline the sale of their personal information or to know what data the business has collected about them, among other things. Although not as stringent as GDPR, it can still charge heavy penalties for non-complying businesses.

- **Gramm-Leach-Bliley Act (GLBA)**: Enacted in 1999, it deals with companies that provide consumer loans, financial advice, and other financial products. The law requires that companies explain their data sharing and protection policies to consumers along with putting in controls to protect consumers' data that these types of companies have.

- **Payment Card Industry Data Security Standards (PCI-DDS)**: This is not a government regulation per se but an independent body; the PCI Security Standards Council enforces this for companies that accept, store, or transmit credit card data. An interesting thing about PCI-DDS is that it even applies to businesses that use third-party vendors for their credit card processing. So, it is up to the business to ensure that the vendors they use for payment processing comply with PCI-DDS.

- **Nevada's Senate Bill 220**: This came into effect in 2019 after Nevada followed California's lead in enacting the bill. Although it has similar provisions to the CCPA, one key distinction is that individuals under the Nevada bill cannot take legal action against companies, but the attorney general can impose fines for non-compliance.

In the coming sections, we will discuss in more detail the need for privacy laws, understand the difference between data privacy and security, and delve into more details of GDPR and CCPA.

Understanding the need for privacy laws

Unbeknown to many, the right to privacy is part of Article 12 of the **Universal Declaration of Human Rights** (**UDHR**), which means that it is a basic human right to have privacy. Technological advancements in the last few decades have made it easier for governments and corporations to exploit data and use it for surveillance or commercial purposes, respectively. This was especially brought to light when Edward Snowden blew the whistle on the **National Security Agency's** (**NSA's**) spying programs. This highlighted the need for legislative bodies to have oversight and governance to ensure programs such as these don't poach an individual's right to privacy.

An example of private entities using consumer data to benefit commercially is the Cambridge Analytica scandal, which used the data of Facebook consumers without their consent to influence voting in the US 2016 elections. With stringent privacy laws in place and their enforcement in full effect, private corporations know where the boundaries are and what the repercussions could be should they violate them.

People when they are young sometimes post content online that may not be deemed appropriate and reduce their chances of employment later in life. Another aspect of this is the posting of explicit and intimate images of people by former romantic partners for the purpose of exacting revenge. This can potentially lead to destroying a person's life. Having privacy policies in place provides a way to remediate and prevent these types of incidents from happening. The GDPR's *right to be forgotten* law gives individuals the ability to request the complete removal of their information from the entity that is storing their data.

Freedom of expression is another right that is protected because of privacy laws. Imagine being tracked for everything that you say or write and then that information being used against you by employers, banks, or other public institutions. Having privacy laws protects this freedom of expression and also gives you control over your data. They let you decide where, when, and how your data can be used and prevent your data from being exploited by powerful corporations and individuals.

Another aspect of freedom of expression is the right to engage freely in politics. Privacy laws protect that right by allowing you to vote based on your political viewpoint without any negative repercussions. This is the reason why vote casting is considered confidential and you are not obliged to tell anyone who you voted for, including your employer. This is also very important for family members as well where one member may not necessarily agree with the political viewpoint of another and vote differently.

A fundamental value to function in society is trust. Privacy laws help form and grow that trust. What bank would you choose to do business with? One that sells your data for commercial reasons to a multitude of data gathering companies that sell it to interested parties or one that has policies and procedures in place and is transparent with you about how they protect and treat your data? That's one reason why laws such as PCI-DDS exist, to protect your personal data from being misused as well as protecting your financial information. You may have noticed many websites prompting you to subscribe by entering your email and displaying a message to the effect that your data is never sold but only used for such and such purpose. They are trying to be transparent with you and assure you that your data is not used for anything other than the stated purpose.

In the next section, we will review the difference between data privacy and security.

Securing data versus the privacy of data

It is important to understand the difference between data security and privacy. They are not the same but are interlinked and crucial for an organization to protect data. It may be worth mentioning that protection is not the sole responsibility of the IT department, but rather a holistic, organization-wide approach is needed with proper training and accountability so everyone feels and acts in ways that can ensure the protection of data.

Data security is concerned with protecting your data from unauthorized access and malicious use. The way this is achieved varies from organization to organization and depends on the volume, type of data, and other factors that will drive the need for appropriate tooling and procedures. Data privacy, on the other hand, deals with policies and processes that define how you can collect, use, share, and discard data that is in your purview. Compared to data security, it is more universal since the laws apply to a wider base. However, there may be laws or rules that are imposed on certain industries or associations that the business is part of. For example, the PCI Security Standards Council is a private entity, but it imposes rules regarding data that member organizations must follow to gain or maintain their compliance with the standard.

Understanding the business risks

As a data architect, you must be cognizant that when organizations start collecting and processing personal data, there are inherent risks that the organization is undertaking that must be properly understood to put risk mitigation strategies in place. It is your responsibility as a data architect to point these out so appropriate team members (for example, the privacy law officer) can be pulled into these conversations so the risks are discussed and appropriate action is taken to address them.

Keep in mind that the privacy laws are not there to stifle businesses but rather to attempt to balance the need for data by businesses versus respecting and protecting individuals' data privacy. Here are a few common risks that businesses are generally exposed to when dealing with personal data:

- **Lack of control around data access**: Some organizations lack control around who can access personal data and whether it's required for them to access it based on their job function; that is, access to personal data must be based on a *need-to-know* basis. This also ties into ensuring processes are in place that when the authorized individual leaves the company, their access to personal information is discontinued immediately to prevent any untoward data incidents.

- **Lack of processes to deal with requests**: Privacy laws such as GDPR require organizations to remove personal data as part of the *right to be forgotten* clause of the law. Not having processes in place to respond to or completely remove the information as required by the law can result in the organization being exposed to heavy penalties.

- **Transparency around sharing data**: Some laws require that the organization must spell out how the personal data collected is used, including sharing with third parties. Failure to do so can result in the company being found to be in violation of the law.

- **Responding to data loss**: Companies usually will tend to disclose whether there has been a theft or unauthorized access of personal data, but some laws mandate that victims are informed in a timely manner. This requires the company to have the appropriate processes and procedures in place to react to such situations.

- **Application and system vulnerability**: Insufficient security around systems and web applications, whether on-premises or in the cloud, can result in data breaches. There has been a number of breaches in the last few years, some involving very large, well-known businesses. For example, about 148 million users were impacted when a breach happened at Equifax in 2017. In a breach at Adobe in 2013, about 152 million users were impacted because encryption was weak and although passwords were stored with encryption, password hints had been stored in plain text.

  Another aspect of this is to protect data not only at rest but also in transit between systems and applications. There are technical standards that when fully complied with can ensure the secure transmission of data.

- **Collect more data than needed**: Organizations should focus on collecting only the data that is required. The more data you collect, the more responsibility you take to ensure that the data is properly stored and processed. If a business offers chiropractor services, it can collect data for the patient that is used for diagnostic purposes, but if it decides to collect data about the family of the patient, it then has more data than it needs to ensure is properly protected. The rule of thumb should be to only acquire data that you truly need for your business process. If you anticipate needing the data in the future, your business processes and technical architecture should be designed in a way to acquire and protect that additional data properly.

- **Using data for things other than its purpose**: When collecting data, ensure that your organization is fully transparent and clear with the individual on how the data will be used. Using data for one purpose but then repurposing it for something else can represent a compliance violation. Privacy laws usually require the extent of personal data collection and how it's used. Laws such as GDPR require that when requested, the organization must inform the requestor of all the information it has on the individual. This obviously requires policies and procedures in place to ensure responses are given in a timely manner because failure to do so can result in non-compliance with the law.

Now that we have discussed the importance of data privacy and why it's important for businesses, let's do a deep dive into GDPR. Privacy laws such as GDPR and CCPA are complicated and require specialized expertise and tools to properly implement in organizations. The following discussions are not meant to be exhaustive but should be viewed as a means to introduce you to some of the key components of the laws and set a foundation for deeper discovery at a later time.

Global Data Protection Regulation (GDPR)

For a number of years now, Europe has led the way with privacy laws. It introduced the initial EU Data Protection Directive that came into law in 1995 that required companies and organizations to properly protect personal data and have a clear, legitimate use for that data. Recently, though, in 2018, a more comprehensive privacy law called **GDPR** came into effect. GDPR is more comprehensive in nature than its predecessor and significantly expands the rights of individuals to privacy and obligates organizations that meet the defined criteria to comply with this law.

Its primary purpose is to give individuals control of how their personal data can be used and to consolidate and provide a single privacy act to make it easy for organizations to implement it. It is worth noting that GDPR applies to organizations beyond the borders of the EU as long as they are dealing with data belonging to EU citizens, which means that whether the organization has a physical presence in the EU is irrelevant. Violating GDPR laws can result in hefty fines of 20 million euros or 4% of annual global revenue, whichever is greater depending on the extent of the breach and the damage it caused.

In the next few sub-sections, we will try to understand what GDPR requires, and then in another section, we will discuss the CCPA.

Understanding GDPR terms

Before we can do a deep dive into understanding what GDPR requires and how we can use Salesforce for compliance, let's first understand some of the terms used in GDPR:

- **Data subject**: A person who can be identified from some attribute such as name, location data, or social security number.

- **Personal data**: Any and all information related to a data subject that is associated with that data subject, for example, age, gender, or physical address.

- **Sensitive personal data**: Personal data associated with a data subject that identifies their political views, religious affiliation, health information, or ethnicity, for example, a member of such and such party, or a fingerprint scan.

- **Controller**: This is an entity that determines the purpose of processing personal data. For instance, an employer collecting data for the purpose of providing employment to an individual becomes the controller of that data.

- **Processor**: Any entity that processes personal data based on the direction of the controller. For example, Salesforce becomes the processor of data when the employer enters the demographic details of the candidate into Salesforce.

- **Pseudonymous data**: This is considered data that cannot be tied to a data subject without tying it to additional information that is stored elsewhere. For example, when the candidate visits the company pages, the website tracks the candidate and stores their IP address, which, when linked with other information available about the candidate, can result in identifying the data subject.

Let's discuss the key principles that form the underlying requirements of GDPR.

The underlying foundation of GDPR requirements

There are many requirements in the GDPR privacy law. Understanding the underlying principles will help you understand the essence of these requirements and, to an extent, the intent of the law. Keep in mind, though, that you should consult with a qualified person who has the necessary knowledge and experience in this area before interpreting the law yourself. Fines for violations under GDPR are hefty and negatively impact the reputation of a business:

- **Fairness and transparency**: Organizations must process personal data fairly and transparently. In our earlier example of the candidate applying for a job, the employer must be transparent on what information is being collected about the candidate and also how that information will be used by the employer.

- **Purpose of data collection**: This relates to collecting personal data only for the specified purpose and it cannot be used for any other purpose other than the expressed explicit purpose stated at the time of data collection. For example, a data gathering company that sells data for individuals gathers candidate data for a job posting. The personal data collected is for hiring purposes and therefore cannot be sold for commercial gain.

- **Data minimization**: This principle states to collect personal data only to the extent that it is needed and relevant to the stated purpose. For example, the employer cannot ask whether the candidate owns their home, what vehicles they drive, and their plate numbers as those details are not relevant to the decision-making process in most cases. A common example of this is phone apps where some of those apps require more access than is needed for the purpose of the application.

- **Accuracy**: Personal data must be accurate and kept up to date. For example, the candidate gets the job in our example and 6 months later, moves to a new home. They send an email to HR informing them of their new address. The company must ensure that the address gets updated in their systems. Doing this in a timely manner is important because the employee may have moved to a tax-free designated zone and the local tax authority must be informed of that change.

- **Deletion of data**: Personal data must only be kept for as long as the need is there for the original purpose. As stated earlier, repurposing the data for some other use without consent is not allowed. For example, if the prospect was interviewed and not given the job, their data with the company must be removed.

- **Data security**: This principle states that organizations must implement appropriate technical and organizational measures to protect personal data from unauthorized access and use. Depending on the sensitivity of the data being collected, it recommends the use of a few techniques such as encryption, pseudonymization, and anonymization. When using the pseudonymization technique, GDPR requires that the additional data that can be used to identify the subject is stored separately. Search for *AOL search data leak* for an example of how the pseudonymization of data without proper safeguards caused a data breach leading to some people getting identified from their search history. Here is a story that New York Times ran back in 2006: `https://www.nytimes.com/2006/08/09/technology/09aol.html`.

Definitions

Anonymization: This involves completely removing attributes from the data subject that can identify a personal subject. A key aspect of anonymization is that the data subject cannot be identified in any way if the data is further processed.

Pseudonymization: This involves removing personal data and replacing it with pseudonyms, hence the term pseudonymization. While anonymized data can never be restored to the original state, pseudonymized data is different and with further processing can be used to identify the data subject.

Encryption: This involves converting the original representation of data into an alternative form that is then accessible by authorized parties only. Although data can still be intercepted during transit, encryption provides the assurance that it cannot be read by the interceptor due to the need for encryption keys that allow the message to be read.

In the next section, we will discuss the key rights of the data subject.

Rights of the data subject

GDPR provides rights to data subjects that they can use to control the usage of their data by data controllers. These rights can help us to understand the GDPR law better but also assist us with thinking about a technical plan on how to implement the requirements stemming from these rights in Salesforce:

- **Data access**: This gives the data subject the right to confirm with the data controller whether their information is being processed. The controller then must provide details about how the data is being processed, the purpose of processing, and whether it has been shared with third parties.

- **Objection to data processing**: This gives the data subject the right to object to the processing of their data, especially if it's being processed for marketing purposes.

- **Data rectification**: This gives the subject the right to request corrections to the data that is being processed by the controller.

- **Restrict processing**: The data subject can request that the data controller halts the processing of their data, at which point the controller is obliged to action the request and ensure data processing stops.

- **Data portability**: This gives the data subject the ability to request access to their data in structured, commonly used formats so they can transmit it to another company or store it for their own record-keeping purposes.

- **Data erasure**: The data subject can ask the controller to stop processing and remove their data in certain situations, such as when the data subject withdraws their consent or the original purpose of the data has been served and it's no longer needed.

Let's look at where we can start to implement a GDPR compliance program.

Complying with GDPR

Salesforce has committed to complying with privacy laws and has worked closely with EU authorizers to ensure compliance. This is evident by the certifications that Salesforce has received from a multitude of organizations certifying that Salesforce is compliant with some of the well-known privacy laws, such as GDPR and **Health Insurance Portability and Accountability Act (HIPAA)**, among others.

Organizations that are starting out must remember that Salesforce is the data processor and they are the data controller. This means that they have responsibilities as a data controller that must be understood and, as a result, processes put in place for compliance with the law:

- **Building the team**: Salesforce recommends starting off with the executives and getting their buy-in to comply with GDPR. The risks of not complying and the consequences can be highlighted to ensure that risks are properly understood and appreciated. After you have identified that your organization is subject to GDPR, this is probably the most important step. This is because gaining compliance takes substantial financial investment and requires staffing resources so the buy-in from leadership is of utmost importance.

  Then comes the step to form the core team, which can be done by appointing a key person who is accountable for delivery and then having each of the departments designate one or two people for the initiative. This forms the core team, which can then identify project champions within their respective areas that will serve as advocates and potentially as testers as the changes are implemented.

- **Current state assessment**: Once the team has been formed, analyze your existing privacy policies and documentation because there could be areas where synergies exist with what GDPR requires and what you have already implemented. The next step is to make an inventory of all the data stores that have personal data stored in them. Keep in mind that this analysis of personal data also needs to account for the employee, candidate, customer, vendor, and prospects. You want to capture the data store, the type of data being stored, the origin of that data, the usage of the data, who has access to it, how it is secured, any integrations with other systems including third-party systems, and how long it's kept in the system.

  A word of caution here is that large companies have siloed technology tools and sometimes departments or teams decide to use tools that are easy to sign up and can be set up by a business team member effectively bypassing IT. That's why it is important to have representation from each business area, otherwise these undocumented shadow IT systems can unnecessarily jeopardize the company's reputation and financial standing.

  Identify high-risk activities involving data processing from the inventory you created. Carry out a data protection impact analysis to determine the actions needed to ensure that the personal data is properly protected.

> **Data Protection Impact Analysis (DPIA)**
>
> DPIA is required under GDPR whenever an activity is undertaken that is considered a high risk to personal data. DPIA is conducted before the activity is undertaken so the organization can understand and proactively take proper steps to protect personal data. It is also used as evidence that the organization is taking steps to comply with GDPR.

- **Establish controls**: Salesforce recommends creating a roadmap of operational and technical changes required to implement controls and processes for data protection. We already discussed DPIA earlier but some other artifacts and processes to ensure compliance include the following:

  a) **Privacy notices**: These are meant for data subjects and should clearly inform the subject of the personal data being collected.

  b) **Usage limitations**: These are controls put in place to ensure that the personal data is used solely for the original purpose that was identified at the time of acquiring the data.

  c) **Security**: These are measures implemented to prevent unauthorized access, use, and the modification or disclosure of personal data.

  d) **Data subject rights**: These are processes put in place to respond to requests from the data subject. These could be requests for complaints and requests for data or the rectification or deletion of personal data of the data subject. It also includes managing the preferences of the data subject.

  e) **Vendor management**: It's important to manage contracts with vendors, affiliates, and other third-party providers to ensure that their collection and use of personal data is legal and falls within the boundaries set by GDPR.

  f) **Incident response**: These are processes to respond to security breaches, including taking remediation steps and informing the affected parties as required by GDPR.

  g) **Training**: This should be planned early on with the view that employees and external parties whose personal data is shared understand the need for privacy policies, how they have been implemented, and the consequences to the company should the law be violated. Tools can be provided to report misuse of data or to seek clarification on activities related to data processing.

- **Audit frequently**: Once you have implemented the processes and tools to comply with the law, it is important to conduct frequent internal audits to ensure continued compliance. Many organizations will find that they are subject to multiple privacy laws and it is best to have an internal auditor trained in privacy law to conduct your audits so problems can be spotted before they materialize.

- **Document compliance**: Once the initial baseline has been established and the processes and tools are in place, the organization can start to document compliance activities. These can be in the form of DPIAs, data inventory, a data processing register, and other artifacts and documentation related to compliance. The organization may also decide to appoint a **Data Protection Officer** (**DPO**) who is responsible for overseeing the organization's data protection strategy and its implementation so that the organization is compliant with GDPR.

  Most organizations choose to do periodic DPIAs or audits to ensure that the data protection program continues to be compliant. This is especially important as new sources of data come into existence and volumes of data being collected are growing exponentially.

Now that we have learned the important terms and the principles of GDPR, it will be easier for us to assist in implementing these in our organizations within the context of data architecture and also to provide guidance to other stakeholders such as developers and analysts.

Let's discuss the other privacy law, which was recently introduced in California, the CCPA.

California Consumer Protection Act (CCPA)

The US passed the Privacy Act in 1974, becoming one of the first countries in the world to adopt a privacy law. This act restricted federal agencies in the use of data collection. Given the governance system in the US, individual states can also pass laws governing the use of personal data for their residents.

The US state of California passed a privacy law recently called the CCPA to protect the private data of its residents. The CCPA came into effect on January 1, 2020, and gives California residents much more control over the collection and use of their personal information. We will look into some of the specifics of the law later in this section. What we need to understand is that it gives consumers the right to know what type of personal information a business is storing about them and whether the business is sharing their personal information and with which entities. It also has other provisions that give consumers the right to access or request the removal of their personal information.

Let's look at some of the terms that CCPA uses in the next section.

Understanding CCPA terms

Let's look at the terms that are used in CCPA to better understand the discussion that will follow. These terms, although they look very simple and are commonly understood, have very specific meanings in the eyes of the law. These terms and the later discussion around the specifics of the law are listed here as a general reference and not legal advice. Always ensure you consult with a qualified person who is trained and has the necessary experience:

- **Business**: CCPA defines any entity that either has an annual revenue of $25 million or more or collects information on 50,000 users annually or earns more than half of its revenue from selling personal information as being subject to this law. It must be noted that business here refers to any entity anywhere in the world that is dealing with California residents' personal information.

- **Consumer**: A person who is a natural resident of California.

- **Personal information**: Any information that identifies or could be reasonably linked to a particular consumer. This includes commercial, biometric, internet, or other electronic network information, and geolocation data.

- **Processing**: Any operation performed on personal data, whether manual or automated.

- **Service provider**: The entity processing data on behalf of the business and to which the business has disclosed personal data of consumers for a legal purpose agreed to in a contract. This means that a business does not need to collect personal information from consumers for the law to be considered applicable. If a business receives personal information from another business and falls under the definition of the business, then regardless of how that personal information was obtained, the business will still be subject to CCPA.

Let's look into some of the details of the law from the perspective of a business.

Key requirements for organizations

In this sub-section, we will discuss some of the key requirements for businesses to be compliant with CCPA:

- **Honoring consumer rights**: The CCPA imposes certain obligations on businesses that include responding to disclosure requests, honoring opt-out requests, and responding to data deletion requests, among other provisions of the law. The law also imposes requirements on businesses to develop two or more methods for consumers to submit requests.

  It should be noted that consumer requests for the deletion of personal data need to be carefully analyzed before fulfilling the requests in cases where the data may be required by law enforcement. In these types of cases, the business is not required to accede to the consumer's request.

- **Consent**: The law requires businesses to provide clear and conspicuous links for consumers to opt out of the sale of their personal information. The business must make it such that creating an account is not required for opting out of the sale of their personal data.

- **Training**: This requirement ensures that businesses must provide adequate training to their personnel involved in handling matters related to CCPA and providing information to consumers on how to exercise their rights under CCPA.

- **Disclosure**: This requires that businesses must disclose the categories of personal information collected before or at the time of collection of the information. The disclosure must be detailed, encompassing the categories of personal information collected, categories of sources from where information is collected, the purpose of information collection, and any third parties that will be accessing the collected information.

  The law also requires that businesses provide this disclosure on their public privacy policy page. If a page is not maintained, then the disclosure must be made on the website and these disclosures must be updated annually. These disclosures must also be made available to individual consumers when they request access to them directly by contacting the business.

- **Vendor compliance**: The CCPA law requires that service providers handling personal information must also comply with the law. The law stipulates that the business must sign a contract with the service provider requiring them to limit the processing of the data to the business purpose of the contract. It also requires the service provider to certify the contract and state that they understand the restrictions and will comply with them.

As mentioned earlier, these are not all the provisions of the law and as you can probably appreciate by now, the law has exceptions and nuances that require specialized expertise in law.

Now that we have looked at the key requirements for the business to comply with CCPA, let's review some of the rights of individuals under the CCPA.

Consumer rights

The Privacy Act's scope was to govern the collection, use, and dissemination of data by federal agencies in the US. The CCPA's mandate is to enhance privacy rights and consumer protection for the citizens of California. Let's briefly review these rights one by one:

- **Right to know**: Under this right, the consumer is entitled to receive clear and transparent information about the categories and types of personal information the business is collecting, and the purpose this data is being collected for. This must be done prior to or at the time of collection of the personal information. A salient feature of this right is that the identification of the third parties that this data is shared with must also be disclosed. This closes a big loophole where, previously, third-party identity was not required to be disclosed and it could be anyone's guess how many, and which, third parties had access to your data.

- **Right to access**: Under this right, consumers can request that a business discloses the categories of personal information that the business has about them, categories of sources from where the personal information is collected, the purpose, third parties that the personal information is shared with, and specific data elements such as email addresses and phone numbers that the business holds about the consumer.

  It should be noted that while this right may seem straightforward and disclosing this information will not be hard, challenges will arise with unstructured data where personal information may exist, for example, texts and emails.

- **Right to opt out**: Consumers have the right to request businesses stop selling their personal information with the general rule being that the sale of data on children under 16 are prohibited except in certain situations.

- **Right to request deletion**: This right grants the consumer the ability to request that the business deletes their personal information. Of course, there are exceptions under the law when the business doesn't have to comply with these requests. For example, the business detects a security incident or the prosecution of those who partake in malicious activities such as fraudulent, deceptive, or malicious activity.

- **Right to equal services and pricing**: This right ensures that the consumer is not treated differently in terms of being charged a different price or a change in the quality of service if the consumer has exercised their rights under the CCPA.

Now that we have looked at the key consumer rights under the CCPA, let's look at some considerations for implementing CCPA in your organization.

Implementing CCPA

CCPA is a relatively new law that was passed a couple of years ago at the time of writing this book. It has gone through many amendments and more changes are expected to be made by the California Attorney General as time passes. This poses a challenge for businesses as they have to be vigilant and keep up to date with new changes as they get introduced in the law.

I would suggest starting off by following the same steps that are recommended in the *Complying with GDPR* section, tailoring them to fit your needs. The key is to have an expert resource who can guide you throughout this process.

Now that we have looked at GDPR and CCPA in more detail, in the next section, we will look at how these can be implemented and what tools Salesforce provides to assist in enforcing these privacy laws.

Salesforce tools for implementing privacy laws

We have reviewed GDPR and CCPA privacy laws but there are others as well. For example, the **Personal Information Protection and Electronic Documents Act (PIPEDA)** in Canada or **Personal Information Protection Act (PIPA)** in Japan. The underlying principles for these laws are the same, that is, balancing the needs of businesses for data so they can provide products and services versus protecting consumers' data and giving control to consumers on how they want their data to be used.

Given that Salesforce is used globally by a multitude of companies in different industries, Salesforce provides tools on the platform that can be used to meet these privacy requirements rather than specific solutions for each law. This provides more flexibility as no two businesses operate the same way and some businesses may not be subject to these laws.

We will briefly review these tools, using examples to gain a better understanding, but note that the tools used for each platform may be different. For example, the implementation for data deletion requests for Commerce Cloud will be different than a deletion request for Sales Cloud. In the following discussion, we will be looking at a Sales Cloud example because that is more commonly used, and the intention is to not have an exhaustive discussion here but rather provide pointers on how to go about complying with the laws. You will need to work with your privacy officer as an architect to understand the law's requirements and then implement the solutions appropriate to your business and the platform you are using. Let's take a look at some of the requests related to privacy laws and how they can be handled within Salesforce:

- **Personal data deletion requests**: Privacy laws will usually require that you delete data when it's not needed for the original purpose it was intended for or a customer requests that it is deleted. Make sure that you consider all sources where the customer's personal data may be, for example, full copy sandboxes or developer sandboxes that may have been seeded with production data (data for sandboxes should be anonymized unless there is a real business justification to have production data).

  When a delete request is received, consider all the records that could hold personal data. If it's a prospect, start with the lead record, contact, tasks, calendar events, and any freeform text fields. Add-on packages such as CPQ or additional features such as Sales Cloud Einstein will require special consideration as merely deleting data from records in Sales Cloud will not remove it from them. For example, in CPQ, you would need to delete records from additional objects such as `Quotes`, `Contracts`, `Invoices`, and `Orders`.

- **Consent management**: Consent management is tracking your users' requests on how they want to interact with your organization. This includes honoring opt-out requests or removing data when consent is withdrawn after being given initially.

  For these types of scenarios, ensure that you have searched through contact and lead records and remove personal information in the fields. These typically include phone, email, and mailing addresses. **Email Opt Out** and **Do Not Call** fields are present on the `Lead` and `Contact` objects. These should be checked. Care should be taken that merely checking these fields will not preemptively stop sending emails that are sent via custom processes, for example, if you don't use a dedicated marketing tool and use Lightning Flow and email prospects. You will want to ensure that your processes check these flags and act appropriately.

If you are using Sales Cloud Einstein and your customer doesn't want you to use their data in machine learning models, there is a custom field, `AI_HasOptedOutProfiling__c`, that you can create on the object that has personal information and mark it as **TRUE** for the specific customer record. This will ensure that the customer's data is not used in machine learning models. If you are using Salesforce Inbox, Einstein Activity Capture, or Einstein Automated Contacts, you can simply exclude the email under **Setup** and then **Data Policies**.

- **Data processing restrictions**: This relates to restricting the processing of customers' data. This can happen in cases where the customer finds out that their data is incorrect and requests that the company stops further processing the data. For example, a customer finds out that there is a problem with their credit report and calls the credit management agency to request them to put any further processing on hold until the data has been corrected.

  In cases like these, you can export the data out of Salesforce using the **Data Export** feature or your tool of choice for exporting data and delete the record if needed from Salesforce. If that is challenging due to technical reasons, consider putting some kind of a flag that gets checked whenever the data is used by another Salesforce application or if it is integrated with an external system. This will prevent the record from being processed.

- **Data requests**: Some laws require that you provide data to customers when they request it. An example of when this could materialize is when a prospect decides to stop any further communication on the opportunity and asks for access to the data the organization has about the individual. In some cases, law enforcement or courts may request access to data that the business is holding.

  These types of requests can easily be catered to by using **Data Export**. For features such as Salesforce Inbox or Einstein Activity Capture, you will need to create a case with Salesforce Support to request access to read receipts for emails sent to customers or feedback that was provided by a sales rep for Einstein email insights.

As discussed in this section, there is a multitude of different scenarios that can materialize and require flexibility on the platform to ensure that they can be catered to without disrupting the regular operations of the business. To make it easy for organizations to manage these privacy policies and comply with them, Salesforce introduced a tool called **Customer 360 Privacy Center**. We will briefly discuss that in the next section.

Customer 360 Privacy Center

As mentioned earlier, the core focus of Customer 360 Privacy Center is to make it easier for organizations to comply with privacy laws. It does that by de-identifying the data, deleting it, or enabling the portability of data after a customer request has been received. As customers become more conscious of data privacy, data portability is becoming more important as customers will migrate to platforms that offer superior data privacy protection with comparable functionality.

Customer 360 Privacy Center also provides organizations with the ability to set up policies to manage the retention of customer data in the organization and also allows setting up the anonymization of data at the record or field level to comply with *right to be forgotten* requests.

The Privacy Center tool can also be used to securely transfer personally identifiable information to your customer. The tool's data portability feature includes a policy creator that can identify and compile where the personal information of a customer exists. Then an API can be used to generate the file that has this data and share it with your customer.

As discussed here, Customer 360 Privacy Center can simplify complying with privacy laws using a single tool rather than having to worry about compliance as your org updates. Another benefit is that since the tool is managed by Salesforce, they will keep it updated as the laws evolve.

With the knowledge covered in this section, you can kickstart conversations on what to implement in terms of these privacy laws in conjunction with Salesforce but also consult with your legal department to confirm your understanding and what you are implementing. Salesforce provides tools that can be leveraged to assist in compliance but don't underestimate the importance of defining and improving business processes as well. The best technology will fail if the business process it is intended to support is not defined or if it is defined, it is not streamlined.

Putting it all together

Let's put all the learnings of this chapter in a case study and see how these learnings would be practically applied. We are working with a hypothetical company called, **Alpha Mobility Services** (**AMS**), which is a large global telecommunications company providing mobile and internet services to both B2B and B2C customers in 31 countries.

AMS has grown naturally as well as via acquisitions, resulting in a multitude of CRM, marketing, and ERP systems within its technology landscape. The data architect team has worked to consolidate the various CRMs into Salesforce and Salesforce is now globally used. The company uses multiple web-to-lead forms to capture data from prospects and create lead records in Salesforce. A team of **Sales Development Representatives (SDRs)** also creates leads in the system and routes them to the sales team.

AMS has upward of 3 million leads and 1 million opportunities in its system. For support purposes, AMS has implemented Service Cloud and uses communities to support customers. It also has a Social Customer Service setup that allows customers to open cases with the company via Twitter and Facebook. It also uses web chat, allowing customers to create a case when the regional customer support center is offline. The last count revealed that there are a large number of open cases in the system. A preliminary analysis concluded that some of these were attributable to duplicate cases that were erroneously created.

Problem

Various teams that use the system have been complaining for months now about incomplete data that is critical for marketing or sales teams finding out that contact records are stale and not reliable except for new customers that have been onboarded. In some extreme cases, sales reps have reached out to a contact only to find out that they have moved and are not with the company anymore. This is causing delayed sales cycles, reduced upsell opportunities, and difficulty retaining customers, leading to higher customer churn rates that are much higher than the industry average.

Duplicate data is rampant in Salesforce, leading to a single customer having their billing and order data spread over multiple accounts. This causes issues with any meaningful reporting related to customer spend, retention, and where the company should focus its energies to increase revenue. Due to this and the data quality issues mentioned earlier, automated processes that run are also aggravating the situation since the automations are working off of data that is not very reliable. A data architect has been hired to present a plan and implement a governance structure to rectify these issues.

The solution approach

The new data architect has had initial meetings with different business teams as well as the management team to understand the issues and what could be causing them. The data architect has also had implementation documentation on the CRM consolidation project and the initial setup document when Salesforce was implemented 7 years ago shared with them.

Armed with all this information and after reviewing the documentation, the data architect plans to approach the problem in two steps. Step 1 will be to conduct an assessment of the current state and document and present the assessment report. Step 2 will be to fix existing issues and put governance processes and tools in place to prevent and minimize data quality issues in the future.

Step 1 – assessing the current state

The data architect wants to ensure that there is a clear scope defined for what's included in the assessment. Based on the information gathered so far, they put together a scope document outlining the boundaries of the assessment, the exit criteria, the assessment team, the approach they will take to conduct the assessment, and any assumptions and constraints that you have identified so far.

Once the scope document has been reviewed and approved by the management team, the data architect conducts a stakeholder analysis exercise identifying the business users, their interests and influence on the project, and the best ways to communicate with these users.

The architect has already reviewed the provided documentation and plans to conduct 1:1 meetings and run some surveys with the identified users. After reviewing the survey results and the notes taken in these meetings, the architect decides to create a business requirements log that will have all of the requirements identified along with the pain points that the users mentioned.

The data architect prepares the assessment report outlining the pain points, the business requirements, and the suggested approach to eliminate the pain points and meet the business requirements. The architect has also suggested some metrics associated with measuring data completeness and accuracy that can be used to measure success in the next phase.

Step 2 – fixing current issues and implementing a plan

The data architect has recommended a de-duplication tool on an immediate basis to fix the existing duplicate records. The recommended tool also has the functionality to set up duplicate rules that will help prevent new duplicate records from being created. Another tool has been recommended by the architect to enrich the data from data management companies that provide data enrichment services.

The data architect has put together a vision document that outlines the business objectives of the governance plan, the approach, the teams, and the responsible roles to see the plan through success. They have also suggested some metrics to ensure success is continuously measured throughout.

The data architect is also working with the internal communications and training teams to devise a plan on how to communicate the value of data and emphasize that data is everyone's responsibility. In parallel to that, the architect worked with the Salesforce administrators to identify opportunities to streamline page layouts and introduce validation rules so data is correctly entered at the source. Another critical aspect that the architect noted was that there was a lack of proper backup and recovery strategy for Salesforce. The architect has recommended a tool for that and suggested an approach to the Salesforce admins to ensure that backups are taken regularly and restores can be done when needed.

The data architect has engaged the enterprise architect team to put in place a process to ensure that a business architecture for the existing landscape as well as a roadmap is defined. It was found during these discussions that business requirements and enhancement requirements for existing Salesforce applications were not recorded in a central place. To fix this problem, the architect has recommended implementing a business backlog along with a recurring meeting with business users to prioritize the backlog and report on progress.

With these changes in place, the architect has created several Salesforce reports and uses reports by the tools implemented to gauge the quality of data and reports these along with the agreed-upon KPIs to the management team. Phase 1 of the project is complete, and users are already reporting increased satisfaction with the data they are working with along with a decrease in duplicate records, which they were frequently coming across earlier. With the data enrichment tool in place, contact and lead records have more up-to-date and accurate data in them, reducing the time sales reps had to spend earlier to find that information.

Summary

We have discussed a lot of topics in this chapter. We started off with enterprise data governance and explained what it is and what's different about it with respect to data management. My hope is that our discussion on data governance benefits and the risks of not having it provided you with a deep understanding and appreciation of its importance to any organization regardless of its size. We also highlighted why metadata management, an essential component of data governance, is important and how not having effective governance around metadata management can hinder our ability to govern data efficiently.

Once we understood the importance of data governance, the next logical step was where we go from there and that's what was covered: assessing your current state of data governance. We discussed some challenges with current state assessments, and I provided practical steps that you can take to conduct a successful assessment exercise. We ended the section by discussing some common metrics that can help you evaluate your current state and also set targets for the future state.

In the final section of the chapter, we discussed privacy laws in detail. My hope is that after reading that, you have developed an appreciation of how critical these are to businesses not only for compliance reasons but also for protecting the customer's information and to establish trust in them. Because we live in a global economy, GDPR and now the CCPA are probably the most commonly applied laws. GDPR because it covers the massive economic region of the EU, and the CCPA because it is one of the largest economies in the world. Additionally, we discussed tools and techniques that you can use right away in Salesforce to design and implement compliance with these laws.

In summary, this chapter should have provided you with the knowledge and the tools needed to implement data governance initiatives, what they entail, and how they can be implemented. Starting off with the suggested approach for the current state assessment will enable you to focus on the areas that need the most attention. Data privacy laws are becoming more important and our discussion on those should give you the confidence to have those conversations and implement them at your organization.

In the next chapter, we will discuss performance on the Salesforce Platform and the different tools that are available for monitoring performance, and how we can use them to design solutions to ensure that our applications are scalable and performant.

Questions

1. **Precision Printing** (PP) has been having severe data problems and they have recently hired a data architect to help them clean up their sales master data. The architect ran reports and after analyzing the data, presented a report that pointed out major problems with the data. Thousands of records were identified as duplicate or incomplete. What steps can the data architect recommend to clean up the data and maintain it in a good state? (Choose three answers)

    a) Hire interns and task them with identifying duplicate records and deleting them manually.

    b) Use a third-party tool to validate the data.

c) Implement duplicate management rules to detect duplicates and present warning or error messages to the user.

d) Evaluate the security design and adjust the sharing rules, if needed.

2. Frugal Budgets is a global clothing company and has decided to implement a data governance plan to monitor and improve data quality. What steps can the data architect recommend to achieve this goal? (Choose two answers)

a) Implement a Lightning Flow process to query records and identify duplicates, then send a report to the administrator.

b) Implement data quality dashboards to visually show the quality of data to the users.

c) Evaluate the field data type and ensure it fits the purpose of the field; for example, if an email needs to be captured from the user, a field of the email type should be used rather than text.

d) Develop a custom solution that implements Apex triggers to make callouts, then compare and update the data from external data validation sites.

3. **Precision Printing (PP)** has a global customer base with about 45% of its customers based outside of the EU. A data architect has been hired to develop a plan for data governance in Salesforce. What should the data architect include in the data governance plan? (Choose two answers)

a) The data dictionary

b) Data quality metrics

c) Roles and responsibilities

d) A list of all Salesforce flows in the org

Further reading

- *European Union Privacy Law Basics*: https://trailhead.salesforce.com/en/content/learn/modules/european-union-privacy-law-basics/get-to-know-eu-privacy-law

- *California Consumer Privacy Act (CCPA)*: https://trailhead.salesforce.com/content/learn/modules/california-consumer-privacy-act-basics/

6
Managing Performance

In previous chapters, we have talked a lot about data management and governance. That all made sense, but if the applications you build on the platform are slow or crash under heavy loads, you will not build a trusted relationship with your users, whether they are internal or external customers accessing applications through the Salesforce Experience Cloud.

In this chapter, we will start by exploring the topic of performance within Salesforce and understand why performance-related issues happen in the first place. Of course, we need tools to determine whether we are, in fact, facing performance issues and whether we require further diagnosis. So, we will discuss some of the tools that are available to further investigate and resolve issues.

Once we have built a foundation around the causes using the tools available, we will look at the things that we can do to improve performance on the platform. Since performance can be impacted by a wide variety of factors, and therefore a wide range of activities can be undertaken to improve them, we will cover some of the more common performance improvement techniques that we can use to improve it. A very important aspect of performance management is ensuring that you have tested your applications before they get into the production environment. So, we will have a thorough discussion on the importance of performance testing and how to conduct such tests successfully on the Salesforce Platform.

Once you have brought your application up to an acceptable level of performance, you want to make sure that it continues to run in an optimal manner, which requires an understanding of performance monitoring, so we will wrap up the chapter with a discussion on monitoring the platform.

The key topics that we'll cover in this chapter are the following:

- Salesforce Platform performance
- Performance tools
- Improving performance
- Conducting performance testing in Salesforce
- Monitoring performance

So, let's dive right into understanding performance on the Salesforce Platform.

Salesforce Platform performance

Over time, data in your organization will grow. If this growing data is not managed properly, it can cause issues, including performance issues, storage limits, and low adaption of the system. One of the best ways to manage data over the long run is to incorporate data archiving and data management practices as part of every new implementation. When this is not done, data archiving and stewardship activities become afterthoughts and require more work to implement. This is regardless of factors including having sufficient storage for the next few years, good performance, a lack of performance-related complaints from customers, or thinking that you will never hit the limits.

Good architecture means thinking ahead about performance and minimizing, where it makes sense, the use of available resources. In this section, we will review why performance matters and some of the more common reasons that cause performance issues. We will also be reviewing performance-related tools and how to execute performance tests on the Salesforce Platform.

Let's try to first understand why it's important to keep an eye on the performance of your organization.

Importance of performance monitoring

Salesforce is used widely across sales and marketing organizations, and it's become a critical business platform. With its ease of use and the capabilities provided to extend the platform, it is used by a wide arrange of teams. From Support to Sales operations, Finance to Legal and **Human Resources** (**HR**), different teams use it to conduct their business on the platform.

The Salesforce AppExchange store also provides a massive 3,000+ business applications portfolio that also makes it easy to tailor the platform to multiple different use cases. Another reason why it's widely used is the numerous integration tools that can be hooked up with the platform. And because the platform is widely used, many **Independent Software Vendors** (**ISVs**) have built easy-to-use connectors that can quickly and easily integrate their products with Salesforce.

All of these present a great opportunity but also a challenge because of the need to maintain a performant business platform. This is especially true on the new **Lightning Experience** (**LEX**) **User Interface** (**UI**), which is heavily dependent on client-side processing and, overall, it is more dependent on network quality for providing an optimal user experience. Generally, **Software as a Service** (**SaaS**) and **Platform as a Service** (**PaaS**) are harder to monitor because the infrastructure is not owned by the customer. Tools such as networking and application monitoring tools, for example, capturing packets for analysis, don't work outside of your own environment. Thankfully, some tools can assist in pinpointing these types of issues. We will review some of these tools later, but now, let's understand the reasons why it's important to monitor performance on the Salesforce Platform in the first place:

- **Revenue generation and productivity**: Sales teams need to be continuously selling and, to achieve that objective, organizations typically spend significant amounts of capital to implement and configure Salesforce, so it's tailored for their business. Many organizations also invest in third-party tools such as AppExchange applications to make their sales teams as effective as possible. Besides technology, organizations spend time training their sales representatives in perfecting their pitches and slide decks and offering call script guidance and myriad other tools to help them close deals. Technology and these tools, along with optimized business processes, result in a well-oiled selling machine. A performance problem in Salesforce can severely impact the productivity of your sales team, which could potentially lead to lost revenue.

- **Trust**: If you have a system that's slow frequently, or on which users cannot do their day-to-day activities, soon you will have unhappy users who will lose trust in the system. Users talk with each other and share their experiences and once a negative trend starts to develop, it is not easy to reverse it. Having processes and tools in place to ensure the system performs at an optimal level is crucial to ensuring a continued positive return on your organization's investment.

- **System health**: Issues related to performance usually point to underlying issues that should be reviewed and rectified. If not rectified, these can affect other areas of the application or increase the effort required to extend the application. For example, a report is running slow and the architect, after investigating, finds out that the organization has many complex sharing rules. Each time the report is run, the sharing rules must be evaluated, thereby slowing down a report that otherwise would have performed well. Another area that this could impact is if your customer has integrations that run on a nightly basis to bring in data say from an ERP. Having complex sharing rules can slow down the process because the system has to recalculate data access. This can be a problem in very large global orgs where users are logged in and using the system in multiple time zones. In these situations, other techniques can be used to ensure a smooth data import and minimize the impact on users.

- **Service Level Agreements (SLAs)**: System performance is important not just from the perspective of internal users, but also of customers. Your SLAs with customers outline the response times and the level of service the customer can expect to receive. If your org is non-performant, your customer SLAs can be adversely impacted. For instance, in a large car dealership, a commitment is made to customers that their vehicles will be serviced within a certain period, and if that time period is missed, then an automatic 15% discount is applied to the entire bill. Salesforce is used to manage work orders and submit orders for auto parts. Let's say a technician is attempting to query the parts for a specific make and model so they can order them, but the system is slow, which is taking the technician longer than expected to order relevant parts. As a result, work will not get completed on time and cost the company revenue in the form of the 15% discount it now has to give to the customer.

- **Continuous improvement**: Organizations try to compete and maintain their competitive advantage and use different techniques to do so. Proactively monitoring your performance enables you to ensure that mistakes made in the past are not repeated and lessons learned in the past are incorporated for future design and build. The net result of this is an overall improvement in customer service and an assurance for internal users that the organization is taking data seriously and is vested in it.

Now that we have looked at the reasons for monitoring performance, in the next section, we will review why performance issues happen in the first place, followed by a discussion on some of the tools that can be used to measure and improve performance.

Reasons for performance-related issues

We established earlier that Salesforce is a critical business application and is increasingly used for more business functions than just CRM. There is a multitude of factors that could impact performance and affect business operations and therefore, we must understand these factors.

The first thing to do when your users report a performance-related issue is to check the Salesforce Trust site and ensure that the problem is not on the Salesforce side. You can also subscribe to alerts from this site. To check the status of your instance, visit `status. salesforce.com` and enter your instance ID as shown in the following steps. First, let's review the steps to find your instance ID:

1. Navigate to **SETUP** and then **COMPANY INFORMATION** to find your org's **Instance** ID, as shown in the following screenshot:

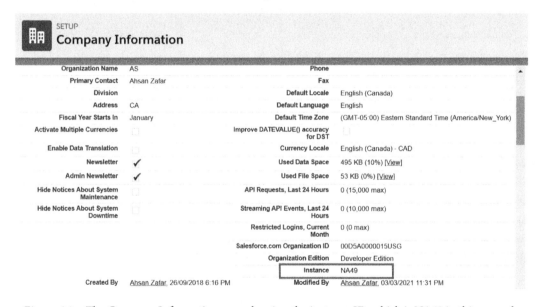

Figure 6.1 – The Company Information page showing the instance ID, which is NA49 in this example

2. Once you have the instance ID, go to `status.salesforce.com` and enter your instance ID:

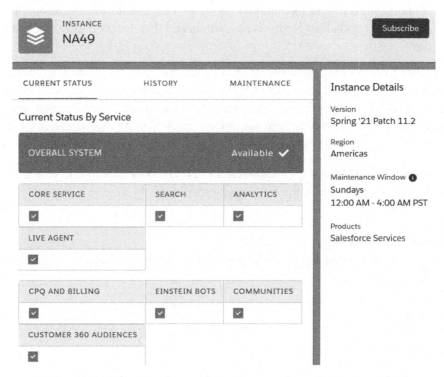

Figure 6.2 – All features are operating without any issues for instance NA49

You can also click on the **HISTORY** tab to see historical records for any issues that have arisen on this instance, and the **MAINTENANCE** tab shows the patches and releases applied on the instance, including upcoming releases. This can be a very helpful tool for planning purposes ahead of each release, as well as planning for in-flight or upcoming projects.

One challenge with performance issues is that there is a wide spectrum of factors that can impact performance, and therefore it is important to narrow things down quickly to the most likely culprit. A good way to start on that is to cast a wide net and ask questions such as the following:

Does it affect everyone who is using Salesforce?

- Are users in different locations experiencing similar performance issues?
- What browsers are they using?
- Is the performance issue experienced while using other browsers?

Having the answers to these questions can help you narrow down the issues to the two or three most probable possibilities, which can then be explored further. Let's look at the reasons for performance-related issues:

- **Leisure network traffic**: Many users these days carry devices that connect to the office wireless access points and stream high-definition video and audio, which can result in the office networking bandwidth getting constrained. A way to mitigate this could be to provide a separate access point for these users so leisure network traffic passes through that access point and critical applications, including Salesforce, can run on the regular network, leaving plenty of bandwidth free. You will need to determine a way to prevent users' devices from getting on the network; this can usually be done through **Media Access Control** (**MAC**) filtering so only authorized MAC addresses can get on the regular network.

> **MAC addresses**
>
> A MAC address is a unique identification number that uniquely identifies hardware on the network. Every MAC is unique in a network and no two MAC addresses will ever be the same. This is ensured by the nomenclature used for MAC addresses, a topic outside the scope of this book. Read more about MAC addresses at `https://www.pcmag.com/encyclopedia/term/mac-address`.

- **Bandwidth quality**: Low bandwidth can be a problem and your users will notice if you try to resolve it, but adding more bandwidth to fix performance-related issues will not always result in desired outcomes. This is because the quality of the bandwidth is also important. An increase of a few percentage points in package loss can impact performance in a noticeable way.

- **Location**: Salesforce has several hundred instances globally where all the orgs are run from. Your proximity relative to the instance that hosts your org can also be a factor in performance-related issues. If the physical distance is significant and there are many hops to get to the instance, this can result in slow performance. Salesforce instances are spread throughout the world in multiple regions and the org is assigned by Salesforce based on where the users are located. Before signing up, you should consult with your account executive if you would like your org to be in a region where most of your users will be based, rather than in the region where the contract will be executed.

> **Hop**
>
> *Hop* is a networking term that refers to the number of network devices a packet has to pass through to reach the destination. These network devices can be routers, switches, repeaters, and so on.
>
> Each device receives the packet, processes the information in it, and then forwards it on to its destination. Each time a device does that, this takes time and can have an impact on the performance when millions of packets are transmitted. In Windows, you can use the `tracert` command in **Command Prompt** to see the number of hops. For example, from my laptop to `salesforce.com` is 9 hops.
>
> Keep in mind that a lower hop count doesn't necessarily mean a faster connection because other factors contribute to the connection speed as well.

- **Inefficient configuration or code**: Performance issues can also be caused by incorrectly configured applications or code that is sub-optimal. These can be a massive drain on system resources, thereby impacting performance. If a problem keeps happening in a specific Visualforce page or a Lightning component, you will want to review the code and ensure that it follows best practices. Another possibility is an incorrectly configured application. Earlier, we discussed the example of sharing rules. If there are too many sharing rules, that can slow down reports or data queries in general because every time a query is executed, the system has to run the sharing rules to ensure that the data security is protected in line with these rules.

- **AppExchange packages**: Many AppExchange packages add business value to your processes, but some of the packages also communicate back and forth with the ISV servers and can impact performance. For example, if you are using a digital signature solution and install the managed package, there may be bandwidth being utilized by the package, resulting in poor performance. Admins should frequently review and assess managed packages to ensure they are still useful and provide the value that they were initially installed for in the org.

- **Browsers**: The unsung heroes of the cloud world, browsers play a critical role in users' experiences. As a browser is used over time, it accumulates a lot of data. This can include the browser accumulating a large number of cookies and caches resulting in an impact on performance. It is also recommended to have the browsers updated to the latest release, as browser vendors are continuously releasing new patches to fix not only security vulnerabilities but also to improve performance.

  Using browsers that are supported by Salesforce is another important factor. For example, an organization was using Internet Explorer 11 and kept running into issues and therefore, users started to use Google Chrome. The issue was that whenever users ran into problems with Salesforce or in general, corporate support teams would not provide support since Internet Explorer 11 was the supported corporate browser.

Running multiple browser windows at the same time or having multiple tabs open in the same window can seriously downgrade performance. This is because each window and tab that is open consumes memory and **Central Processing Unit (CPU)** cycles.

Another aspect of browsers is the ability to add plugins and extensions. I recommend disabling all plugins and extensions during diagnoses if a specific user is reporting a problem. This can easily be done by opening the browser in **Incognito** or **Private Browsing** mode.

- **Technical debt**: This can play a significant part in slowing down performance if a close eye is not kept on it. Simply defined, **technical debt** is the debt you take on when expediently delivering solutions. Pay attention to the word *debt*, which means that it needs to be paid back promptly or it will demand payment with interest. Technical debt is not necessarily a bad thing as long as there are processes and tools in place to ensure the technical debt is taken care of.

  Technical debt in the world of Salesforce includes anything from abandoned custom fields, workflow processes, reports, and triggers, to workarounds put in place to meet business requirements. When Salesforce provides a solution to fill a gap in its solution, usually as part of its three releases per year, or the organization decides to go for a third-party solution or improve its own solution, on many occasions, the old solution or workaround is left as is in the org, contributing to technical debt. As time passes and technical debt accumulates, if no action is taken, users will start seeing performance issues.

- **Hardware and software requirements**: There are certain hardware and software requirements that are needed in order for Salesforce to run optimally. For example, 8 GB of RAM is recommended to run LEX. The minimum required is 5 GB of RAM, but depending on your application's need for resources, users may experience performance problems due to minimum RAM requirements. Performance issues can be caused by these requirements not being met. Salesforce will not block customers from using unsupported software and hardware, so this should also be checked so that potential hardware and software problems can be ruled out right at the beginning of the diagnostic process.

- **Network topologies**: Some customers, due to the nature of their business, may have very strict requirements in terms of which **Internet Protocol (IP)** addresses their Salesforce org can be accessed from. Sometimes, they will require their users to log in to Salesforce via a **VPN (Virtual Private Network)** and that can cause network traffic delays because all communication has to be tunneled through the VPN.

- **API limits**: Almost every Salesforce org has some type of AppExchange package installed or integration with another system. For larger orgs, sometimes there can be tens of AppExchange packages installed along with many other integrations. All the integrations and some of the AppExchange packages, depending on what the app is about, utilize API calls. Since Salesforce imposes limits to ensure quality for other customers on the instance, there are limits placed on these calls. Hitting the limits means that you either wait for 24 hours to pass (the period after which the limits get reset) or purchase additional API calls from Salesforce. The interruption caused by API limits is a serious problem as it can impact direct revenue-generating activities or customer service. For example, if your marketing automation tool cannot communicate with Salesforce, then any high-value leads coming into the tool cannot be pushed over to Salesforce.

> **Governor limits**
>
> Certified managed packages are managed packages that have passed the security review for AppExchange. They have their own set of governor limits in addition to the customer's org limits. For example, the per transaction DML limit in the customer org is 150; a certified managed package will get its own 150 DML limit per transaction. Refer to the Per-Transaction Certified Managed Package Limits section at this link: `https://developer.salesforce.com/docs/atlas.en-us.apexcode.meta/apexcode/apex_gov_limits.htm`.

Now that we have discussed the reasons for performance-related issues, in the next section, we will discuss some of the tools that can be used to address performance-related issues.

Performance tools

There is a multitude of tools that are available to monitor and diagnose performance-related issues. The discussion in this section is not meant to be exhaustive, detailing each tool that is available and its capabilities, but rather providing pointers so you can understand and put them to use when you run into performance-related issues.

It must be mentioned that for business-critical applications, performance must be placed at the forefront right from the outset. It's not a good practice to design an application and leave performance considerations to the end, or worse yet, until the app goes into production and users start to report problems. This is the reason that performance tests should be performed to gauge the application's ability to scale up to the higher threshold of the range of the number of expected users. We will discuss performance testing and how to conduct it for Salesforce in more detail in the *Conducting performance testing in Salesforce* section.

Let's discuss some of the tools at our disposal to monitor performance in Salesforce.

URL suffixes

This is a technique to view your page load times for LEX. It is done by adding `?eptVisible=1` to the end of the URL. For example, when I add this to the **Account** page for a specific record, the result shows me that the page was loaded in **4.49** seconds. We will discuss the details related to LEX performance in the *Performance in LEX* section.

We can see in the top right of *Figure 6.3* that the **Account** page took **4.49** seconds to load:

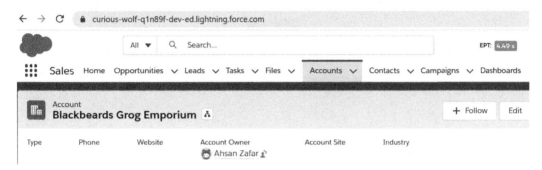

Figure 6.3 – The EPT (Experienced Page Time) value is shown as 4.49 seconds

This is a handy tool to quickly get some preliminary data on how the page is performing without going through any extensive setup.

Speedtest

This is a test to measure performance and provides different metrics to gauge **JavaScript (JS)** speed and the connection speed to Salesforce servers. To use this, simply append `/speedtest.jsp` to the URL while logged in to your org. For example, in my case, I have `https://curious-wolf-q1n89f-dev-ed.my.salesforce.com/speedtest.jsp`.

Then, on the resulting page, run the test. As shown in *Figure 6.4*, this produces the Octane score, the download and upload speeds, and other pertinent information. In this case, the Octane score is well below the minimum score required by Salesforce, so the user should expect to experience performance issues:

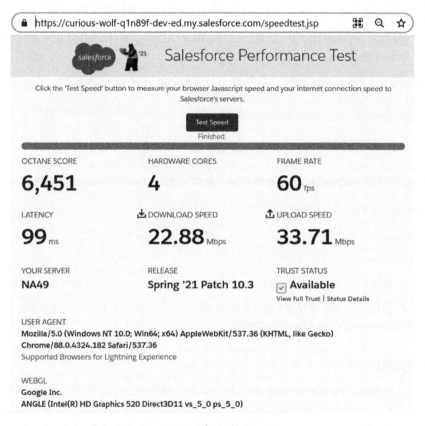

Figure 6.4 – The Octane score

As seen in *Figure 6.4*, Speedtest has other information that is useful for troubleshooting, such as upload/download speeds, instance ID, and other pertinent details relating to the browser and the operating system.

> **Octane score**
>
> The **Octane score**, developed by Google, is a measure of how JS in the browser is performing. Higher Octane scores correspond to faster load times. It is important to note that the Octane score factors in hardware and the type of browser as well. Salesforce requires a minimum Octane score of 20,000 and recommends an Octane score of more than 30,000 for optimal performance.

Salesforce Optimizer

This is a free tool from Salesforce that can be run either as a PDF report or as an app and provides details on a bunch of metrics covering usage, unused fields, custom code, reports, and dashboards. Not only does the tool scan and highlight problematic areas in your org, but it makes recommendations on how to solve those issues. It also provides an estimate of the effort of rectifying each issue that's analyzed, along with additional resources if you drill down into the item, as shown in *Figure 6.5*. The report or the app can be run from **Setup** by searching for Optimizer.

I prefer running the app since it covers more features than the report and provides a sorting feature with which you can sort the list view. Salesforce recommends running this report or app at a regular cadence. This can enable you to catch issues before they materialize. *Figure 6.5* shows the results after Salesforce Optimizer has been run:

Salesforce Optimizer
Results

55 items • Sorted by Status • Last run 28/02/2021 2:14 PM

Feature	Type	Estimated Effort	Status ↓
User Logins	User Management	< 30 minutes	Immediate Action Required ⚠ red ⚠
Insecure Default External Access Levels	Improve Org Security	> 2 hours	Immediate Action Required ⚠ red ⚠
Pending Release Updates	Improve Org Security	> 2 hours	Action Required
Unassigned Roles	User Management	< 30 minutes	Review Required
API Versions	Custom Code	1 - 2 hours	Review Required
Profile Assignments	User Management	1 - 2 hours	Review Required
Incomplete Chatter Profiles	Usage	< 30 minutes	Review Required
Inactive Chatter Users	Usage	30 - 60 minutes	Review Required
Multiple Apex Triggers per Object	Custom Code	1 - 2 hours	Review Required
Field Usage	Fields	30 - 60 minutes	Review Required
Unassigned Custom Profiles	User Management	< 30 minutes	Review Required
Unused Reports	Reports And Dashboards	< 30 minutes	Review Required

Figure 6.5 – Results from the Optimizer app

You can drill down into each item and view the results in more detail along with the estimated effort and additional resources to help you rectify the issue.

Salesforce Shield's event monitoring

Salesforce Shield is a set of security tools that provides an extra layer of security and governance in Salesforce. One of the tools is called **Real-time Event Monitoring**, which gives access to real-time data on performance and other metrics such as security and usage data on the platform.

Event Monitoring is an API-only tool, meaning that it can be accessed via the API, and the key object in the tool is `EventLogFile`. This means that the data can be easily imported into application monitoring tools such as Analytics or Splunk for easier consumption.

You can use the Salesforce **Event Log File (ELF)** browser app (`https://salesforce-elf.herokuapp.com/?_ga=2.82989334.1271813283.1614356382-1891424622.1607399861`) to access and download event log files. The data can then be visualized using your tool of choice for data visualization. The following screenshot of the browser shows the results filtered down to a single event type of **API**:

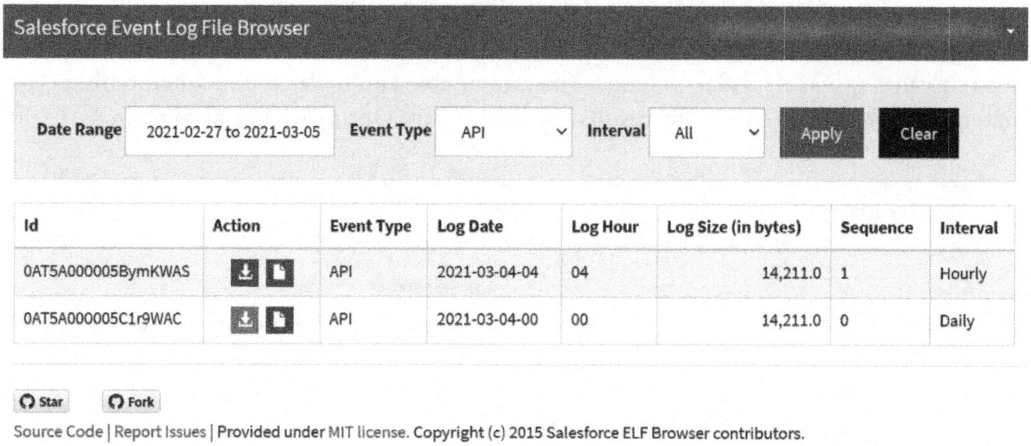

Salesforce Event Log File Browser

| Date Range | 2021-02-27 to 2021-03-05 | Event Type | API | Interval | All | Apply | Clear |

Id	Action	Event Type	Log Date	Log Hour	Log Size (in bytes)	Sequence	Interval
0AT5A000005BymKWAS		API	2021-03-04-04	04	14,211.0	1	Hourly
0AT5A000005C1r9WAC		API	2021-03-04-00	00	14,211.0	0	Daily

Star   Fork

Source Code | Report Issues | Provided under MIT license. Copyright (c) 2015 Salesforce ELF Browser contributors.

Figure 6.6 – All the logged API events for a week in the Event Log File Browser

Here is a screenshot of a log file downloaded from **Event Log File Browser**:

	A	B	C	D	E	F	G
	EVENT_TYPE	TIMESTAMP	REQUEST_ID	ORGANIZATION_ID	USER_ID	RUN_TIME	CPU_TIME
	API	2.02103E+13	TID:17799340000c627ff9	00D5A0000015USG	0055A000006L6x5	24	7
	API	2.02103E+13	TID:17799340000c627ff9	00D5A0000015USG	0055A000006L6x5	14	7
	API	2.02103E+13	TID:182427400009f2a802	00D5A0000015USG	0055A000006L6x5	22	18
	API	2.02103E+13	TID:300595000070b04506	00D5A0000015USG	0055A000006L6x5	8	4
	API	2.02103E+13	TID:300595000070b04506	00D5A0000015USG	0055A000006L6x5	4	3
	API	2.02103E+13	TID:463390000083f97c2e	00D5A0000015USG	0055A000006L6x5	4	2
	API	2.02103E+13	TID:51712700005790e83e	00D5A0000015USG	0055A000006L6x5	68	52
	API	2.02103E+13	TID:570254000099a027ff	00D5A0000015USG	0055A000006L6x5	80	63
	API	2.02103E+13	TID:7450210000d1094500	00D5A0000015USG	0055A000006L6x5	4	3
	API	2.02103E+13	TID:19956120000561e55b	00D5A0000015USG	0055A000006L6x5	69	32
	API	2.02103E+13	TID:19956120000561e55b	00D5A0000015USG	0055A000006L6x5	31	10
	API	2.02103E+13	TID:19956120000561e55b	00D5A0000015USG	0055A000006L6x5	12	6
	API	2.02103E+13	TID:21393930000aab16a8	00D5A0000015USG	0055A000006L6x5	9	5
	API	2.02103E+13	TID:40400020000369a9fe	00D5A0000015USG	0055A000006L6x5	61	47
	API	2.02103E+13	TID:417069000008ab8461	00D5A0000015USG	0055A000006L6x5	47	35
	API	2.02103E+13	TID:4170240000b067095	00D5A0000015USG	0055A000006L6x5	62	46
	API	2.02103E+13	TID:119769530000a57cc9	00D5A0000015USG	0055A000006L6x5	4	3
	API	2.02103E+13	TID:121062250000ad691d	00D5A0000015USG	0055A000006L6x5	47	29

Figure 6.7 – A sample log file showing the details logged by the Event Monitoring tool

> **Note**
>
> Some blank columns have been hidden in the preceding screenshot for brevity and the screenshot has been cropped for improved legibility.

You can also determine which applications are using the API calls by combining the results from the event log files and associating them with the IP address of the calling app in Salesforce. Here is a sample login history record pulled from Salesforce:

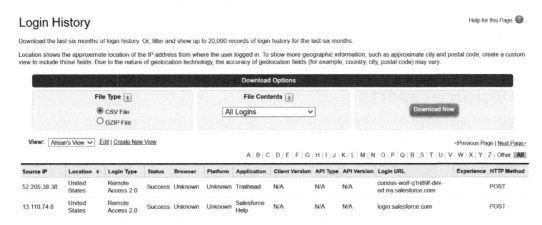

Figure 6.8 – Login information from Developer Workbench

Source IP can be combined with **CLIENT_IP** in the event log file to get granular information – for example, about the applications that are utilizing the most API calls, the timings when the API calls are made, and other useful information that can be gathered. This is especially useful when the given application is not specified in the login history or **CLIENT_NAME** is unknown in the event log file. *Figure 6.9* shows a row from the log file showing that the **Account** object was queried (in the **METHOD_NAME** column):

API_TYPE	API_VERSION	CLIENT_NAME	METHOD_	ENTITY_NAME	ROWS_PR	REQUEST_	RESPONSE	DB_BLOCI	DB_CPU_TIME	TIMESTAI	USER_ID_DERIVED	CLIENT_IP
P	50	Workbench/51.0.0	query	Account	39	751	7052	34	10	2021-03-(	0055A000006L6x5QAC	35.173.67.53

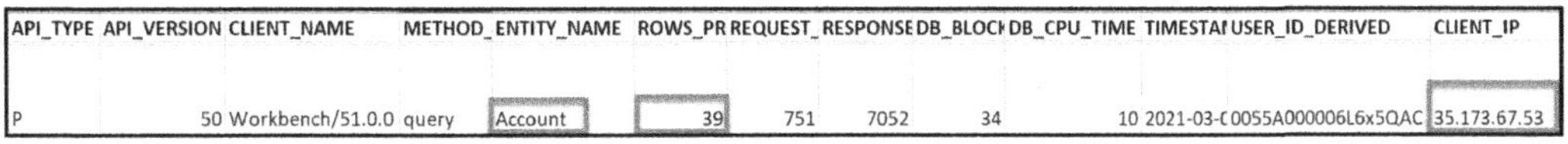

Figure 6.9 – Sample record from the event log

In *Figure 6.9*, the total number of rows processed is shown as 39 (in the **ROWS_PROCESSED** column, the full column heading is not shown), while also showing us the IP address of the origin.

Let's now continue to review other tools that we can use for monitoring Salesforce.

Salesforce Page Optimizer

This is a tool specifically designed to monitor the performance of Salesforce Communities. It is provided as a plugin for Google Chrome and provides actionable insights into how the page is performing. We will discuss this in more detail later.

Salesforce Lightning Inspector

This is another Google Chrome extension that helps to diagnose performance bottlenecks. It can be used to inspect different aspects of an application, such as events that fired and client-side storage details. The **Performance** tab shows details of how long components are taking to get executed and where the potential bottlenecks are.

Salesforce reports

Salesforce has out-of-the-box tools and reports that can be used to monitor the limits on API calls. We established earlier that API limits can create serious issues for business-critical applications that rely on external systems via integrations or AppExchange packages.

Out of the box, you can use the **System Overview** page, which shows the API calls for the last 24 hours as seen in the next screenshot. You should also consider setting up API usage notifications that send an email every *x* number of hours when the API usage reaches a certain threshold. The system keeps on sending emails until the API usage goes below the specified threshold:

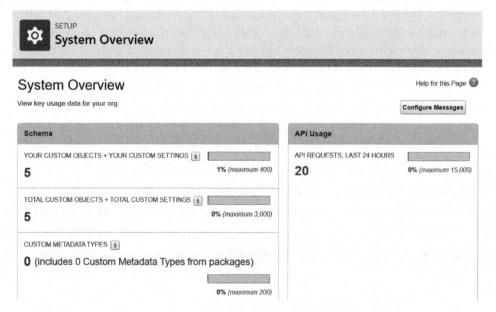

Figure 6.10 – The total number of API calls made in the last 24 hours; in this case, 20

Another way to review the usage is to run a report called **API Usage Last 7 Days**, which shows the usage for the last 7 days as seen in the following screenshot. This report is only available in the **Classic** view:

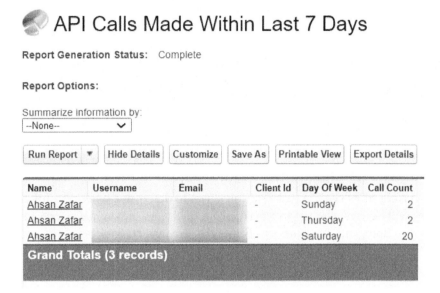

Figure 6.11 – The report is showing the number of API calls that have been made in the last 7 days

These reports can be a useful tool to gain insight on how APIs are being used in your org and whether any proactive intervention is required to prevent API limit-related errors.

Query Plan tool

This is used to access query plans for **Structured Object Query Language** (**SOQL**) and **Salesforce Object Search Language** (**SOSL**) queries, reports, and list views to optimize them for performance. This is a valuable resource at your disposal that you can use to proactively avoid problems or quickly rule out SOQL queries as the cause of performance issues. The Query Plan tool is accessed from the Developer Console and helps in tuning SOQL queries. You can use the tool to understand the different query plans and whether your indexed query filters will be used by the Query Optimizer or whether it will perform a full table scan.

> Query plan
>
> A **query plan** is essentially the map showing a sequence of steps that can be used to access data from the database. The Query Optimizer, upon submission of a query, evaluates some of the different approaches it can take to fetch the data and returns the plan with the least cost. This means that the returned plan will get the data in the least amount of time.

Since most custom code-based applications use SOQL, this is a very handy tool to test how your SOQL queries will perform. Let's also understand what a full table scan is before we deep dive into the Query Plan tool.

Full table scan

A **full table scan** is when the database table is scanned row by row and every row is examined to check whether it matches the query's `where` clause. Performance-wise, this is an expensive operation, and the use of filters is encouraged in SOQL queries:

```
SELECT name FROM Account WHERE name = "Star Wars Innovations";
```

The filter is the part after the `where` clause in the SOQL query. The `name = "Star Wars Innovations"` part is the filter, which will cause the index to be used since the name field is indexed in the `Account` object.

There is a certain set of criteria that Salesforce uses to determine whether a full table scan or an index will be used, leading to a performant query. As shown in *Figure 6.12*, indexes play a key role along with the number of rows that are expected in the query result:

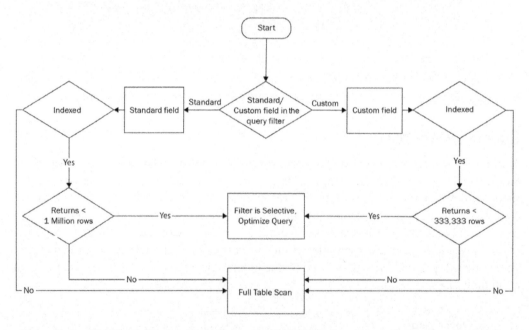

Figure 6.12 – High-level diagram showing the criteria that Salesforce uses to determine whether the query filter is selective, or whether a full table scan will be used

The Query Optimizer determines a query to be selective when it has a selective filter in it. Selective filters help the query engine in terms of how it gets the results, whereas a non-selective filter (and therefore, a non-selective query) will require that a full table scan is performed, which is a costly operation. This is determined by the following:

- The filter has a standard or a custom field.

- Some standard fields are indexed automatically. These are as follows:

  - Primary keys (**Id**, **Name**, and **OwnerId**)

  - Relationship fields (lookup or master-detail fields – **CreatedById**, and **LastModifiedById**)

  - Audit fields (**CreatedDate** and **SystemModStamp**)

  - Record types for standard and custom objects

- If a **Custom** field is set as **Unique** or **External**, it is automatically indexed.

- Once it is determined that a filter is indexed, the number of rows returned is then determined. For standard indexed fields, 30% of the first 1 million records and 15% of the remaining records are determined. If this is fewer than 1 million rows in total, then the filter is selective and used by the optimizer.

- For custom indexed fields, 10% of the first 1 million records and 5% of the remaining records are considered, and if this is less than 333,333 rows in total, then the filter is considered selective and used by the optimizer.

- If an AND operator is used in the filter, then the query targets less than the following:

  - Twice the index selectivity thresholds for each filter

  - The index selectivity thresholds for the intersection of the fields

- If the OR operator is used, then the query targets less than the following:

  - The index selectivity thresholds for each filter

  - The index selectivity thresholds for the sum of those fields

- If the LIKE operator is used and doesn't have a leading wildcard, for example, LIKE 'Star%', the Optimizer samples the first 100,000 rows for selectivity.

Salesforce has an upper limit on how many records would be indexed in the table and the 1 million records for a standard index and 333,333 records for custom indexes are reflective of that limit. If all indexes in the filter are standard, then the standard selectivity threshold is used, otherwise, the custom selectivity threshold will be used.

Let's look at some examples to determine whether an index will be used in the following SOQL queries.

Example 1

Here we have a filter clause on the **SystemModStamp** field, which is indexed:

```
SELECT name FROM Account WHERE SystemModStamp >
2019-01-01T00:00:00Z
```

The details pertaining to the object are given in the following table:

Total Records in Object	4,000,000
Filter has Indexed Field	Yes
Records Returned	500,000
Selectivity Threshold	750,000
Number of Records Returned is Lower than Threshold	Yes
Query is Selective	Yes

Figure 6.13 – Criteria that will be used by Salesforce to determine whether the query is selective

The query is selective in this case because the selectivity threshold will not be exceeded when the query is run.

Example 2

In the following example, a custom field is being used as the index. Notice that the selectivity threshold is much lower for queries having custom index fields:

```
SELECT name FROM Account WHERE LastEmailedDate__c  >
2019-01-01T00:00:00Z
```

Figure 6.14 shows the details of the object and how the query will behave:

Total Records in Object	4,000,000
Filter has Indexed Field	Yes
Records Returned	200,000
Selectivity Threshold	250,000
Number of Records Returned is Lower than Threshold	Yes
Query is Selective	Yes

Figure 6.14 – Selective query with the selectivity threshold met

Once again, the query is considered selective because the number of records returned is much lower than the number of records in the selectivity threshold.

Example 3

In the following example, the use of two filters with the **AND** operator causes the query to be selective:

```
SELECT name from Account where RecordTypeId = 'xxxxxxxxxxxxxxx'
AND LastEmailedDate__c  > 2019-01-01T00:00:00Z
```

Figure 6.15 shows the behavior when two filters are used in the query, causing it to become a selective query:

Total Records in Object	4,000,000
Filter has Indexed Fields	Yes
1st Filter Returns (RecordTypeId = 'xxxxxxxxxxxxxxx')	200,000
2nd Filter Returns (LastEmailedDate__c > 2019-01-01T00:00:00Z)	300,000
Records Returned	150,000
Selectivity Threshold	800,000
Record Returned Lower for Individual Filter and Lower for Intersection of Filters	Yes
Query is Selective	Yes

Figure 6.15 – Multiple filters having indexed fields results in the query becoming selective

In this example, multiple query filters were used, both of which had indexed fields, resulting in a lower number of records being returned than the selectivity threshold, and thus making the query selective.

Example 4

In the next example, the use of two filters with the OR operator causes the query to be selective:

```
SELECT name from Account where RecordTypeId = 'xxxxxxxxxxxxxxx'
OR LastEmailedDate__c  > 2019-01-01T00:00:00Z
```

Figure 6.16 shows the result of a query using the same number of rows used in the earlier examples, but with an OR operator:

Total Records in Object	4,000,000
Filter has Indexed Fields	Yes
1st Filter Returns (RecordTypeId = 'XXXXXXXXXXXXXXXX')	200,000
2nd Filter Returns (LastEmailedDate__c > 2019-01-01T00:00:00Z)	300,000
Records Returned	200,000
Selectivity Threshold	250,000
Record Returned Lower for Individual Filter and Lower for Intersection of Filters	No
Query is Selective	No

Figure 6.16 – Criteria used to determine whether a query is selective when the OR operator is used

We've learned that although, individually, the filter returns a lower number of records (200,000 and 300,000, respectively), when combined, they exceed the selectivity threshold limit and therefore the query is not considered selective.

In the next section, we will review how we can understand the results from the Query Plan tool and used those to adjust our queries for better performance.

Interpreting results from the Query Plan tool

Now that we have run some queries in the previous section, let's run a query and understand how the tool works. *Figure 6.17* shows the result of a Query Plan that was run on the Account object that returned a single record. Let's analyze closely what the various numbers mean:

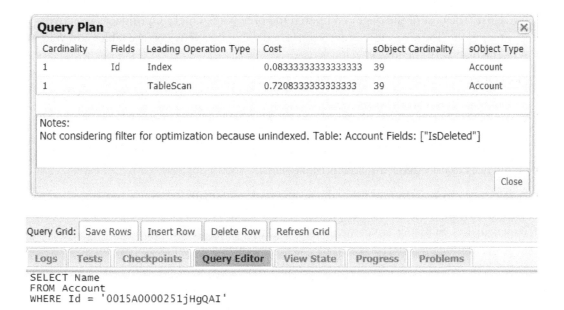

Figure 6.17 – The Query Plan tool

This query is selective as seen from the result when the Query Plan tool is run. If the value in the **Cost** column is above *1*, this means that the query is not selective. In this case, the index will be used since the filter is considered selective.

Let's go through some definitions of the columns seen in the Query Plan tool result in *Figure 6.17*:

- **Cardinality**: Estimated number of records returned by the leading operation.

- **Fields**: The indexed field(s) used by the Optimizer. In our example, the **Id** field is shown because that is the field used by the Optimizer.

- **Leading operation type**: Primary operation type used by the Optimizer to optimize the query. Some values include the following:

  - **Sharing**: Salesforce will use an index based on the sharing rules associated with the user running the query.

  - **Index**: The query will use the index on the queried object.

  - **TableScan**: Will query all rows in the table.

  - **Other**: The query will use optimizations internal to Salesforce.

- **Cost**: The cost of the query compared to Force.com's Query Optimizer's selectivity threshold. The cost value is derived from database statistics on the tables and values. The plan with the lowest value is used.

- **sObject cardinality**: Approximate record count for the queried object.

- **sObject type**: Name of the queried object.

The plan is only shown for operations that are supported, including operations such as NOT EQUAL TO, comparisons with null values such as Name = ' ', leading wildcards, or references to non-deterministic formula fields.

It is important to keep in mind that due to the multitenant-driven architecture of Salesforce, the platform has its own SOQL Query Optimizer that considers multi-tenant statistics. Statistics are gathered on a nightly basis, but the Optimizer can also perform dynamic pre-queries which has its results cached for an hour. Salesforce's Query Optimizer also keeps track of candidates for customer indexes internally and automatically creates one-column indexes that it determines could help with selectivity.

Note that soft-deleted records can have a significant impact on query performance, so the IsDeleted = false filter may be used in your query. This will exclude all the soft-deleted records. Keep in mind that the deleted records count toward statistics, so make sure that you have a process to hard-delete records.

When a field is indexed in Salesforce, that may not necessarily mean that it is available right away – rather, it can take up to 15 minutes for the index table to be updated by the indexing server because it executes asynchronously. This is important because say you have a large table, and by working with Salesforce Support, you determine that a custom index would help. The index is created on the field, but the performance is still slow. It could be because the index table has not been updated yet.

Now that we have reviewed some of the tools that can be used for monitoring, let's look at the techniques we can use to improve application performance.

Improving performance

We have looked at a variety of tools that can be used to diagnose and monitor performance-related issues. The next obvious step is to fix these performance bottlenecks depending on where the issue is. The technique or the tool to rectify the problem will also be different. For example, if there are multiple triggers per object, page performance could get impacted, and to fix this, you will need to refactor the code to use a single trigger per object. Another example that we will review later as well involves using multiple Process Builder flows on a single object – fixing that would require determining the tool that will provide optimal performance.

Let's look at some of the actions we can take to improve performance once we have identified the issue. This should not be taken as an exhaustive list, but rather as pointers that can help you quickly improve the performance of your application. For example, multiple actions can be taken to improve Visualforce page performance, but I mention only a couple of them in the following sections.

Browser caching

This is a simple setting from the UI that can significantly improve page performance by avoiding extra server calls by securely caching the most frequently used data on the client, that is, a browser. This setting is turned on by default and Salesforce discourages turning it off. Some exceptions to this include situations where the company's security policy doesn't allow the caching of secure data, and in sandboxes when you want to immediately see the effects of your configuration or code changes without emptying the cache.

Using a Content Delivery Network

A **Content Delivery Network (CDN)** is a collection of server-based infrastructure that speeds up the performance of websites. When a website is loaded, the images and other content hosted with the website get loaded as well. If you are accessing the website from a different continent than where the website is hosted, you will see latency and a delayed response compared to a user located within the same city or region as the web hosting.

With a CDN, the content is copied to servers across the CDN, which then serves from the closest location to the customer visiting the website. This helps in reducing response times to the customer and provides a great customer experience. In Salesforce, static content from the Lightning Component framework and other applications is served from Akamai's CDN servers located across the world. This results in improved application load times as static assets, including image files, **CSS (Cascading Style Sheets)**, JS, and font files, and other libraries are cached and served to the user from the most appropriate CDN location. Using a CDN doesn't cache any metadata or data in your org.

Network issues

Once you have run some basic commands such as traceroute or ping and notice something that requires further investigation, involve your networking team right away to perform a more in-depth investigation. Don't delay involving your team if you have gone through all the things related to Salesforce and have ruled out the fact that a Salesforce-related issue is causing performance issues because that will delay the incident resolution process. The networking team will need time as they won't have answers right away and will need to troubleshoot on their end, and only once they have found the root cause can they then start the remediation process.

However, by running the `traceroute` or `ping` commands, you can give them a jump start. So, let's take a slightly deeper look into these commands and what information they reveal.

Ping

This is a widely used command to check whether there is connectivity with the host, which in our case is the Salesforce server. The command sends four packets to the server and if the server responds with four packets, then that means connectivity exists and there is no packet loss. If the server doesn't respond, then that could mean that there is an issue with the server. Let's look at an example to understand this better. If we ping `login.salesforce.com`, we can see in *Figure 6.18* that the server at this location responded and there was no packet loss:

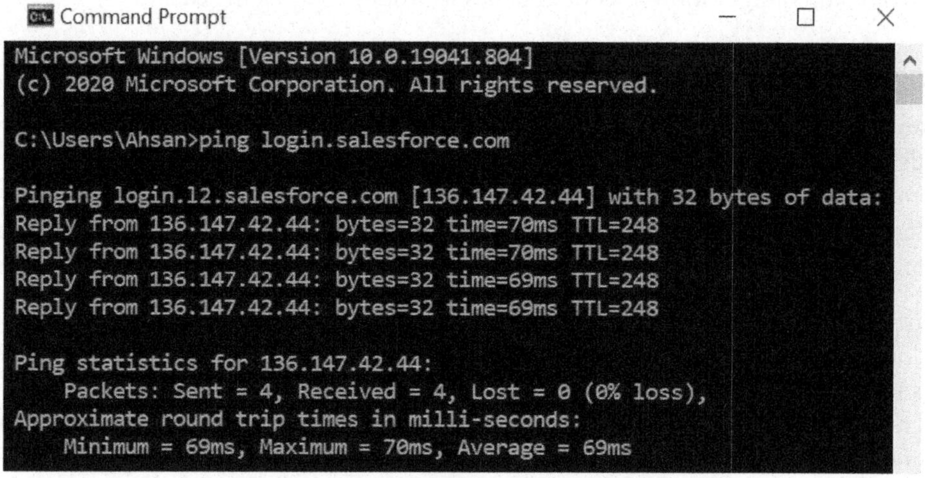

```
Command Prompt                                    —    □    ✕

Microsoft Windows [Version 10.0.19041.804]
(c) 2020 Microsoft Corporation. All rights reserved.

C:\Users\Ahsan>ping login.salesforce.com

Pinging login.12.salesforce.com [136.147.42.44] with 32 bytes of data:
Reply from 136.147.42.44: bytes=32 time=70ms TTL=248
Reply from 136.147.42.44: bytes=32 time=70ms TTL=248
Reply from 136.147.42.44: bytes=32 time=69ms TTL=248
Reply from 136.147.42.44: bytes=32 time=69ms TTL=248

Ping statistics for 136.147.42.44:
    Packets: Sent = 4, Received = 4, Lost = 0 (0% loss),
Approximate round trip times in milli-seconds:
    Minimum = 69ms, Maximum = 70ms, Average = 69ms
```

Figure 6.18 – Server response of a ping operation

As in *Figure 6.18*, the server at `login.salesforce.com` responded, and therefore, there is connectivity between our devices and the server.

If the same number of packets were not received as were sent, or the packet loss amounts to more than 10% of the total packets that should have been received, we would know that packet loss has occurred and that further investigation is required. The **Round-Trip Time** (**RTT**) is the cumulative time it takes for a data packet to travel to the destination and then return to the sender.

Salesforce's recommendation is to capture `ping` results with multiple packet sizes and durations. Running the following commands is recommended:

```
ping -f -n 25 -l 1200 login.salesforce.com
ping -f -n 25 -l 1300 login.salesforce.com
ping -n 25 -l 1400 login.salesforce.com
```

Run the same set of commands but with your instance as the destination. For example, if your org is on NA111, then run the commands as follows:

```
ping -f -n 25 -l 1200 na111.salesforce.com
ping -f -n 25 -l 1300 na111.salesforce.com
ping -n 25 -l 1400 na111.salesforce.com
```

The -n switch indicates the number of echo requests to send, with the default of 4, and the -l switch indicates the buffer size, so when we state 1200, that means 1,200 bytes of data should be sent. Make sure to let the previous command finish before running the next one. Ensure that you save the results for your internal networking team as well as the Salesforce Support team.

If we were to ping a location that doesn't exist, we will get the output as shown in *Figure 6.19*. Sometimes, firewalls block `ping` requests due to security reasons, resulting in total packet loss, in which case it cannot be definitively established that the server is down:

```
C:\Users\Ahsan>ping aliens.com

Pinging aliens.com [2600:3c02:1::2d4f:f40e] with 32 bytes of data:
Request timed out.
Request timed out.
Request timed out.
Request timed out.

Ping statistics for 2600:3c02:1::2d4f:f40e:
    Packets: Sent = 4, Received = 0, Lost = 4 (100% loss),
```

Figure 6.19 – Pinging a location or a device that doesn't exist results in a 100% packet loss

Minimum, maximum, and average RTT numbers that are close to each other indicate there is not much variance over the time of the test, as seen in *Figure 6.18*, but a large variance between the minimum and maximum RTTs would indicate latency issues that require further investigation.

Traceroute

This command is used to track the real-time path of a data packet from the source to the destination. It records all the IP addresses of the network devices it passes through to get to the destination and the time between each hop. As you can imagine, the more routers the packet has to move through, the longer it takes because each device has to process the packet and forward it to the next router.

The `tracert` command, by default, sends three packets to each hop so you will see RTTs per hop in the results. For example, running `tracert na111.salesforce.com` gives us the following result:

```
C:\Users\Ahsan>tracert na111.salesforce.com

Tracing route to na111-ph2.ph2.r.salesforce.com [13.110.36.70]
over a maximum of 30 hops:

  1    17 ms    17 ms    16 ms  192.168.1.254
  2    18 ms    18 ms    24 ms  10.139.190.1
  3    42 ms    43 ms    42 ms  154.11.12.203
  4    73 ms    73 ms    75 ms  six.salesforce.net [206.81.80.33]
  5    74 ms    73 ms    73 ms  eth1-1--spn3-ncg0-phx3.net.sfdc.net [13.110.5.200]
  6    78 ms    70 ms    77 ms  dc11-ncg0-phx3.na111-ph2.salesforce.com [13.110.36.70]

Trace complete.
```

Figure 6.20 – Result of the tracert command run on the NA111 instance

As seen in the preceding screenshot, the destination is shown along with its IP address, and we can see that a maximum of 30 hops will be used in the test. As mentioned earlier, the three numbers in each line represent the time it takes to get to each hop. These numbers are cumulative and do not represent the time it takes for individual packets to travel to the destination. One cause of confusion that perplexes a lot of people running traceroute is that the subsequent hops time are sometimes lower than the previous ones. For example, in *Figure 6.20*, hop 5 took 73 ms, whereas hop 4 took 75 ms. This is because the command sends separate packets for each hop and it's not the same packet that is being tracked from hops 1 to 6. The conditions on the network are constantly changing and therefore it is entirely possible that there was network congestion when the packet for hop 4 was sent versus the packet for hop 5.

Sometimes, you might see asterisks in traceroute results – this doesn't necessarily indicate a problem, but as mentioned earlier, some networks do not respond to these packets (referred to as ICMP packets) due to security or network traffic reasons.

Skinny tables

Database table joins are expensive operations. Depending on how complex the query is, it can take considerable amounts of time and database resources to return results. If you have such a situation, using skinny tables can help speed up the performance. Skinny tables are special tables created by Salesforce that have frequently accessed fields. Remember from *Chapter 3, Understanding Data Management*, where we discussed the Salesforce architecture, all standard fields are stored in a table, whereas all custom fields are stored in another table. For example, if you have custom fields on the Account object, those are stored in a different table and when you run a report containing those custom fields, Salesforce has to do a join behind the scenes and return the results.

When a skinny table is used, standard and custom fields that are frequently used are stored in the table to eliminate the need for expensive joins, as seen in *Figure 6.21*. As the data changes in the source tables, the skinny table is kept up to date automatically without requiring any intervention from the customer. Another advantage of using skinny tables is that the platform will automatically use the skinny table in reports and list views, among others, thereby improving overall performance for users:

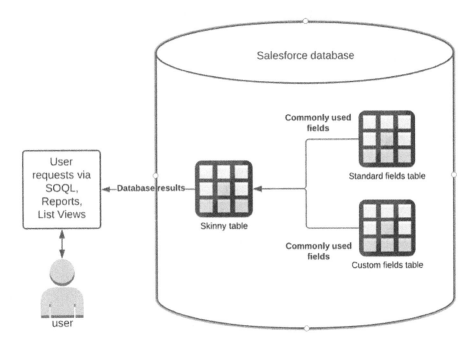

Figure 6.21 – As shown, data for the user is queried from the skinny table directly rather than from the standard and custom fields, thereby avoiding expensive join operations

It's important to note that skinny tables can be used for read-only operations and can be created on both standard and custom objects. There are certain limitations on what types of fields can be created; for example, neither **Roll-Up Summary** fields nor **Formula** fields are supported. The customer cannot create skinny tables themselves, but rather they have to open a case with Salesforce Customer Support to get them created.

There are some limits for skinny tables that must be kept in mind when considering them as a solution. One of the major limitations is that you cannot use them across different objects, that is, each skinny table can only have data from a single object. For example, a skinny table cannot be created for the `Opportunity` object that also has data from the `Opportunity Team Member` object.

You can have up to 100 fields in a skinny table and any time a new field is added to the object, you will need to contact Salesforce to get it added to the skinny table. They also support encrypted fields and encrypted indexes. Skinny tables are copied over to full-copy sandboxes at the time of sandbox creation or refresh, but for other types of sandboxes, a request must be submitted to Salesforce Customer Support.

Query filters, indexes, and negative operators

Ensure that you are using filters in your SOQL query as much as possible as that helps the Optimizer narrow down the records when certain conditions are met. For example, this developer org has 39 `Account` records, so let's try to query all the records and view the query cost. As seen in *Figure 6.22*, the query cost with no filters is greater than 1, which we know is inefficient:

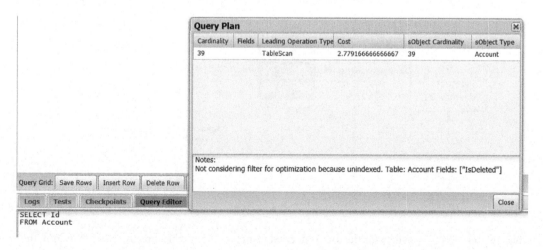

Figure 6.22 – The cost is a high 2.78, which is very inefficient for a query

If we use a filter on the **Industry** field, which is not indexed, and run the query plan again, we see that even though a full table scan is still required, the query is very efficient:

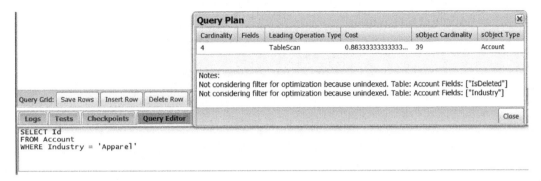

Figure 6.23 – Cardinality shows 4, meaning four records will be returned that have Industry as apparel

Notice how using a filter improved performance. The notes about **IsDeleted** and **Industry** simply mean that these fields cannot be used for optimization because they are not indexed

Indexes will behave similarly and result in even more performant queries. In this example, we are using the **Id** field as an index:

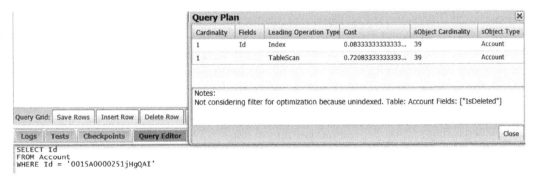

Figure 6.24 – Using an index in the query results in a very efficient query

While looking for opportunities to improve performance, scan your queries to see whether they reference a negative operator such as NOT EQUAL TO (!=) as these can result in very inefficient queries. The following example queries all **Account** records that don't have **Account Site** as null:

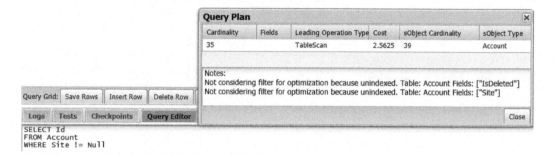

Figure 6.25 – As seen, simply using a single negative operator can cause the query to perform poorly

When looking to improve performance, review your SOQL queries because poorly written queries can cause a significant drag on resources and impact performance for users.

Deleted records in the recycle bin

This seems very innocuous, but deleted records can play a significant role in impacting performance. The reason is that when you simply delete records from the UI or through an API, they are marked for soft deletion, which means they are moved to the **Recycle Bin** and kept there for 15 days or until the size limit is reached. When you run a query, there is an associated overhead from filtering out soft-deleted records, thereby causing performance issues.

Ensure that you don't have a large number of soft-deleted records, which can easily be done by ensuring that the recycle bin is emptied frequently, either from the UI or by using the Bulk API, which has a hard-delete option that removes records permanently from the database. Keep in mind that this option doesn't move the records to the recycle bin, so use it carefully.

Archive

Ensure that data archiving is a component of every project dealing with data (how many projects are there that don't?) rather than an afterthought once you start to run into issues. Orgs that have years and years of data in the database can cause major performance issues. Imagine querying an object that has 500,000 records and the database having to run a full table scan to fetch a few thousand records.

There are multiple ways to archive your data, all the way from building your own custom solution using the Bulk API to using Heroku or deploying a ready-made AppExchange solution. What tool you use will depend on your business and regulatory requirements. The important thing is to understand that not all data is equal, and you will want to carefully analyze and categorize your data and implement solutions to meet your requirements. For example, a small software company may not find it useful to keep quote records that are more than 3 years old, whereas a heavily regulated health insurance provider may be required to keep patient records for a minimum of 7 years.

Lazy loading

This is a feature that is used in Visualforce pages to speed up performance, and if you are still using Visualforce, you can look at implementing this. The idea is that the page first loads essential features so the user can start interacting with it, delaying the rest until the user performs an action, such as clicking a button, or until a brief period has passed, and then the rest of the page is loaded.

Another aspect of improving performance is to enable separate loading of related lists on the page. This is a UI-level setting that enables users to interact with the page while the related lists are still being loaded. This allows the user to interact with the page until all components, including related lists, have loaded, of which there can sometimes be a large amount, especially on the **Account** page. This is because the `Account` object is a key object in Salesforce and a large number of objects usually have a lookup or parent-child relationship with it.

Standard features in Visualforce

Try to use standard features as much as possible unless you have thought through the pros and cons of each approach and the custom approach turns out to be better. For example, you may want to use jQuery for pagination purposes in your Visualforce page, but when the page is loaded, it will take time to query the data and present it on the page, whereas using the standard server-side pagination option might be quicker, but the processing is done on the server side.

The former may be more suitable when the dataset is small, but occasionally there may be a large dataset, and the user is happy to wait for the page to load occasionally. The server-side option, on the other hand, is more appropriate for larger datasets and when the performance of the page is very important.

Use with sharing Apex classes

Apex code, by default, runs in system mode, which means it has access to *everything*: it can access all objects and their fields, and field-level security and sharing rules don't apply. Check to make sure that your classes are using the `with sharing` keyword because that respects field-level security and sharing rules. The net result of this is that smaller result sets are returned, which can help improve performance.

Devices and browsers

As discussed earlier in this chapter, the Octane score is a good measure of the browser's performance. The higher the score, the better the performance is expected to be. Since the Octane score takes into consideration the user's device as well, it is important to confirm that the device supports the minimum requirements required for the smooth operation of Salesforce. If the user's device is running at the minimum recommended hardware specifications, upgrade the device with additional memory and processing power.

Another thing is to confirm that the device is charged or is not being throttled in some way. Devices usually switch to low-power mode when they are close to running out of power or users may have inadvertently changed the settings, causing the device to operate in a low-powered mode.

If you determined in your initial investigation that the issue is specific to a user, check their browser. Currently, Chrome is the most optimal browser for running Salesforce Lightning. I highly recommend not using Internet Explorer with Salesforce LEX as your users will run into many problems. If the browser is Chrome, then check for its version and whether the version is supported by Salesforce.

Disabling any extensions or plugins in the browser can also help with performance significantly as they actively consume memory and processing resources. If nothing works, then restarting the browser can also help with performance-related issues as resources that are tied up by previous processes are freed.

Visualforce pages

You should have standards on where most development is going to happen, be it Visualforce or Lightning. But considering that Visualforce is the older UI and a lot of custom development has been done in Visualforce, I suggest revisiting the previous release notes and determining whether the custom functionality provided by the Visualforce page is now available through out-of-the-box functionality or by using declarative tools.

When you have to resolve a performance-related issue on an immediate basis for a Visualforce page, I suggest reviewing **View State**. **View State** is an encrypted string that stores a collection of values comprising field values, controller state, and components' state in a hidden form element. Very large view states require large amounts of processing time because the string has to be serialized/deserialized and encrypted/decrypted depending on the type of request.

If you notice the issue is with the size of **View State**, you can reduce the number of variables that are included in **View State** by declaring them as `transient`. Doing this will not include these variables in **View State**, but make sure these are variables that are not needed for maintaining the page state. If **View State** is large because controllers and controller extensions have a large number of fields, consider filtering out any extraneous fields that might not be needed.

Debug mode

Salesforce uses the production mode by default that optimizes and minifies JS code to reduce its size. This means that the JS code in the browser is obfuscated, and this only applies to framework code – custom code is never minified and obfuscated. This debug flag should always be turned off in production because otherwise, it can significantly slow down performance for the users it has been turned on for.

Page redesign

Having many fields on the page can also impact performance, so you want to make sure that only fields that are actually used are available on the page. Use tools such as **Field Trip**, for example, to identify fields that are not frequently used and remove them from the page and eventually from your org.

Keep a minimal number of fields that are deemed most important on the primary page and less used fields on another tab. Do the same for components, placing them on second or even third tabs if they are not the most important. The reason is that components that are on the primary page are rendered at the time of initial page load, whereas other components are loaded on demand.

If you notice many related lists on the primary page, move them to other tabs. Salesforce recommends having fewer than three related lists on a tab. For the primary page, place the most important related lists on it.

Solution tool selection

Not every tool is created equal and that means you must be cognizant of the tool that you are using to deliver your solution. The performance of a Workflow Rule versus a Lightning Flow may be different and can be a factor in deciding which tool to use. This is a design-time consideration, but it can break your business process down the road as volumes increase or more automation is put in place.

I want to explain this point in depth because usually, we don't pay much attention to how the choice of our tool is going to impact performance, and our decision making in most cases is limited to whether the solution choice is declarative versus being code-based. To illustrate my point, let's use an example of simple automation that is used to update an **Account** record when an opportunity has been won. We will update the **Type** field from **Prospect** to **Customer – Direct**. As our tool of choice for this example, we will define **Workflow Rule** and **Lightning Flow** and measure the performance using the **Developer Console**.

Before we set up the workflow rule, let's first ensure that our debug log levels are set up appropriately. Follow the next steps to turn on debug logs:

1. Navigate to **Setup | Environments | Logs | Debug Logs**.

2. Set up the debug level details as shown in *Figure 6.26*. Once you have set up the debug level, make sure to turn on debugging by updating the start and stop times and ensuring that you have debugging turned on for the correct user:

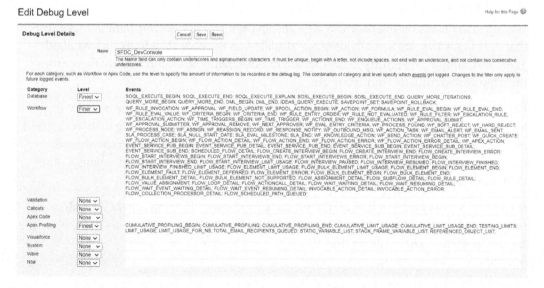

Figure 6.26 – Note the level of detail for each debug element; by default, other categories are turned on as well, but we want to focus on performance results, so we turned on Database, Workflow, and Apex Profiling

Here is how the workflow rule is set up. There is one action associated with the workflow rule that updates the **Type** field on the associated **Account** record to **Customer – Direct**. *Figure 6.27* shows the setup of the the workflow rule:

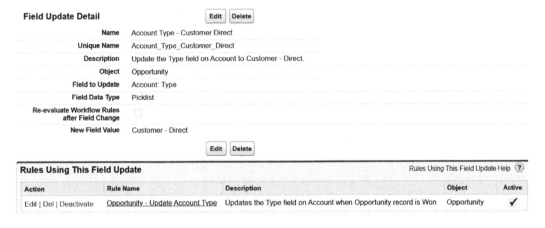

Figure 6.27 – Workflow Rule setup

In the following screenshot, we show how the **Field Update** action has been set up:

Field Update Detail	Edit	Delete

Name	Account Type - Customer Direct
Unique Name	Account_Type_Customer_Direct
Description	Update the Type field on Account to Customer - Direct.
Object	Opportunity
Field to Update	Account: Type
Field Data Type	Picklist
Re-evaluate Workflow Rules after Field Change	☐
New Field Value	Customer - Direct

Edit	Delete

Rules Using This Field Update   Rules Using This Field Update Help ⑦

Action	Rule Name	Description	Object	Active
Edit | Del | Deactivate	Opportunity - Update Account Type	Updates the Type field on Account when Opportunity record is Won	Opportunity	✓

Figure 6.28 – The setup of our Field Update action

Debug logs are on, and the workflow rule has been set up, so go ahead and update the opportunity to **Closed Won**. Check the **Account** record to ascertain that the **Type** field has been correctly updated. Once that has been confirmed, go to **Developer Console**. In **Developer Console**, click on the **Logs** tab, as seen in the following screenshot:

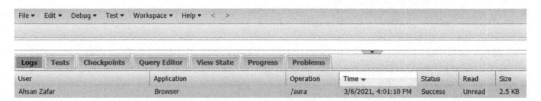

Figure 6.29 – The transaction has been logged

Double-click the log record, which will open the **Execution Log** page (not shown here). Once the log has opened, go to the **Debug** menu, click on **Switch Perspective**, and then click on the **Analysis (Predefined)** option, as shown in the following screenshot:

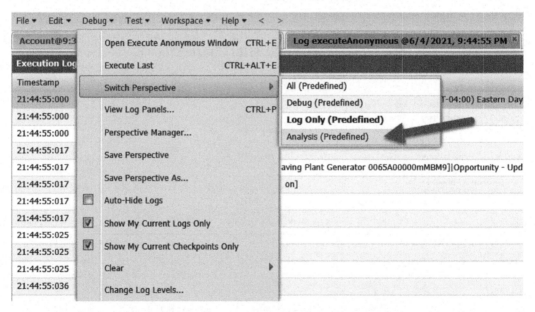

Figure 6.30 – The Switch Perspective and Analysis (Predefined) menu options

On the **Analysis (Predefined)** perspective, click on the **Performance Tree** tab:

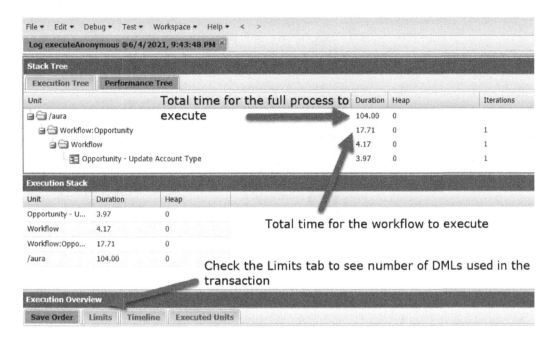

Figure 6.31 – The results from our transaction

You can see that the total process time was **104 milliseconds (ms)**, while the Workflow Rule tool took **17.71** ms to execute. There were no DMLs executed as part of the process, so the **Limits** tab (second half of the page) has no information.

Let's now work on the Lightning flow and set up the same process. Here is what our Lightning flow definition looks like:

Figure 6.32 – Lighting Flow that fetches the Account record ID and then updates the Type field when the Opportunity record is set to Closed Won

Now, let's do an update on an Opportunity record, but before that, make sure that the workflow rule we created earlier has been deactivated and the debug logs are turned on. Following the same process as we did for the workflow rule, we see the following results:

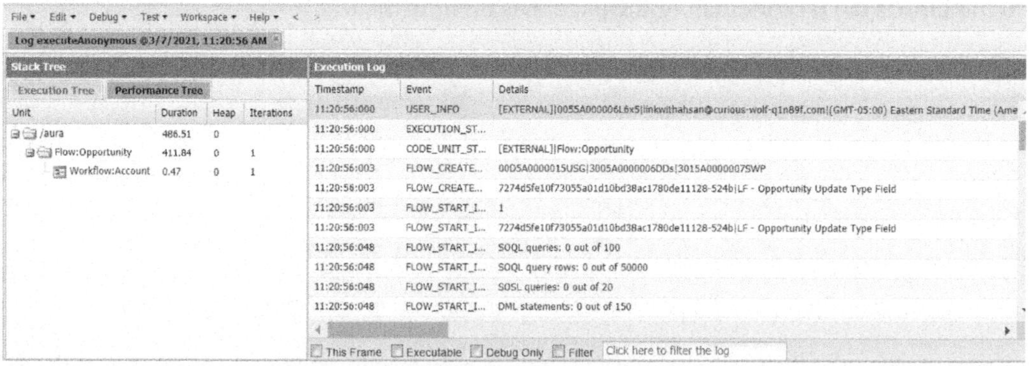

Figure 6.33 – The result showing the time it takes for the Lightning flow to update the Type field on the associated Account record

The results are astonishing: the workflow rule took **17.71 ms** to complete, whereas Lightning Flow took **411.84 ms** to give us the same result. Lightning Flow took approximately 23x longer to update a simple field on the `Account` object.

Imagine, if you had a complex business process that involved multiple DML statements, SOQL queries, and other operations, how this number could change. This is what I mean by not all tools are created equal. If your users are complaining of performance issues, this is one area that you cannot ignore and must take into consideration when troubleshooting.

We compared a workflow rule with a Lightning Flow, but the same principle applies to other tools as well. Should you use a trigger, a Process Builder, or perhaps an asynchronous queueable process to deliver your solution? These are the kinds of questions you want to ask yourself during the design phase, but also during troubleshooting if you find out that Lightning Flow is taking too long and letting it run is no longer an option. You may have to resort to other options immediately to ensure that business operations continue to run with minimal interruption.

Performance in LEX

The first interface of Salesforce was the Salesforce Classic interface that was geared more toward data entry and retrieval. As web technologies matured over the last few years, Salesforce decided to develop and release a new interface based on web standards and one that was geared toward providing a platform for developers to build rich applications that are responsive and performant.

A salient feature of LEX is that the bulk of the work is done on the client side, that is, your browser. Pages are loaded progressively component by component to reduce load times. This is different to Salesforce Classic, where the page was generated by the server and then rendered in the browser. Because LEX is based on modern web standards that promote component-based designs for reusability, a Lightning component in Salesforce can call child components.

As LEX does more processing on the client side, it is sensitive to the environment of the user and the performance of the application can be impacted by a few factors. The hardware that the user is using and the browser have an impact on the user's experience.

Another factor is the quality of the network that the user is on because data has to move between the user's browser and Salesforce servers. Increased network latency will cause the performance to be slow. We have discussed some of these causes in earlier sections, but we should be cognizant by now that performance-related issues in LEX are more dependent on the user's machine compared to Salesforce Classic.

Technical requirements for LEX

LEX is becoming the norm in more and more organizations and those organizations that are still using the Classic interface will eventually need to migrate from that interface to LEX. I briefly want to mention the minimum as well as the recommended requirements from Salesforce for an acceptable user experience. Keep in mind that these values should be used as guidance only and that you should do testing with users in different regions to ensure that they can perform their roles with acceptable levels of performance when using business applications on the Salesforce Platform.

For the minimum requirements, Salesforce recommends the following benchmarks:

- A network latency of 200 ms or less
- An Octane score of 20,000 or greater
- A download speed of 1 Mbps or greater
- 5 GB of RAM with 2 GB available for browser tabs

Salesforce's recommended configuration is as follows:

- A network latency of 150 ms or less
- An Octane score of 30,000 or greater
- A download speed of 3 Mbps or greater
- 8 GB of RAM with 3 GB available for browser tabs

These benchmarks are for desktops and laptops. The minimum required benchmark numbers for tablets and phones are different and should be referenced in Salesforce's documentation.

In the next section, we will go into more detail on **Experienced Page Time (EPT)**.

Understanding EPT

Page load time in Lighting Experience is measured by EPT. This is the time it takes for the page to load so it is available to the user in a useable state where they can meaningfully interact with the page. This sounds simple but there are nuances to what EPT actually is.

We discussed earlier that the key difference between Salesforce Classic and LEX was that pages are generated by the server in the former, whereas in LEX, pages are made of components that are rendered progressively. Progressive loading means that the component might load other sub-components later, so knowing exactly when the page is available to the user is not straightforward.

Other factors that can impact this metric include error handling, caching, and implementation details of the page, which, if not handled properly, can negatively impact EPT.

To accommodate these factors, Salesforce calculates EPT as the time from the page start until no more activity has happened for 2 frames (roughly 33 ms). Accounting for these two frames allows any asynchronous calls such as **XML HTTP Request** (**XHR**) activity, storage activity, or other client-side work to complete.

In the next section, we will look at Experience Cloud and what can be done to ensure optimal performance for your external-facing websites hosted on Salesforce.

Salesforce Experience Cloud

Experience Cloud is the new rebranded name for Community Cloud and refers to external-facing websites that your customer or partners may use. Ensuring that they are performant is critical from a revenue as well as a reputational perspective. It is said that customers usually spend less than 15 seconds on a website page before leaving it. This means that you have less than 15 seconds to capture their attention and have them spend more meaningful time on your website, preferably leading to a purchase (assuming it's an e-commerce site).

Imagine if a potential customer visited your website and the product page was taking too long to load or it crashed – the prospect will most likely leave rather than wait for the page to load and will go to your competitor instead. In the *Conducting performance testing in Salesforce* section, we will look at Costco's example, which is estimated to have cost the company around $11 million in revenue with just a few hours of outage.

Salesforce provides the **Page Optimizer tool**, which can analyze your site and identify potential issues that might impact performance. The Page Optimizer is a downloadable Google Chrome browser extension. The tool shows the network performance of the page, evaluates the pages based on the web standards used in the Lightning framework, and suggests actions that can help improve page performance.

The number of customizations you have on your Experience Cloud site, along with the number of page views per month, logins per month, and traffic patterns are some of the common causes of performance issues on Experience Cloud sites.

The recommendation is to ensure that you have run scale and performance tests on your site before going live as very heavy loads on the site can cause performance issues. Heavy use of Apex, SOQL, and SOSL can also cause slowness on the site, so try to stick with using standard features as much as possible.

We discussed earlier the use of CDNs, which can improve the performance and scalability of the site due to static resources and other frequently accessed content getting offloaded onto these networks. Another feature that Salesforce offers is the use of waiting rooms, which allow users to be queued into a waiting area and then slowly passed into the main website in a controlled manner. This allows sites that experience heavy spikes in traffic to manage this load properly without the risk of slowdowns or crashing under the load.

In this section, we extensively covered the reasons why performance issues happen and looked at the multitude of tools at our disposal to monitor performance in Salesforce. Utilizing these tools, we can methodically rule out the reasons why these issues may be happening and arrive at the root cause.

In the next section, we will discuss performance testing your Salesforce implementation.

Conducting performance testing in Salesforce

The Salesforce Platform serves several billion transactions per day and is designed to be highly scalable. Given that Salesforce provides its platform as a service, they conduct extensive testing and monitoring to ensure that their platform can withstand the load that can be placed on the infrastructure.

Performance testing has two components:

- **Stress testing**: Stress testing is used to measure system performance under extreme conditions using loads that are beyond the maximum expected load. The goal of stress testing is to determine the maximum limit the system can stretch to without crashing.

- **Load testing**: Load testing, on the other hand, is measuring the performance of a system under expected loads. The goal here is to ensure that acceptable levels of service can be provided, or if there are formal SLAs, that they can be met.

An application that doesn't perform well under heavy loads can crash the system and potentially cost an organization millions of dollars in lost revenue. In 2019, the Costco Wholesale website crashed for less than a day on Thanksgiving. Business Insider reported that the crash cost the company about $11 million in lost sales. This is just one example, but the costs can be enormous both in terms of financial and reputational losses.

Unlike traditional on-premises systems where performance testing was an essential part of the software engineering process, since Salesforce proactively monitors its cloud services, we don't have to worry about whether the system will scale or not. The Salesforce Platform has proven itself to be scalable beyond doubt; in 2013, a staggering 1.3 billion transactions were executed on the platform every day. That number is much higher today; to be fair, the Salesforce Platform will perform, but would the custom solution that you built in-house using your developer resources perform? (Note that if you are using out-of-the-box features and have only lightly customized the system, you will not reap huge benefits from investing time and resources in conducting a performance test.)

Where performance testing matters is when you have custom applications with relatively complex business logic running for a large or even a limited number of users. In these scenarios, you can get peace of mind by deciding to do performance testing to ensure that the application will not crash. You may decide to just focus on stress testing the application to understand its limits.

Another reason you may want to consider performance testing your application is to test integrations. In many cases, Salesforce is integrated with several systems, especially **Enterprise Resource Planning (ERP)** systems, and, depending on the integration, large volumes of data can be pushed to Salesforce. For example, in a quick sales type environment, the inventory system may have to push large volumes of inventory data into Salesforce every hour. You will want to ensure that Salesforce will still perform well when that integration is running and hundreds of users are actively using Salesforce. Large volumes of data import or export can also strain the system and impact performance. This is another area where you want to do a performance test and ensure that the system is capable of handling large data loads.

We must be cognizant of the fact that Salesforce is a multi-tenant environment and the resources, including software and hardware, are shared across hundreds of clients. Performance testing in general is resource-intensive and involves large volumes of data. Therefore, proper care should be taken to ensure that your testing will not hog the resources. Salesforce has robust monitoring mechanisms in place to ensure fair resource use and can throttle your usage if abnormal activity is observed.

There are several reasons why Salesforce's **Site Reliability (SR)** team may throttle the system. Normally, these are applied automatically when a certain threshold is exceeded. The most common reasons for triggering a throttle include inefficient SOQL queries, a high number of inbound synchronous requests, or even asynchronous jobs. Performance testing is another reason why the org may get throttled. Salesforce has instituted a process to coordinate performance testing that includes getting prior approval from the Salesforce team. Refer to the *Performance Test FAQs* help article that goes into more detail on the roles and responsibilities of both the customer and Salesforce for performance testing. You should never, under any circumstances, conduct a performance test in a production environment and should always use a sandbox, preferably a full sandbox, for performance testing.

In the next section, we will look at how to approach performance testing on Salesforce applications.

Approaching performance testing in Salesforce

Performance testing must be done in a very well-planned manner, ensuring that the scope of the testing is known, and that the goals of the tests are clear. Here is an approach that you can use to successfully conduct a performance test.

Planning

The first thing to do is to plan the performance test. Be very specific on what exactly you want to test and measure. Is it the page load times that are being tested? Does it include API testing as well? You will get the most value by narrowing down your tests to the most critical aspects of your business application. These can be pages in the application that run complex business logic and have been performing relatively slowly compared to other pages during unit testing or functional testing.

Test model

Once you have identified the requirements in the planning step, the next step is to define the test model. The test model defines the multitude of variables that will need to be defined and loaded to mimic reality. Let's discuss some of these for more clarity.

Certain transactions occur more frequently than others; for example, creating an order happens less often than searching for contacts, so your test distribution will need to have a good number of scenarios for search testing. Think time is another factor and is defined as the time between when the user receives the last packet of data to the point that they take the next action on the website, for example, clicking **Next** on the page. If your scripts are running test steps right after one another, that wouldn't be realistic because human users generally take a break, process the information, and then proceed to the next step. Therefore, it would not be realistic to run automated tests that don't consider think time because your conclusions from the performance testing will not be accurate.

Usage patterns are another factor that must be considered, taking into account when the system is expected to be used the most. For example, visitor numbers for Thanksgiving sales are going to be much larger than the number of visitors on any other day.

You should also consider the fact that Salesforce is not a regular website where content is served and users interact with it in different ways. Rather, as we mentioned earlier, when a LEX page loads, multiple things happen, and merely measuring the page load time using regular tools will lead to inaccurate conclusions. That's the reason why Salesforce recommends using EPT as the metric for measuring performance for LEX as well as Experience Cloud. The reason is that EPT considers the unique underlying architecture of LEX in which individual components can communicate with the server. By using EPT, we can be sure that we are getting an accurate page load time.

You can also measure the server side of things with Salesforce, but as mentioned in the *Conducting performance testing in Salesforce* section, that is less important because the platform is proactively managed for performance and scalability. If you still need to test performance, **Shield Event Monitoring** provides detailed metrics that can be used to gauge performance. If you don't use this, you can also use the Developer Console to get some of these details, but they won't be as detailed as the measures available from Shield Event Monitoring.

With Salesforce, you will be interested in measuring the throughput and response times. **Throughput** is defined as the number of units of work that the system can process in a given amount of time. Examples of throughput are the number of records created in a minute, and the number of searches per hour. **Response** time is defined as the amount of time it takes for the system to process the request. Examples are the number of milliseconds it takes to generate a document from a document generation tool, and the number of milliseconds it takes to load a page.

Test plan

Define the test strategy and plan and include the test cases and tools that will be used for the test. The test plan will also need to have details related to environments that will be needed for testing and where all the test defects will be logged. You also need to ensure that you have sufficient resources to cover all aspects of testing, and this should be in the test plan.

Ensure that you have considered the schedule for when the tests will be performed, the scenarios that will be tested, the success criteria, and the responsibilities of the resources that will be part of the test. One tip that I find useful is to include a one-pager system-level diagram that shows the different systems that will be part of the test. These will show your different load-generating servers, your Salesforce org, and other systems that may be used in testing, such as a visualization system for visualizing test results. This diagram helps in communicating with internal stakeholders and Salesforce.

Don't go overboard with what needs to be tested, but rather spend the time thinking through where you will get the most value from. If you have 10,000 users and a mission-critical application being launched that will only be used by 500 concurrent users and will grow to a maximum of 1,000 concurrent users in 5 years, there is little value in load testing the application by simulating 10,000 concurrent users. If, for any reason, you cannot simulate the test by having 500 virtual users, you can engage a few users to conduct the tests and then extrapolate the results.

Salesforce recommends doing performance testing in a full sandbox, which is identical to the production environment in terms of data, but the data is *point in time*, meaning that since it is cloned at a given point in time, any changes in production after that point are not reflected in the sandbox. Another thing to keep in mind is that although the full-copy sandbox is similar to production, it is not identical with respect to the infrastructure it is hosted on.

Once you have finalized your decisions for the tools and the test cases that are in your scope, you will then want to develop the test scripts that will be run during the testing. Your test cases must take into consideration the realities of how actual users will be using the system so that the results are as close to reality as possible. The previous test model discussion will help you in determining which factors you would need to consider for your test scripts.

Test execution

In this step, you will execute your test scripts and record the results. Make sure to coordinate your testing with Salesforce. They will want to know the details beforehand, including who the key contact is that Salesforce can reach out to in case of any problems, your expected **transactions per second** (**TPS**), any details about the tests and the tools to be used, and so on. The Salesforce team cannot validate your testing strategy or provide debug services for any problems that may happen during test execution.

TPS

TPS is the number of transactions executed per second. For example, if 10,000 users are running a single (1) business process that has 2 transactions in it in 1 hour, then the TPS would be the following:

10,000 x 1 x 2 = 20,000 per hour

TPS is 20,000/(60*60) = ~ 5.5 transactions, rounded up to 6

Salesforce recommends setting that to double for testing purposes, that is, 12 transactions per second.

Distributing results and rectifying problems

Once you have run through the test scripts, it's time to distribute the results. Aggregate the results for easier understanding and to prevent any misinterpretation of the results. If I am not presenting the results to a live audience, I like to provide an explanatory note for each table and graph so the reader can review the results with a better understanding of the context.

With the wealth of testing data that you will have, there are going to be areas that will need to be improved. We reviewed techniques to improve performance in an earlier section. Here, I would suggest using the Pareto principle and focus on solving those performance constraints that will reap the biggest benefits. For example, if the opportunity page is too slow and takes a long time to load, then prioritize that over a Visualforce page that is extremely slow but used by a handful of internal users for keeping track of the company's fleet. Since the former is used by the sales team and is directly tied to revenue, solving that performance constraint should take priority.

In the next section, we will discuss some of the key attributes of a successful performance test.

Conducting a successful performance test

In this section, I want to review a few things that you can do to ensure a successful performance test. These are not in any specific order and are meant to be used as guiding principles, following which you will be able to ensure a comprehensive and successful performance test with your Salesforce implementation:

- **Coordinating with Salesforce**: Your test will generate a lot of data and the spike will get noticed by the monitoring teams at Salesforce, so it is never too early to open a case and start sharing your test plan with them. Not only will this increase the chance of you getting your desired dates for testing (yes, you present a schedule to Salesforce, but they have the final say in agreeing or disagreeing with the dates), but your correspondence with Salesforce can also help you to identify any gaps and work on those before you start your testing.

- **Governor limits**: We know governor limits are in place to ensure that no one customer hogs resources, depriving others in the same instance of reasonable performance expectations from their Salesforce subscription. Performance testing can trigger governor limits, which is a good thing to know before you find that out in production, but it also makes the testing complicated. What you want to do is check your code and ensure that any potential areas where governor limits may get triggered during testing are taken care of before conducting your performance test.

- **LEX**: If you are testing LEX, make sure that you have appropriate tools to test the LEX interface. This is because LEX cannot be tested headlessly, unlike the Visualforce interface. It will require a tool that can test the **GUI** (**Graphical User Interface**).

> **Headless testing**
>
> This is a method of testing where browser UI testing is conducted without the *head*, meaning that there is no browser interface, and the tests are run behind the scenes. This saves on resources that would otherwise be needed; for example, in a real browser window, memory is required to run the operation and the more tabs or windows you have open, the more memory you will need. This skews upward the results of the performance testing.
>
> In LEX, headless testing using traditional load testing tools is not possible because a large chunk of the work is done by the browser and components can have child components that may communicate with the server. New tools such as Flood Element, in conjunction with Puppeteer, can now enable headless testing of LEX.

- **Experienced resources**: There is a multitude of testing that is done in the software industry, and having expertise in one type of testing doesn't necessarily translate into having expertise in other kinds. For example, a test lead that has extensive experience in large-scale off-the-shelf **ERP (Enterprise Resource Planning)** systems may not necessarily know how to set up and conduct performance testing. Make sure you have the right expertise for the job because that plays a significant role in the success of your testing.

- **Load generation**: If you are testing the LEX interface, then, as mentioned in this section, you will need a tool that can do that. But for performance testing, you will also need to set up load generating servers that will generate the data that the tool can test with. Ensure that your load generation setup is compatible with the tool and can produce a sufficient load to adequately conduct a performance test.

- **Test with different browsers**: When testing the LEX interface, make sure you have considered different browsers that users may use in real life. In the example I mentioned earlier, an organization may have Internet Explorer as their corporate supported browser, but users may be using a different browser, so if you test with Internet Explorer only, your test may run and return results, but will not be realistic.

- **Multi-tenancy challenges**: Because the environment in which Salesforce is run is shared by many customers and Salesforce doesn't provide statistics on benchmark numbers of the environment, your performance results could vary widely depending on the time of the test, the load on the instance, and so on. To overcome this hurdle, you can run tests at different times, initially with a single user. That data can then be averaged to use as a benchmark for full-on performance testing. That should give you a good idea of what performance will be like in production.

  When changes or bug fixes are introduced to the environment, make sure to take new measurements to ensure that you are comparing your performance testing results with the new values.

We have learned the approach that we can take to performance test our applications in Salesforce and what steps we can take to ensure that the performance tests we conduct are successful and meet the business goals. It can be a costly and time-consuming exercise to set up the resources to conduct performance tests, but by following these guidelines, you can reduce the risk of failure and increase your chances of success.

In the next section, we will look at monitoring, the available tools, and what to monitor to ensure your org keeps running smoothly.

Monitoring performance

In this section, we will discuss the tools that we can use to monitor our Salesforce orgs proactively. Remember our discussion from *Chapter 3*, *Understanding Data Management*: preventing a problem from happening costs $1 compared to remediating it once it has materialized, which costs $10. If the remediation doesn't happen in time and a failure happens, it could cost $100 to fix. In the next section, we will discuss what to monitor, and in the subsequent sections, we'll look at some of the tools that are available for monitoring your Salesforce org.

What to monitor?

There are tens of benchmarks to measure, but are there a few that we can measure that will provide the most value to us? The short answer is yes; you can track and monitor performance on the following metrics. For some of these, you will need to consult your networking team to suggest the best tools available for the job. Be prepared to explain how Salesforce works, its multitenant architecture, and the fact that organizations don't get direct access to the underlying databases and application servers:

- **Page load time**: This is an obvious one as usually, users will start to complain as they see their pages take longer to load. LEX pages are made up of multiple components and when reviewing the results, you would want to see the component load sequencing along with the load time. This is important from a diagnostic perspective because then you can assess which component is causing the issue. The issue can be any number of things, such as network latency, third-party host issues, or CDN issues.

  You can run automated tests for Salesforce pages to record the page load time (EPT in LEX). There are tools now that can log them, send alerts if they are below a certain threshold, and run scheduled reports for trend analysis. These tests can provide detailed data on the execution time for each component, the sequences in which the component was loaded, and other details about the component.

- **Network**: These tests provide details about the performance of the network layer. These details include latency, packet loss, the number of hops, and other data such as communication between network devices as the packet travels from the source (client's web page) to the destination, that is, the Salesforce servers.

Another aspect of this test is collecting **Hypertext Transfer Protocol (HTTP)** performance data, which includes the **Domain Name Service (DNS)** resolve time, the time to negotiate **Secured Socket Layer (SSL)** connections, and server response codes. For mission-critical applications, monitoring these and getting alerted when problems start to arise is very important. For example, a ferry company using Salesforce as a crew scheduling system needs to ensure that for legal compliance purposes, the ship is staffed with appropriately skilled crew members. Once the scheduling is complete, the terminal from where the ship will sail needs to then print that and ensure that the crew has checked in and is ready to sail. If they have issues connecting with Salesforce due to networking issues such as latency and packet loss, that can lead to severe problems, including delaying the sailing time and potentially getting hit with penalties in cases where the service is considered essential.

- **User experience**: You can also proactively collect performance data from the users' perspective, meaning gathering stats such as wireless signal performance, for example. This can also include users from a certain geographical area that may be experiencing issues, or it could be a remote location that doesn't have high-speed internet service. This data can then be viewed for any specific locations that need attention, or perhaps be shared with the network team so that they can take corrective action before users raise any tickets related to performance issues.

We have learned about the important data points that we can monitor as far as performance is concerned. With this knowledge and the tools we have discussed in this chapter, an effective strategy can be developed to diagnose and fix performance-related issues.

Summary

We started the chapter by discussing the importance of why we should be concerned with performance in the first place. I hope that this will give you food for thought regarding why it's a bad idea to start developing a solution in Salesforce without properly thinking through design and architectural considerations. The Salesforce Platform is powerful and allows customers to build applications that shorten the software development life cycle time, but that strength turns into a weakness when solutions are haphazardly put together.

Our discussion of the reasons why performance issues happen in the first place is hopefully a checklist that you can use to ensure that the applications or integrations you are building don't have those problems. A challenge with performance issues is that they show up over time, but knowing why they happen will let you avoid most of them in the first place.

We extensively discussed a variety of tools that are available to us for improving performance, along with some principles that we can use to ensure acceptable application performance. Know these tools and play with them in a sandbox or developer org to understand their strengths and weakness so when the time comes, you know the right tool to use for the job.

Performance testing is not generally discussed in Salesforce circles, but it can be a very valuable tool to gauge whether you will run into performance issues in the production environment. Even though its focus is limited, for large organizations where applications are rolled out to thousands of users or more and in situations where the org is very complex and there are doubts about how it will perform under load, performance tests are useful. They should especially be used for external customer-facing Experience Cloud sites to ensure that the site will perform within acceptable ranges when under a significant load.

In the next chapter, we will discuss the topic of large data volumes, which is becoming a hot topic since organizations are growing their data exponentially and need ways to manage it appropriately.

Questions

1. **Precision Printing (PP)** has a large number of records in the `Opportunity` object and users have been complaining of reports taking a very long time to run, and list views taking even longer to load. What can the data architect suggest to improve the performance of these reports and list views? Choose two answers:

    a) Ask the users to check their internet and upgrade to higher-speed connections.

    b) Reduce the number of fields queried in the list views.

    c) Schedule the reports to run automatically so users don't have to wait for them to complete.

    d) Analyze the reports to determine which fields are most commonly used in reports and list views. Contact Salesforce Customer Support and get a skinny table created on the `Opportunity` object.

2. PP is deploying an application for its 50,000+ Salesforce user base. The architect assigned to the project has raised concerns that performance tests should be conducted before the application is rolled out in production. Working with the **Quality Assurance (QA)** lead and the project manager, what are some of the considerations that the team needs to consider for performance testing in Salesforce? Choose two answers:

    a) Performance testing must be conducted on a Salesforce-provisioned sandbox especially designed for performance testing.

b) Salesforce must approve the test methodology and test cases must be submitted before running the tests.

c) There is no need to do performance tests because the application will get tested automatically in the production environment. A team can be available on standby to resolve any issues as they arise.

d) Prior approval must be sought from Salesforce when conducting performance tests on the platform.

e) A full-copy sandbox can be used for performance testing because it is close to the production environment with respect to hardware and, when the sandbox is created, it can have the same data as the production environment.

3. **Data Combinations** (**DC**) is a data analytics firm that relies on Salesforce for its sales and marketing processes. DC has heavily customized its sales application. The firm is currently using the Classic UI, but planning to migrate to LEX soon. Users have been reporting very slow page loads for `Account` record pages. What can the architect suggest to improve the situation? Choose two answers:

a) Tell the users to be patient as migrating to LEX will solve most of these performance issues.

b) Run a report to analyze how frequently the fields on the page layout are used. Remove the fields that are not used from the page layout.

c) Enable lazy loading by implementing a button on the page layout with a component that queries data from an external source rather than loading it when the page loads.

d) Contact Salesforce and ask them to create custom indexes on fields that are visible on the page layout.

Further reading

- *Technical Requirements for Lightning Experience*: `https://help.salesforce.com/articleView?id=sf.technical_requirements.htm&type=5`

- *Introduction to Performance Testing*: `https://developer.salesforce.com/blogs/2020/09/introduction-to-performance-testing.html`

- *Performance Test FAQs*: `https://help.salesforce.com/articleView?id=000335652&type=1&mode=1&language=en_US`

- *Under the Hood: How the Salesforce Platform Handles 1.3+ Billion Transactions per Day*: `https://developer.salesforce.com/blogs/engineering/2013/10/under-the-hood-how-the-salesforce-platform-handles-1-3-billion-transactions-per-day.html`

- *Experience Cloud Performance and Scale Best Practices*: `https://help.salesforce.com/articleView?id=sf.networks_perf_scale_best_practices.htm&type=5`

Section 3:
Large Data Volumes (LDVs) and Data Migrations

In this section, you will learn about LDVs – what they are and how to use them in searches and SOQL queries. Topics related to loading LDVs will also be discussed, with examples demonstrating how to load data efficiently without running into issues. In the final chapter, best practices for migrating data and the use of APIs will be discussed.

In this section, the following chapters are included:

- *Chapter 7, Working with Large Volumes of Data*
- *Chapter 8, Best Practices for General Data Migration*

7
Working with Large Volumes of Data

In this chapter, we will discuss working with big data in Salesforce. Salesforce has been in use by organizations for a long time, and more and more organizations have moved from the implementation and stabilization phase to a more mature growth stage where the focus is on leveraging features introduced during the implementation phase to increase revenues and reduce costs. Business growth means data is growing as well and it needs to be managed properly to prevent any disruption to the business.

We will take a brief dip into different types of databases and then dive right into **Large Data Volumes (LDVs)**, a topic that piques my interest because of the unique challenges associated with it. We will look at what defines an LDV scenario and also discuss how we can avoid these scenarios when possible. And when we do find ourselves working with LDVs, we'll see some of the considerations to take into account to be successful along with the techniques to optimize loading or integrating LDVs.

There is no need to always do a point-to-point integration involving a middleware with Salesforce: that's where Salesforce Connect and external objects come into play. We will review external objects, their limitations, and the benefits of using external objects. And when you are working with very large volumes of data going into hundreds of millions of rows or billions of rows of data, big objects come to the rescue. We will discuss the benefits of big objects and the considerations for them before wrapping up this chapter.

The topics covered in this chapter include the following:

- Revisiting databases
- **Large Data Volumes (LDVs)**
- Salesforce Connect and external objects
- Introducing big objects

By the end of our discussion, we will understand the options available to us when it comes to big data and also which option to use given the use cases we are working with.

Revisiting databases

Before we dive deep into LDVs and some associated topics, let's take a brief history trip. Understanding relational and non-relational databases will help us understand the different types of solutions that are available with Salesforce and assist us in determining which one to use depending on requirements. In the early days of modern computing, tapes were used for storage, and the first digital-tape storage system, IBM's Model 726, could store **1.1 MB (megabytes)** on a single reel of data. For comparison purposes, these days, a tape cartridge can hold up to **15 terabytes (TB)**. Model 726 was a non-relational database in that it was free-form records linked together.

Then came relational databases, which offered a more organized approach to store, retrieve, and search data. Data was stored in multiple tables in keeping with normalization principles and logically linked together using unique identifiers called **primary** and **foreign** keys. Refer to *Chapter 2, Understanding Salesforce Objects and Data Modeling*, for a more in-depth discussion on normalization with the help of examples.

Relational databases

Relational databases provide an optimal medium for transactional and analytic applications and are widely used today as storage backbones for **Enterprise Resource Planning** (**ERP**) systems, **Customer Relationship Management** (**CRM**) systems, and analytical applications. The following four characteristics, abbreviated as **ACID** (**Atomic, Consistency, Isolation, Durability**), of relational databases make them ideal for these purposes:

- **Atomic**: Relational databases have a very robust transaction control mechanism built into them. This means that if a transaction fails at any time, it will be rolled back, switching values to earlier values to ensure that data remains accurate. This prevents some values in the database from being partially updated while others are left untouched because of transaction failure. A common example used to demonstrate atomicity is the transfer of funds from one account to another in a bank. The atomicity attribute ensures that the full transaction, that is, debiting one account and crediting the other, is completed, otherwise the full transaction has to fail to keep the database in a consistent state.

- **Consistency**: This means that checks and constraints that are defined in the database are satisfied for every transaction. For example, if a column in a table has been defined to hold integer values, the database shouldn't allow a transaction to insert characters or **Binary Large Objects** (or **BLOBs**, which are used in Oracle databases usually to store images and audio files). Another example is when the customer's name is required in a table that holds customer master data. Any time a null value is entered and a save attempted, the constraint defined on the column will kick in and prevent the save from completing.

- **Isolation**: This attribute is related to transaction visibility to other users and processes of the system. It ensures that a transaction accessing the same data is not running concurrent to another transaction. This is important: let's say a bank account has a balance of $1,000 and two transfers are initiated to transfer $200 each to two different accounts. These should be two individual transactions, but if they run concurrently, both will read that the balance is $1,000, whereas the second transaction should have read the balance as $800 (after the first $200 has been transferred to the other account).

- **Durability**: This attribute is related to ensuring that once a transaction has been completed, the results of the transaction must survive any system malfunctions. There are measures that database administrators can take to ensure that their databases are durable, including taking regular backups of data, and modern databases, such as Oracle and SQL Server, have built-in mechanisms to cope with catastrophic failures and still maintain data durability.

Now that we have reviewed relational databases, let's take a look at non-relational databases in the next section.

Non-relational databases

You can probably guess from the name that non-relational databases do not use relationships (take primary, foreign keys as an example) as in relational databases, and therefore do not use tables with columns and rows.

Non-relational databases use storage that is optimized for the type of data that will be stored in the database. For example, if it's **JavaScript Object Notation (JSON)** data that will be stored, a document data store that is optimized for JSON storage may be appropriate. Non-relational databases are usually referred to as **NoSQL** databases. This is because they don't use SQL for querying data and other methods are used to query data. Let's briefly discuss some NoSQL databases:

- **Columnar data stores**: This type of store looks deceptively similar to a relational database, but it stores data in a denormalized format. These databases have column families (similar to tables in relational databases) that have rows that have columns. Values in these columns are essentially tuples of key-value pairs. The column family holds columns of data that are logically related and usually queried and manipulated as a unit. *Figure 7.1* shows an example of a column family:

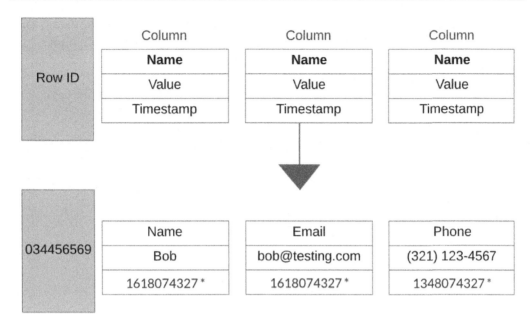

*timestamp in UNIX time

Figure 7.1 – Example of a columnar database

In a columnar database, not all columns need to be populated, and the number of columns for each row can be different as well. In the preceding example, just one row is shown:

- **Key-value data stores**: These databases store data as key-value pairs, with the key acting as an identifier and the value being the data that is being stored. The value is stored using an appropriate **hashing function**. Without going into a more in-depth discussion around hashing, which is outside the scope of this book, a hashing function simply converts an input of variable length to a compressed numerical fixed-length output using a mathematical function. An example of a key-value store is shown next:

Keys	Values
123	('Hi', 'Bob', '544-3434', 10000)
343	('Hello', 'John', '434-9241', 5751)
569	('Howdy', 'Tim', '979-3111', 50311)

Figure 7.2 – Example of a key-value database

Key-value stores are optimized for querying data using keys and, unlike relational databases, they are not suitable for retrieving data using non-key values.

- **Graph data stores**: This type of data store manages entities, which is the data itself, but also the relationships between these entities. Entities are called **nodes**, whereas the relationships are called **edges**. This type of database places relatively more emphasis on how entities are connected to each other compared to relational databases. This type of database allows for extremely fast queries to understand complex entities and their relationships (nodes). *Figure 7.3* shows an example of a graph data store:

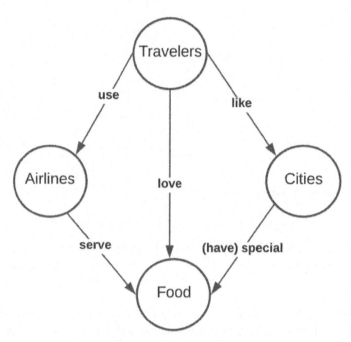

Figure 7.3 – An example of a graph database showing nodes and edges for travelers

Operations to access nodes and their edges are very efficient in graph data stores and are commonly used for use cases where large amounts of data exist and complex relationships need to be explored. For example, financial systems that are designed for fraud detection use graph data stores to analyze beyond the individual data points and form reasonable conclusions.

- **Document data stores**: These data stores are designed to store named string fields and values in an entity called a **document**. The format these documents use is JSON format and provides flexibility so that every stored record can be different than the other. *Figure 7.4* shows an example of a document data store:

```
[
    {
        "year"   : 2020,
        "make"   : "Tesla",
        "model"  : "Model S",
        "info"   : {
            "Parts sourced from" : [ "Mexico", "China", "Brazil"],
            "First delivery date" : "2010-01-07T00:00:00Z",
            "Consumer product rating" : 7.2,
            "image_url" : "http://imageURL_ModelS"
            }
    },
    {
        "year"   : 2021,
        "make"   : "Lucid",
        "model"  : "Air",
        "info"   : {
            "Parts sourced from" : [ "Mexico", "China"],
            "First delivery date" : "2021-03-07T00:00:00Z",
            "Consumer product rating" : 8.1,
            "image_url" : "http://imageURL_LucidAir"
            }
    }
]
```

Figure 7.4 – A sample document store for electric vehicles

These types of data stores are suited for use cases where the rigid structure that a relational database provides is not very important. Rather, the flexibility to store and retrieve data as documents is preferred, such as in the case of high-traffic websites that allow users to create profiles.

Whether it's a relational or non-relational database, each has its own strengths and weaknesses that would make it appropriate for certain use cases. Non-relational databases are suitable for storing large amounts of data with little structure. Because a minimal structure is required, they offer more flexibility to changing business conditions. Where more structure, complex business logic, and ACID transactions are needed to ensure accuracy, completeness, and data integrity, a relational database is definitely a better architectural choice. The Salesforce platform uses relational databases as its foundational data store, but there are other services where it makes use of non-relational databases.

You may not have to play a role in deciding whether to use relational or non-relational databases, but understanding the idea behind them enables us to interact with them in a more meaningful way since we understand their strengths and weaknesses. This is especially applicable since most of us, if not all of us, use cloud-based services in one way or another. Now that we have a better appreciation of the different types of databases and understand the critical role they play in providing the services that we use, let's dive into LDVs.

Large Data Volumes (LDVs)

LDVs in Salesforce don't have a strict formal definition, and if you ask an experienced architect what constitutes an LDV scenario, more than likely the answer you will get will be, *It depends*. The reason is that you could have an LDV scenario even with a much lower number of records than the general guideline that Salesforce provides. The general guideline is that once you have more than 1 million records in any object, you have an LDV scenario and you may start seeing the implications of LDVs.

Although the number of records is a consideration in determining whether an LDV scenario exists, that is not the only consideration. There could be several other factors that could create an LDV scenario even when the number of records is less than the generally recommended threshold, which is more than 1 million records. These factors include the following:

- **Transaction volume and complexity**: This is related to how much data is moving in and out of the organization. If you have integrations that are syncing data with external systems such as an ERP, and hundreds and thousands of records are being transferred into the system, that may not meet the recommended guidelines of an LDV scenario. But let's say you have three of these integrations that run at the same time – now you would have exceeded the general guideline limits of an LDV.

  Another aspect is the complexity of the transactions. An integration that brings in and updates account records from an ERP is going to run much quicker than an integration that brings in product data from the ERP and forms bundles on the fly in Salesforce CPQ. Similarly, when data is being transferred out of Salesforce, a simple export of opportunity data is going to be much quicker than an integration that updates the ERP with contract, order, or quote data from Salesforce.

- **Data skew**: We will discuss the different types of data skews and why they impact performance in a later section.

- **Org complexity**: The complexity of the org in terms of numbers, the complexity of sharing rules, and the role hierarchy can have an impact and create an LDV scenario. Consider a scenario where, when records are inserted into the `Account` object, there are no sharing rules versus when an integration runs, and the org has complex Apex sharing rules. In the second scenario, each time the record is inserted, record visibility has to be determined, which can cause issues when a large number of records are being processed.

The number of records by itself is obvious, but also a combination of the factors we discussed here will result in an LDV scenario. This should highlight the importance of properly analyzing your org before finalizing an integration or migration approach. Failure to do so can result in issues down the road that will be both costly and time-consuming to fix. Let's understand the implications of LDVs if they are not properly accounted for in the architecture.

Knowing the implications of LDVs

You will likely see the effects of LDVs assuming they were not properly accounted for in the architecture. Here are some of the critical impacts when a system is not optimally architected considering LDV scenarios. This is one of the reasons why, when you are implementing enhancements or new applications in Salesforce, it is critical to ask questions, understand the answers, and design things based on the anticipated growth of data for the next 3–5 years.

- **Reports and list views**: These will most likely be the first things you hear from your users when you have hit an LDV scenario. Reports and list views will start to slow down, and users will complain about how a report used to run in a few seconds and now it takes forever to run it. Worse yet, these may start to time out because of the volume of data that the database has to sift through to return results.

- **Search**: Search results are going to take much longer if the search engine has to query millions of records. This is another area where users will quickly figure out that something is amiss and that it takes much longer than usual to return results. This is especially evident if a custom UI is being used for a search and the search engine has to query multiple objects and multiple wildcards are used.

- **SOQL**: Lightning components or Visualforce pages that use SOQL to return results will start to slow down or run into query timeout issues when the query has been running for more than 120 seconds. Regardless of whether the query runs for so long, you should always write optimized SOQL queries that return results quickly without having the user wait for a very long time.

- **Sharing calculations**: Sharing rules are calculated whenever record ownership is updated. With LDVs, this can take a long time to run. This needs to be considered, especially for scenarios that involve data migration or integration, because as new records are inserted or existing records have their owners updated, sharing calculations will run automatically and, in an LDV scenario, slow down the system.

- **Related lists**: Users would start to notice slowness on a related list for some records. This is related to ownership skew, which we will discuss later, but this can happen in scenarios when the detail side in a master-detail relationship has a large number of records. For example, a fast-paced **Business to Consumer (B2C)** company has hundreds of thousands of customers and some loyal customers have frequent orders that have resulted in a large number of records getting generated in the Order object. A company such as Amazon, which has customers that use Amazon Prime and order almost every single item from their online store, could end up having hundreds of thousands of records in the Order object. The related list on the Person Account record can take a long time to load.

We have taken a detailed look at the multi-tenant architecture of Salesforce, but let's review that and the search architecture from the perspective of LDVs.

Multitenancy and search architecture

In *Chapter 2, Understanding Salesforce Objects and Data Modeling*, we took a detailed look at the multitenancy architecture of Salesforce. Refer to that chapter to refresh your memory, but in a nutshell, multitenancy is a way of providing services to multiple unrelated customers using the same hardware-software stack. A software layer or a runtime engine separates each customer's customizations and data from being viewed or accessed by another customer. At runtime, the engine materializes virtual tables by considering the customer's metadata.

Whenever you create a new Salesforce application using standard or custom objects that then have standard or custom fields, Salesforce does not create a physical database table for, let's say, the custom object with the fields in it as columns on the table. This would not be scalable as hundreds of tenants are usually hosted on an instance and would require immense resources to manage the database changes being made by the tenants. Rather, the platform manages virtual database structures using a set of metadata, data, and pivot tables (tables that define relationships, unique fields, and indexes).

There are a multitude of places in Salesforce where the **search** feature is used, with perhaps the most common being **Global Search**, but it's also used when doing lookups and duplicate record processing. Searching architecture in Salesforce is based on its own data store and is optimized for search.

Knowing how the underlying architecture works will help us understand why we cannot do certain things that were at our disposal with traditional databases. For example, you can optimize the underlying **Structured Query Language (SQL)**, run database statistics at will, or create indexes to optimize database performance. You could also run index update jobs after a large volume of data was loaded if it was deemed important to make the data available to users right away.

With Salesforce, because it's a shared environment with multiple tenants, we don't have access to the underlying database and have to plan our integrations and data migrations properly. For example, a search on the platform runs every 15 minutes and could take a long time to complete if a large data migration was just performed. We will need to time this appropriately if a 24/7 call center of an organization is reliant on it. Similarly, database statistics are run on a nightly basis on the platform, which means that your SOQL queries may be slow if you try to access data following an LDV migration.

Let's review some key considerations when migrating or designing integrations for LDVs.

Considerations for integrating or migrating LDVs

Several considerations must be kept at the forefront when designing LDV integrations or migrations. This is because, although requirements for LDVs are not much different than a typical integration or migration, the caveat lies in understanding the impacts of LDVs, so mitigations can be incorporated in the design to avoid running into issues. Some of these considerations also apply to non-LDV integrations and migrations but are mentioned here because they have a large impact on LDVs.

A greenfield versus a brownfield org

A greenfield org is an org that is brand new, and you are setting it up from scratch. Usually, when they are starting with Salesforce, organizations set up CRM, the org slowly evolves over time, and other applications are built on it. A brownfield org, on the other hand, is one that is already live and is in active use for business operations.

An LDV migration in a brownfield is more complicated than a greenfield org. The reason is that you have more factors to consider, the first and foremost being minimizing any disruption to ongoing business operations. LDV operations can take a long time to run and can have a visible performance impact, which can impact operations. As an example, the last thing you want to see is, while your LDV process to load *Case* records is running, your customer support users waiting for *Case* records to open while they are with the customer on the phone.

With greenfield orgs, you don't run into these types of issues and have a lot more flexibility to run your LDV operations. Always make sure of and think through the implications from a users' perspective of running LDV operations. Many businesses have critical applications running on the Salesforce platform and the `Account` object is the center of the universe in the Salesforce ecosystem. This is because it is used by almost every application that's built on the platform and any LDV operations impacting Account records will slow down the system for everyone on the platform.

When working with a global brownfield org, another challenge is time zone differences. LDVs can take a lot of time depending on how much volume is being loaded, but you may find it challenging that downtime is required to run your operations. One time zone where users may be offline may not necessarily mean that it's a good time to load data because users in a different time zone may be in the middle of their data fully utilizing the system. To prevent these types of issues, LDVs can be run on weekends, but that can still be challenging if you have a 24/7 call center running on the platform.

Data modeling

As mentioned in the last section, the Salesforce data model has the `Account` object as the key object and other objects are related to it via master-detail or lookup relationships. When migrating from other systems, ensure that you have an understanding of the source system's data model. This is because, contrary to your assumptions, the source system may have a different data model than you were expecting. For example, in Siebel, the `S_PARTY` table is the main table that has contacts, users, employees, and accounts (companies). Other records and other tables are extended from it to identify whether the record belongs to an employee, contact, or user. As seen, the data model is different than what you have in Salesforce, and understanding the data model will help you in determining what transformations will be needed to successfully load the data.

Keep in mind that the Salesforce platform is optimized for read operations, contrary to traditional databases, which are optimized for write operations. This means that you would want to pay attention to denormalizing the data as much as possible. For example, an account may have multiple addresses, such as billing, shipping, and legal. In a traditional-type database, these are stored in a separate table in a primary-foreign key relationship, but in Salesforce, the `Account` object has shipping and billing addresses on it. You will want to create new fields for additional addresses that you want to store on the object.

An overlooked benefit of denormalization is that it reduces the number of records that would need to get loaded and therefore results in a faster and more performant load and requires less validation in terms of the total number of rows that need validation. From our preceding example, let's assume that there are four types of addresses – billing, shipping, legal, and sold-to addresses. These would be four records in the address table, but in Salesforce, we would just create the additional two addresses on the `Account` object, thereby reducing the number of rows to load from four to one. The following diagram shows an example to demonstrate this:

ID	Name
1	Precision Printing
2	MPath Logistics

Account table

ID	Type	Address
1	Sold-to	123 Main St, Vancouver BC
1	Billing	1 Mission St, Vancouver BC
1	Shipping	2411 Royals Road, Vancouver BC
1	Legal	541 Sheppard St, Toronto ON
2	Billing	...

Address table

Figure 7.5 – Example showing how addresses would be stored in a normalized database

The **Type** column in the **Address** table is usually another table that has all the address types defined, but that are combined here for clarity's sake. When the data is denormalized and ready to be loaded into Salesforce, the **Address table** will not need to be created as a separate object, but rather the different address types will get created on the `Account` object.

Figure 7.6 shows the equivalent of *Figure 7.5*. As can be seen, the different types of addresses are stored with the account name and other relevant details about the account (not shown here for the sake of brevity):

ID	Name	Billing Address	Shipping Address	Sold-to Address	Legal Address
1	Precision Printing	1 Mission St, Vancouver BC	2411 Royals Road, Vancouver BC	123 Main St, Vancouver BC	541 Sheppard St, Toronto ON
2	MPath Logistics	234 Quadra St, Chicago IL	234 Quadra St, Chicago IL	77 Jasper Ave, Calgary AB	901 Bay Street, Toronto ON

Figure 7.6 – Visual representation of how different types of address will be stored on the Account object in Salesforce

We have seen how data modeling is important and how normalized versus denormalized creates transformation requirements that must be taken into account when designing data migrations and integrations.

Tooling

Extract, Transform, Load (ETL) tools can extract data from the source system, transform, and then load the data into the destination, that is, Salesforce objects. While these are very useful for most migrations, LDVs can take advantage of integration tools such as MuleSoft. The reason is that integration tools offer a more robust set of functionalities, which makes it easier to migrate or integrate LDVs. For example, ETL tools can transform the data but, in an example where you want to insert a batch and then update it based on a certain criterion, you cannot chain the two with most ETL tools. An integration tool, on the other hand, can easily do that and gives you the flexibility, in our example, to let the insert operation complete and then run the update operation if the previous operation was successful. Chaining events like this can be a big time saver because it takes away the need for manual intervention and allows you to run your batches with more flexibility.

Do not underestimate the importance of chaining because it can be a big time saver and save you from a lot of headaches. The reason is that LDVs are different from regular loads where you are loading a few hundred, thousands, or hundreds of thousands of records. Even if 0.5% of records fail in a batch of 100,000 records, you would need to manually fix 500 records, which is a significant number if not gigantic. With LDVs, a batch of 1 million records that has 0.5% records failing means 5,000, which is a very large volume if it has to be fixed manually. Integration tools provide the capability to re-run failed records and you can orchestrate the flow of steps so the number of records needing any type of manual intervention is kept to a minimum.

When migrating into live brownfield orgs, you may find a need to export existing data from Salesforce, transform it in some way, and then load it back into Salesforce. An integration tool can be handy here as well because once you are comfortable with the setup you configured for the tool, you can automate it. For example, if you were to merge two orgs, org A and org B, where org B will be decommissioned following the merger, the chances are that you have a high overlap between CRM data, in which case you will want to extract data from org A, transform the data, including adding new attributes from org B, and then load it back into Salesforce.

Timing your operation

If possible, consider taking a staggered approach when migrating data rather than relying on a weekend to do it. Loading 10 million cases into Salesforce, along with a million Account records and 3 million Contact records, despite your best efforts, can be a lot of work. Stagger your migration by splitting the large volume of data into manageable chunks. That way, at the time of data migration cutover, you will have a smaller delta of records remaining to be loaded.

As you run the batches in a full copy sandbox, benchmarking the time it takes for your load to run will give you an idea of how long it will take to run the loads in production. This is important because you want to ensure that your communications with impacted users are immaculate and they know what, how, and when to expect the impacts on their day-to-day use of the platform.

Iterate, iterate, iterate...

I cannot stress this point enough: iterate your loads multiple times to iron out any kinks. Start with a *Developer Pro* sandbox and a few thousand records, fix any issues, and reiterate the batch. Incrementally start increasing the number of records and load the data. Once you have exceeded the limit of the number of records in the Developer Pro sandbox, move on to a *Partial Copy* sandbox, which provides 5 GB of storage space. Eventually, you will want to perform any user acceptance testing in a full copy sandbox that is identical to production.

Transformations

As you are well aware, data migrations and integrations are usually not simple to extract and load operations but instead involve significant transformation before getting loaded into the destination. With LDVs, transformation becomes more resource-intensive because of the volume of data. As recommended earlier, transformations should be done outside of Salesforce rather than relying on the automation tools there to speed up the loads and to prevent running into issues.

Transformations can be any number of things, from using formulas to concatenate and create new values to adding missing values or replacing values in the destination based on certain criteria. Another type of transformation that you need to keep in mind is the data type transformation to the field type in Salesforce. By data type, I mean that traditional databases such as SQL Server, Oracle, and others have data types defined for each column of the table in the database, so a column can be decimal, text, or something similar.

In Salesforce, because we don't get access to the database directly, we have field types, so to store a number, whether it's an integer or decimal, you create a new field with the type as **Number**. When you want to migrate a number value from SQL Server, you would need to type case that into a corresponding type in Salesforce.

You will also need to transform picklist values from the source into Salesforce and, similarly, other transformations as per your business requirements. The important point is that there can be significant transformations taking place and the tool should be able to handle the loads without slowing down the overall process.

User involvement and validation

Involve your users who are intimately familiar with the data from the outset of the project. Validation of whether a data load was successful has multiple facets, one of which is to involve your power users who know their data. Set the expectations, timelines, and how much and when they will be needed to validate the loads. It's one thing to know that the total number of records from the source matched the total number of records loaded into Salesforce, but that doesn't necessarily mean that all the data elements came across fine, especially when there is a transformation step in between.

Your users will help find the gaps with respect to fields that appear blank, or strategic accounts that are missing. These records with issues may not necessarily show up in your error logs, but the data is not accurate from a usability perspective. Guide your users to select random samples of data to validate the data, but also focus on the ones that are most critical to the business.

Another way to accomplish validation, depending on the objects, is to validate the aggregate counts or sums of fields. For example, if your business requirement is to load opportunity data for the current fiscal year, then compare the sum of the **Amount** field for all opportunities in the current fiscal year with the values from the source system. This can get hairy if the opportunities cannot be compared 1:1 (due to different **Stage** field values, for example) and may require some additional work.

In the next section, we will discuss that LDV scenarios should be avoided, if possible, in the first place.

Preventing LDV scenarios

OK, the title of this section may sound a bit extreme and LDVs are not a malady either, but the point is that if you can, you should avoid running into LDV scenarios. I want to stress that the criterion discussed in the last section doesn't mean that you should automatically start thinking of an LDV scenario unless it's absolutely needed.

There are ways to prevent an LDV scenario and where it makes sense, they should be employed. To be clear, large orgs will have LDV scenarios and cannot be avoided, but my intent here is to again stress that not every LDV scenario is materialized organically. Rather, some can be outright prevented, for example, when the organization has no archiving strategy in place and has been storing years and years' worth of data in Salesforce, resulting in an LDV situation. In cases such as these, you should give serious thought to moving data off the platform. Let's discuss some of the options available to move data off the platform for better scalability and performance.

Data archiving

Regular data archiving using automated tools can be a good strategy to prevent growing your data massively on the platform. Remember that the core Salesforce platform, although capable, is not meant for storing massive volumes, but rather for optimal transactional loads. Archiving data improves reports, list views, and dashboard performance. It also improves SOQLs because the database has to look up a smaller dataset.

Data archiving can be used to retain older data that is not actively needed but is required to be held either for auditing or regulatory compliance purposes. It can help with keeping only active data in the org that is needed for operations. For example, inactive customer accounts and contacts who have not been subscribers for more than 5 years and haven't responded to marketing campaigns may be marked for archival. Let's briefly look at some of the ways in which you can archive Salesforce data:

- **Middleware-centric**: This leverages a middleware to orchestrate the archival process and store data in a data store. For retrieval purposes, you can either use Lightning Connect or use the middleware to retrieve the data into, say, a Lightning component in Salesforce.

- **AppExchange partner**: Another method is to rely on a third-party AppExchange app to archive the data. There are numerous apps on AppExchange that do this and provide a range of features that can be leveraged to meet your data archiving requirements.

- **Heroku**: Organizations utilizing Heroku can leverage it for archiving data as well. This leverages the Postgres database along with Lightning Connect, Heroku Connect, and custom web services to initiate the archival processes.

- **Big objects**: This is another way of archiving data off from the main Salesforce objects into special objects that are designed to hold large volumes of data, but they also have limitations that must be considered. We will discuss big objects in more detail later in this chapter.

Now that we have reviewed archiving methods briefly, let's continue our discussion on other ways in which we can prevent LDV scenarios.

Deleting

Deleting data that has been confirmed to be of no value to the organization and doesn't require storage due to regulatory or compliance reasons is a good candidate for permanent deletion. This can free up storage and reduce potential LDV scenarios.

What needs to be understood is the difference between soft and hard delete. When records are soft deleted, performance improvements will not be realized because the data is still on the platform and remains in the **Recycle Bin** for 15 days. The platform has to explicitly exclude these records from queries and other operations.

If you know that you won't need the delete, using the Bulk API with the **Hard Delete** option will allow you to delete the records immediately without being stored in the **Recycle Bin**. It is recommended to use this option for deleting large volumes of data and for immediate performance improvements.

Mashups

This is a type of data virtualization where the data is stored on an external system and the application is made available in the Salesforce **User Interface** (**UI**). This essentially creates a loosely coupled integration that is not reliant on any proprietary method to integrate the two applications. The downside is that it is optimal for use cases where small amounts of data are needed in real time.

External object

This is another form of data virtualization where the data is stored in the source system, but using OData connectors, data can be made available in Salesforce on demand. For example, assume that you have order data in Microsoft Dynamics. Rather than integrating Salesforce and Microsoft Dynamics in a traditional integration, you could use Salesforce Connect to link up the two systems. When a user pulls up the order-related list on the Account record, a real-time call is made through the connector and the results are returned and displayed in the related list.

In the next section, we will look at the different ways we can optimize performance for LDV operations.

Optimizing LDV operations

There are multiple ways to optimize the performance of LDV operations and we will cover these in the upcoming subsections. Rather than trying all of these things at once if you are experiencing performance issues, try to implement these techniques and note the performance while continuing to monitor and tweak further as required. This can help you to pinpoint the exact cause of the performance issue and may help solve other similar issues.

Data skew

When you have more than 10,000 child records that are all linked with the same parent record, a **data skew** situation arises. This is undesirable, and the key to preventing data skew is to keep the number of child records per parent below the 10,000 threshold and distribute these new child records across accounts. There are three types of skews:

- **Account data skew**

    Account data skew happens when a large number of child records are associated with the same account record. For example, more than 10,000 opportunity records have the same parent account. This usually happens when a generic account is used as a parent for unassigned contacts. Account data skew can cause the following issues:

    a) **Record locking**: When updating a large number of child records, for example, opportunities under the same account in multiple threads, the same account would need to be locked for data integrity. The locks are held for a very short amount of time, but it is possible that the previous update is still holding the lock and, therefore, will fail the update. Remember in a parent-child relationship that when the child is updated, it also locks the parent record to maintain data integrity in the database.

    b) **Sharing issues**: Depending on sharing configuration, simple changes such as changing ownership on an account may require examining every child record for that account and adjust sharing as well. In a scenario involving a large number of records, this can take a lot of time and cause issues.

- **Ownership skew**

   This happens when a single user owns a large number of records, typically more than 10,000 records. For example, an integration user is assigned all the accounts from the external system. When the skewed owner exists in the role hierarchy, operations such as delete or owner changes cause the system to remove sharing from the old owner and all parent users within the hierarchy, and from users who have access through sharing rules. For this reason, ownership changes are the costliest transactional changes in the system.

   If you do need to assign a large number of child records to a parent record, determine whether you can have multiple parent accounts that the child records can be distributed to, thereby avoiding the ownership skew scenario. Remember that every record in Salesforce should have an owner, irrespective of whether it's a user or a queue.

   In situations where ownership cannot be avoided, the skewed owner can be made such that they don't have a role in the hierarchy. That way, the system doesn't have to make any sharing calculations associated with the skewed user's records.

- **Lookup skew**

   This happens when a large number of records are associated with a single lookup record; for example, you have a custom quote object that has a lookup to a custom facility object that indicates where the repair for the component will be done. If there are an excessive number of quotes associated with a single facility record, you will run into lookup skew issues.

   Lookups are basically foreign key relationships in database terms, and when a record is being inserted/updated, the associated lookup record must also be locked to maintain data integrity. This is the reason why lookup skews are not good for performance.

Lookup skews can still happen even if multiple objects have a lookup to the same object; for example, objects x, y, and z each have a lookup to object a. If record ID ax1 on object a is the parent record for say 50,000 records on object x, 10,000 records on object y, and 20,000 records on object z, you will still have a lookup skew situation. Lookup skews can be avoided by employing some of the following methods:

Improving record save performance – This can be done by doing the following:

a) Increasing the performance of your synchronous Apex code – tune your triggers for peak performance by consolidating code into a single trigger object.

b) Removing unnecessary workflows, process builders, or flows or consolidating into existing trigger code. Keep in mind that these automations lengthen the lock duration, which can cause increased lock failures. Removing or consolidating workflows into Apex can improve performance.

c) Processing only what's required synchronously and moving the rest of the code to asynchronous processing since locks are held for the full duration of the custom code execution.

Distributing the skew – Consider adding additional values to the lookup to avoid the skew or leaving it blank, if possible. This is because lookup issues are caused when many records have a lookup relationship to a single record. For example, a business provides quick budgetary quotes to walk-in customers without taking all of their details and creating an account in Salesforce. A generic account record has been created for this purpose. Over time, as quotes get created under this generic account, a lookup skew situation will arise that can then start to impact performance.

Using a picklist field – If there are a few lookup values, consider using a picklist value. By using a picklist value, you eliminate the locks associated with lookups and, hence, any locking issues.

As can be seen, something as innocuous as a lookup can lead to serious performance issues. This is a good reminder that we need to consider the consequences of our design and design for scalability and performance.

List views and reports

List views and reports are usually the first places where users start noticing performance issues. This is because almost every user of the platform will either have reports, list views, or both, so they can focus on the work they need to do:

- **Limit the number of fields**: The first thing I recommend is to educate your users to use fields on both list views and reports that they truly need. On many occasions, when creating reports, users pull fields on them to get a feel for what data is available but never get rid of them when saving the report. There is much less value in having reports with data that won't be used by users, and not only that, but it also impacts performance as well. The best strategy that I find works is to not just tell users what to do when creating reports but explain the rationale behind why it's important that this is done and how it can impact them down the road.

- **Use filters**: Use filters as much as possible to narrow down the result set for reports. In the last chapter, when we discussed query plans and query costs, we discussed how a table scan is less efficient than using indexes. Try to use fields in your reports and list views as filters that are indexed to ensure performance.

  Also, using relative dates, rather than exact date values, will result in better performance. For example, using LAST WEEK in your list view to filter all the leads from last week will be more performant, all things being equal, than entering **From** and **To** dates.

  The use of CONTAINS, != is also discouraged as it prevents the Salesforce platform from using indexes and therefore negatively impacts performance. If you are unsure about how a report that you are creating for your users will perform, I sometimes find it helpful to write the query behind the report or list view and run it in the query plan. This can give you a sense of how your query will perform in the report or list.

- **Unused reports**: Salesforce provides the ability to schedule reports and dashboards so users can automatically get the report or dashboard emailed to them. Ensure that you do a frequent cleanup of reports and dashboards that are scheduled. In one instance, a shared mailbox used by admins had multiple reports emailed that had been requested as one-time requests from executives, but they were never deleted from the platform.

- **Governance**: Implement at a minimum some level of governance around reports. Report proliferation is a real thing and can get out of control really quickly if not dealt with properly. One way that I find useful is to create report folders for each business department and give users in the department full access to the folder. Alternatively, you can designate 1-2 power users and give them **Manager** access, with the remaining users having **Editor** access to the folder.

SOQL best practices

Every time we press a Visualforce page that shows us some data, runs a report, or runs an interface to update data using Data Loader, chances are that we are querying some data from the database and running a query behind the scenes, whether we realize it or not. Acknowledging that some of the data is also cached for performance reasons, but assuming we run the aforementioned operations first time, a query will be running behind the scenes.

Because the Salesforce platform is multi-tenant and customers don't get access to the database directly, when you run a report, SOQL, and list view, your request is sent to what's called a **Query Optimizer**. This is a layer above the database that then converts your SOQL into a SQL query that the database can understand. The Query Optimizer understands *sharing rules*, including *with sharing*, in Apex classes as these have a direct impact on the results of a SOQL statement or when a report is run. The Query Optimizer is designed to optimize the SOQL into SQL for the database to run. *Optimize* here refers to whether a full table scan or index will be performed as well as the order in which the joins will be performed. Some of the practices mentioned in the *List views and reports* section are applicable to SOQL queries as well and so I won't be repeating them here.

Let's review some of the best practices related to running SOQL queries:

- **Using indexes**: This is very useful for ensuring that your queries will run efficiently. There are two types of indexes in Salesforce – standard and custom:

  Standard indexes include fields such as `RecordId`, fields marked as external IDs, `Name`, `LastModifiedDate`, `CreatedDate`, `RecordTypeId`, `Division`, `Email` (for `Contact` and `Lead` objects only), lookup, and master-detail relationships.

You can ask Salesforce Support to create custom indexes on formula fields and fields containing nulls. **Formula** fields calculate values on the fly and, by default, they don't have indexes, which typically means that a table scan would be required. If you decided to create custom **Indexes** on **Formula** fields, the function that defines the **Formula** field must be deterministic. Examples of non-deterministic **Formula** fields include the following:

- They contain a reference to another field, for example, lookup.

- They reference another **Formula** field.

- They use dynamic dates and time functions, for example, NOW, TODAY, and others.

- They have owner, auto number, division, and audit fields (excluding **CreatedDate** and **CreatedByID**).

- They reference other fields that cannot be indexed, for example, multi-select picklists, currency, long text area fields, and binary fields, including encrypted fields.

Standard fields with special functions, for example, on the Opportunity object, the **Amount** and **TotalOpportunityQuantity** fields.

Null fields are not indexed by default and, therefore, a null field would require a full table scan. A two-column index, including a null field, can be created on request to Salesforce. In this case, the second column can be null, but not the first column.

Divisions

This feature facilitates the partitioning of data, thereby improving query performance. You could have Salesforce enable this functionality and create divisions based on regions, but other values are also allowed. Each record then has a value for the **Division** field. For example, *division* values can be based on regions such as North America, Europe, Australia, and the like.

If you have the **Affected by Division** permission, then your search results, list views, and other functionality in Salesforce provide the option to select the division that you want to return results from. For example, you can only show records specific to a division if, at the time of creating or editing the list view, you specify the division you are interested in. Similarly, you can specify the division in report options to return results from a specific division, otherwise records from all divisions will be shown.

Dedicated integration user

I think most, if not all, companies that are integration heavy and have large volumes use a dedicated integration user for these operations, but I would like to reiterate the need to use a dedicated integration user whenever possible. This helps in identifying who made the changes and whether they are related to these processes, but also helps with avoiding any type of conflicts when an active platform user is doing work in the org and their username is being used for integrations or data migrations.

Setting appropriate org-wide defaults

Salesforce stores access to records in **Sharing** tables. Whenever records are inserted or the ownership changes, the platform has to insert/update these **Sharing** tables. Setting the **Organization-Wide Default (OWD)** to **Private** creates the additional burden of maintaining these **Sharing** tables. It is recommended, if possible and it's a greenfield org, to use **Public Read/Write** settings during data loads and then update the OWD to other settings as needed. This will allow the platform to insert data without inserting records in the **Sharing** tables at the same time.

Parallel sharing rule re-calculations

As organizations grow naturally or through mergers, acquisitions, or a reorganization, expect to see changes to your role hierarchy. And if there are sharing rules that allow access via sharing rules, changes to the role hierarchy mean that rules may need to be updated and re-run.

In LDV scenarios, these rules can take a great amount of time to complete and cause issues such as the process taking a long time to run and users needing access to use the system. If the rules are still running and the tables haven't been updated, users will not have access to the data or may have more access than they should.

The other issue is that due to the way these sharing rules are calculated, there is not much information in terms of how long the process will take to complete, and meanwhile, if Salesforce applies a path or a release is being applied, these processes are aborted and must be re-run again.

Once the parallel sharing calculation feature is enabled by Salesforce Customer Support, the updates happen asynchronously via a background processing queue. This allows for multiple execution threads to be created and placed in the queue, resulting in the quick completion of the process, and since jobs are placed in a job queue, interruptions due to patching or release application don't impact these jobs.

Disabling automation and logic consolidation

A good general practice is to disable automation and data quality tools that you may have set up in the org. These include triggers, flows, process builders, workflow rules, and validation rules. The reason is that they are meant to ensure data quality or transformation. Doing these operations outside of Salesforce when loading large volumes of data will help with preventing timeouts and other performance issues with your org. A good practice commonly adopted is to have some sort of a flag on triggers that is accessible to administrators via **Custom Settings** or **Custom Metadata** types. Just by turning the switch to **Off**, all triggers can be turned off for the duration of the LDV operation. This should be extended to click-based tools, such as process builders, flows, and validations rules as well so that they can be temporarily disabled.

Another factor to consider is the complexity of the org. Does it have multiple workflow rules or process builders on the same object? Is the Apex code properly bulkified? Is there custom code that is heavily dependent on synchronous operations? If the answer is *yes* to any of these, you may want to take the appropriate action by bulkifying Apex code. In other cases, you will want to consolidate the business logic that is on multiple process builders into a trigger. An even better option in an LDV scenario could be to move the processing into an asynchronous model. The idea is to avoid synchronous operations unless they are absolutely needed.

Consolidation can also take the form of reducing the number of automation tools you are using and moving them to a single logical place. For example, if you have a workflow rule, a process builder, a trigger, and a flow on an account, from an LDV perspective, I would recommend consolidating them and moving into a trigger or employing asynchronous techniques if the results are not needed right away by the user.

Deferred sharing rules calculation

When making a large number of changes to roles, territories, public groups, users, and account ownerships that are part of sharing rules, they can automatically trigger a rule recalculation. This recalculation can take a long time to run, especially in LDV scenarios, and impact performance, but that may also lead to time-outs.

For these situations, it is recommended to make all the changes and defer the recalculation of rules to a later time, perhaps when the users are offline or a relative period when there is less load on the org. The deferred sharing rules calculation simply defers the automatic calculation of the sharing rules and requires manual intervention when you have completed your work and are ready to let the calculations run. This feature is not available by default, and you need to contact Salesforce Customer Support to have it available in your org.

> **Group membership and sharing calculations**
>
> Sharing calculations usually have groups to grant access to users. A group in Salesforce can be an individual user or another group of users in a particular role or hierarchy. Groups are used in Salesforce to set up default sharing access, record sharing with users, and so on. Refer to this link to read more about the groups in Salesforce: `https://developer.salesforce.com/docs/atlas.en-us.securityImplGuide.meta/securityImplGuide/users_group_member_types.htm`.

Granular locking

Just like when a child record in a master-child relationship is being updated and the system automatically locks the parent record to prevent any data integrity issues, when roles or group membership updates are done, the entire group membership table is locked. This happens regardless of whether the updates are being through the API or using the frontend. When a large number of updates are being undertaken, as in an LDV scenario, or other integrations are running that update roles or group memberships, you may receive `could not acquire locks` errors.

Granular locking allows group maintenance operations to proceed as long as there are no hierarchical or other relationships between the roles and the groups that are being updated. This concurrency allows for large updates to happen quickly, while preventing any locking errors.

Update versus upsert operations

During an insert or an update operation, a row is simply inserted or updated based on the record ID or an external ID. With upsert, however, the platform has to determine whether a record already exists, and, based on the result of that query, it will either do an insert or an update. It is recommended to not use upserts especially for LDV scenarios as that can result in a quite notable performance degradation.

Roll-up summary (RUP) fields

When doing LDV migrations, you can also defer the creation of any RUP fields once the data has been loaded. This is because, as data is loaded into the system, if you have multiple RUP fields, the platform will try to calculate them as the data is getting loaded since they are calculated almost instantly. To reduce any chances of performance slowdown, it is recommended to defer RUP fields once all the data has been migrated successfully.

There are several measures that we can take to ensure that LDVs in Salesforce can be handled without having to be overly concerned about performance. The key thing is to design for performance and scalability right from the get-go. Performance issues don't manifest overnight, but rather they are the consequences of bad design choices or architectural oversights that accumulate over time and impact performance in the org. With proper planning and architectural design, these issues can be avoided and a scalable, performant solution can be delivered to your users.

Not all data needs to be brought into Salesforce, and there are use cases where the data can continue to reside in an external system but is made available to users on demand. This is where Salesforce Connect and external objects come into the picture. Let's discuss them in more detail.

Salesforce Connect and external objects

We briefly discussed external objects in the LDV section, but let's take a deeper dive in this section. Salesforce Connect is a point-and-click solution to integrate external systems with Salesforce without the need for writing complex code or requiring a middleware to move data across the systems. Data is queried from the external system on demand and made available to users in Salesforce. This way, you can easily integrate ERPs such as Oracle, SAP, or Microsoft, along with several other systems that support the OData protocol.

> OData protocol
>
> Short for **Open Data Protocol**, **OData** is a standard that's used for integrating disparate systems or databases. The OData protocol allows for the easy consumption of the interoperable RESTful (REST) APIs. The standardization of OData is its advantage given that you don't have to worry about the formats of different systems. Since both source and destination systems support the OData protocol, this means that they can communicate easily using an agreed-upon data format.

By using Salesforce Connect, which leverages external objects, users can not only read data from source systems but also write, delete, and update data. I have seen it being used to query and display order fulfillment data that was stored in an Azure database. External objects are like custom objects.

Ways to connect

There are multiple ways in which to use Salesforce Connect, one of which is to use an OData connector. Let's review each of these briefly:

- **OData adapter**: OData 2.0 or 4.0 adapters can be used to integrate with systems that support the protocol. One of the common use cases is in organizations that use both Microsoft SharePoint and Salesforce and want to display SharePoint data in Salesforce. Since Microsoft supports OData, you can integrate the two systems without writing any code or doing any testing.

- **Custom adapters**: There may be cases where the OData adapter may not satisfy requirements and a custom solution is required. In that case, Salesforce Connect provides the flexibility to code your own adapter by using the Apex Connector Framework. This is not as quick as a point-and-click solution that the OData adapter uses, but nonetheless provides greater flexibility to meet business requirements.

Having looked at some of the ways that Salesforce Connect can be used, let's take a look at the benefits of external objects.

Benefits of external objects

External objects are an awesome tool in any architect's toolbox as they provide numerous benefits, including the following:

- **Ease of setup**: External objects can be set up using the UI in Salesforce and don't require any coding skills. This can be a huge time saver and it also makes it easy for Salesforce admins with no coding skills to set up an integration with external systems.

- **Data virtualization**: External objects provide a good mechanism to virtualize data. This means that you could have the data stored in an external system and you can make it available for your users on demand whenever they need it. Storage is expensive in Salesforce and external objects can be used to make data available for your users without storing it in Salesforce.

- **Read and write operations**: External objects provide the ability to not only read the data from external systems, but also the ability to write back into the source system. This is a powerful feature that enables Salesforce users to update another system without ever needing to leave Salesforce.

- **Real-time data**: Another benefit of external objects is that the data is available on demand. Whenever you open a tab that is associated with an external object, a REST call is made to the endpoint and the results are returned in real time. This is a huge benefit for use cases where data is required by users right away but is hosted in external systems. This eliminates the need for a middleware tool to track the records that have been moved and/or are waiting to be moved over to the destination; that is, it eliminates the need for syncing between systems since the data is never stored in Salesforce and is fetched in real time.

- **Standard functionality**: There are some limitations to external objects regarding features such as free text search, record views, and list views, and these will be discussed in the *Considerations for external objects* section. This makes it easier for users to leverage external objects' data because of the familiar UI that they are accustomed to in Salesforce.

- **Mobile data**: External objects' data is also available with mobile devices. So, your users are not limited to viewing the data only when they are in front of their desktops, but rather, they can access external objects anywhere and anytime they have an internal connection.

Let's now take a look at some of the considerations for using external objects.

Considerations for external objects

Since external objects provide a means to virtualize data and are similar to custom objects in some cases, there are limitations to consider before using external objects. Some of these limitations include the following:

- **Limited standard functionality**: Standard functionality that you get with most custom objects is not available for external objects. For example, workflow rules, approval processes, record types, field history tracking, and notes are not available for external objects. That's why it is critical that you have a very clear understanding of the business requirements and the business objective that you are trying to achieve as external objects may not meet requirements and other options may be more suitable.

- **Limited custom fields**: Custom fields, such as auto-number, currency, formula, and master-detail relationship, are not available for external objects. Similarly, if you are planning to do roll-up summary calculations using RUP fields, they are not available for external objects.

- **Reporting considerations**: There are reporting considerations for external objects as well. Since data is fetched in real time from the external system, it can take a while for reports to run. Cross filters are also not supported on external objects. When the report is run, including an external object, a callout is made to the external system that counts toward the total callout limit allowed. For example, for the Enterprise, Performance, and Unlimited editions, 20,000 OData callouts can be made in an hour.

Carefully consider the limitations for external objects before deciding to use them for your solution. For a complete list of limitations, refer to this link from Salesforce: `https://help.salesforce.com/articleView?id=sf.platform_connect_considerations_reports.htm&type=5`.

We have discussed how external objects are a useful tool in our toolkit for making data available in Salesforce without the need for a middleware or writing code. Although a powerful feature of Salesforce, carefully review your use cases alongside the limitations of external objects to ensure that your business needs will be sufficiently met with external objects.

Now, we will review big objects, which are another feature in Salesforce that can be used to store hundreds of millions of records.

Introducing big objects

Standard and custom Salesforce objects are designed to hold hundreds of thousands to millions of records, but organizations are generating new data at an exponential pace. Salesforce customers were no exceptions to this and were generating data at a rapid pace. Originally not designed for massive data volumes, the limits of standard and custom objects were being reached, forcing customers to look at other non-Salesforce options. Managing big data is challenging as it requires a specialized skill set and dedicated infrastructure to manage effectively.

Realizing these challenges and the business needs of its customers, Salesforce released the **big objects** feature a few years ago. Big objects can store millions of records, reaching up to the 1 billion mark and more. This data can then be accessed in the Salesforce platform or by any external application as well. The big object architecture is different from the main Salesforce platform, which most people are familiar with. Big objects run on a non-relational database architecture, which allows for greater scalability and consistent performance.

As we saw earlier in the chapter, non-relational databases are not intended for transactional operations, but instead are optimized for large storage. The big objects architecture is no different and has specialized ways to insert and retrieve data. Regular SOQL queries will not work efficiently with big objects as the query will time out and, therefore, **Async (Asynchronous)** SOQL is used to query big object data.

With this brief introduction out of the way, let's now review the benefits of big objects.

Benefits of big objects

The big objects feature helps resolve specific problems that customers were facing when this feature was not around. Let's try to understand the benefits of big objects:

- **End user experience**: If you have an org with millions of records in objects and users are starting to complain about slow reports, list views, or Apex processes taking a long time to complete, big objects may be the option to look at. You can offload older data from the platform into big objects, thereby improving SOQL performance, which translates into higher internal and external user satisfaction.

- **Learning curve**: Even though big objects have their own quirks with respect to how indexes are created and used in Async SOQL, you can use the API or the UI to create big objects and use Async SOQL to query the data. Async SOQL is very similar to SOQL and if you already have SOQL, transitioning over to Async SOQL is not very difficult.

- **Low-cost storage option**: Compared to storage on the platform, big objects are a cheaper option for storing large volumes of data. Once you have established the process and the tools are in place to automatically archive data, you can be hands-off knowing that you don't have to worry about performance or getting approvals for buying more storage on the platform. Salesforce also uses big objects to store field history data in the `FieldHistoryArchive` object. This object can store field history data for up to 10 years.

- **Analytics**: Reporting on massive volumes of data can be challenging, but with big objects, using Async SOQL can make the job easier. Summarizing big object data into custom objects can enable users to use familiar tools such as Salesforce Report Builder and dashboards for analytics. Additionally, **Einstein Analytics (EA)** supports big object data, so you can use the features of EA to quickly visualize your data.

- **Integrations**: Big objects work with **Platform Events** (**PE**) and this is a big advantage because you can simply publish your event and consume it in big objects. For example, whenever a quote is approved and converted into an order, you can publish order details using PE and insert records in big objects to be used by EA reports.

- **Audit and compliance data**: For businesses in industries that generate gigantic volumes of data and are required to keep them for a certain period for audit or regulatory compliance purposes, big objects provide a lot of flexibility. The data remains within highly secured Salesforce data centers and the solution is scalable, so the organization doesn't have to worry about moving data off of big objects.

Now, let's look into some considerations for big objects. These are important because understanding them and considering them when designing solutions for dealing with big data can impact your choice of solution.

Considerations for big objects

As with anything, there are several architectural considerations to keep in mind when deciding to use big objects. Some of these are as follows:

- **SOQL and Async SOQL**: Big objects can be worked with more effectively as a result of using Async SOQL. This is because these objects are created in a certain way and regular SOQL queries are not optimized to work with big objects.

- **Absence of UI**: Unlike standard and custom objects, once you have created the metadata for your big object, there is no UI screen where your users can go and work with big objects. You will have to create your own custom UI, either using Visualforce or Lighting components.

- **Number of big objects**: You are limited to creating 100 objects, along with a limit on the number of fields that you can create in each object. The number of fields that you can create is dependent on your org's license type. For example, you can create 800 fields on your big object if you have the Performance edition, whereas 500 fields are allowed if you have the Enterprise edition.

- **Salesforce Connect**: Big objects don't support the use of Salesforce Connect and external objects. This means that you cannot store your data in big objects and pull it into Salesforce.

- **Consistency over availability**: Big objects are designed to hold billions of records and are architected in such a way that they deliver consistency over availability. Consistency here refers to the fact that on a multi-node system, every node will provide the exact same response, whereas availability ensures that all nodes will provide a response.

  Since big objects architecture prefers consistency, when working with big objects using APIs, ensure that you have retry mechanisms to rewrite complete batches until you have a response from the API. In practical terms, this means that, unlike other database transactions, where the platform or your code can do rollbacks, there are no rollbacks with big objects and therefore a retry mechanism must be in place for complete batches.

- **Sandboxes**: Big objects are copied when a sandbox is created. However, the data is not, so you will need to populate the sandbox yourself.

- **Fields**: Unlike the wide assortment of fields that you can create on a standard or custom object, big objects have limitations in terms of the types of fields you can create. At the time of writing, the following fields are supported:

  - **Date/Time**

  - **Lookup relationship**

  - **Email**

  - **Number**

  - **Phone**

  - **Text**

  - **Text area** (long)

  - **URL**

  This is an important consideration because if you plan on deploying big objects for, let's say, data archiving purposes and offload data from the platform, you will need to consider any field transformations that may need to happen before the data can be stored in Salesforce. Another important consideration is that big objects don't support standard fields such as **CreatedDate**, **LastModifiedBy**, and **CreatedBy**.

- **Encryption**: If you are storing sensitive data that has been encrypted, big objects don't support that currently and any encrypted data from standard or custom objects will be stored as clear text on the big object.

- **Automation tools**: Big objects are meant to support lots and lots of data, and features such as triggers, flows, and process builders are not supported on big objects because these features are meant for business processes that facilitate transactional systems. And big objects architecture is not meant to be used as a transactional system.

- **Security**: Depending on your use case, this is another important consideration to keep in mind when thinking of using big objects since there are limited security options with it. You can enforce object- and field-level permissions, but sharing rules are not supported. This means that you will have to carefully analyze how user access would be mapped from the platform to big objects.

- **Reporting**: Due to the high volumes that big objects are intended for, currently there is no support for search, reports, and dashboards. However, you have the option to summarize the data in the big object using Async SOQL and move it to a custom object on the platform. Then you can search, report, and create dashboards just like you would do with any other standard or custom object.

Now that we have reviewed the considerations for big objects, let's look at some of the use cases for big objects.

Use cases for big objects

Generally, any time you have large volumes of data that are not actively required for transactional or analytical purposes, big objects can be a good option to use. The key thing is to understand the requirements of the business, including how frequently data is needed, analytics, security, and how the data is going to be accessed. Let's take a look at some use cases for big objects.

Regulatory requirements

Regulatory requirements typically require that you have robust auditing mechanisms in place. And auditing even a small number of fields can generate a lot of data. There is a good reason why Salesforce limits the number of fields on which you can activate **Audit History**. You can generate tremendous amounts of data, for example, with a single Opportunity record, let alone records created from other objects.

Different regulatory bodies have different requirements in terms of how long organizations are required to keep data, thereby requiring organizations to archive it and make it available if and when an audit happens. The banking and health industries are heavily regulated and have stringent requirements for data retention and retrieval.

Big objects can easily meet the demands of these types of organizations as they can be scaled horizontally without requiring the customer to do anything additional on their end and, at the same time, avoid any performance impact on end users.

Archiving

Given that Salesforce is a multi-tenant environment, there are limits imposed on how much storage you can use. With standard and custom objects, you can easily store millions of rows of data, but additional storage is expensive on the platform. Big objects are a good option for offloading data from the main platform to free up space and are a cheaper storage option.

The advantage of big objects is that they are readily available to be used in Salesforce without any expensive integration work. You don't have to worry about authentication or row-level security, and there is one less integration to worry about as big objects eliminate the need for these factors, which are essential for any integration.

You can schedule reports to run frequently, perhaps on a quarterly basis, to determine whether there is certain data that is not being updated and that can be a good candidate for archival. Think of your main platform storage as the primary area where data that is actively used or referenced should reside, whereas big objects are a secondary area where less frequently used data or data that is required to be kept for regulatory purposes should reside. One such example is **tasks** in Salesforce, which are frequently used, and records are created at a rapid pace. Rather than deleting old tasks, you can simply archive them and use them for trend analysis and reporting.

360-degree view of customer

Organizations need to have a complete view of the customer as much as possible. All the touchpoints that customers have with the business' digital assets and any interaction offline with the business are important sources of information for marketing. This can generate large amounts of data, especially in the retail industry, and storing all of that in the Salesforce platform can be a recipe to run out of storage quickly.

Customers are now looking for a personalized experience and this can be provided based on predictive analytics. By bringing your data into one centralized location and leveraging Salesforce Einstein Analytics, you can offer your customers personalized offers based on their preferences or send them a special offer based on certain times of the year depending on their shopping history.

Big data is becoming a reality as customers using Salesforce are generating more data than ever. Following the discussion in this section, you should feel more confident regarding the strategies and the tools that are available to deal with these types of very large data volumes.

Summary

We started off by discussing the types of databases to give an overview of what is out there. We all know that the Salesforce platform is largely built on relational databases, more specifically, Oracle databases, but not everything in the Salesforce ecosystem is hosted on a relational database.

The discussion around determining whether you are in an LDV scenario will hopefully prompt you next time when you are in a similar situation to thoroughly assess the factors that can contribute to LDV scenarios even if the rough threshold of a million records is not met. In addition to that, the considerations for LDVs are not only important for LDV scenarios, but some of the discussion is relevant to general data migration and integration as well. I know that the *Preventing LDV scenarios* section has a provocative title, but the thought behind it is that there are ways to prevent an LDV scenario, again acknowledging the fact that it may not be possible when you have 5 million Account records with 7 million Contact records. Nothing is lost, even if you are in an LDV scenario, as Salesforce provides many options for optimizing LDV operations.

We also looked at Salesforce Connect and external objects. This is probably one of the least-used integration options, in my opinion. Granted, external objects lack features that we are accustomed to with standard and custom objects, but they are a powerful feature that can massively cut the time to get a production-ready integration. Big objects are another feature that is relatively new but has some solid use cases. The next time you are thinking of archiving or freeing up space, consider big objects for their ease of use and the ability to be used with Salesforce Einstein, which makes the data so much more accessible to Salesforce users.

In conclusion, you should feel a lot more confident in dealing with the topic of big data in the context of Salesforce following our deep dive into these topics. You have learned the optimal use cases for each of the different options available to you in Salesforce and, coupled with your business requirements, you will easily be able to make a good choice about which option to go with after carefully considering the pros and cons of each of the available options.

In the next chapter, we will discuss general data migration practices, some of the tools available, and the APIs that Salesforce provides for integration and data loading.

Questions

1. **Precision Printing (PP)** is implementing Salesforce and uses SAP's order management module for order fulfillment. Since the orders reside in SAP, the sales team has no access to order status data. What can the architect at PP recommend to meet this requirement? (Choose one answer.)

   a) Implement a middleware tool that can update Salesforce with order status data whenever there is a change on the SAP side.

   b) Develop a point-to-point integration that uses the Salesforce APIs and update the data whenever the order status changes in SAP.

   c) Configure Salesforce Connect and use external objects to update data in Salesforce.

   d) Hire a data entry clerk to enter data in Salesforce whenever there is a change in order status in SAP.

2. PP started a new B2C division a few years ago and has a global customer base of more than 1,000,000 Account records. PP has a multitude of automation tools running on this object, including multiple triggers, process builders, and flows. For the last few weeks, users have been complaining about reports taking too long to run, to the point that some reports are taking more than a minute to complete. What can the data architect suggest to rectify this problem? (Choose two answers.)

   a) Consider using custom indexes on the object and explore the use of skinny tables by opening a case with Salesforce Customer Support.

   b) Consolidate the triggers into a single trigger to follow best practices.

   c) Delete some of the Account records so that the database has fewer records to read.

   d) Analyze and eliminate some of the unused columns from the report.

3. **Global Cycles and Scooters (GCS)** is a B2C business selling bikes and e-scooters to cycling enthusiasts worldwide. The company is interested in keeping the **Opportunity** field history beyond the 18 months (24 months via the API) that's provided with Salesforce and make the data available through Einstein reports. The company is not interested in purchasing additional capabilities that would allow it to retain the field history for up to 10 years. What can the architect recommend in this situation? (Choose one answer.)

    a) Export the data into **Comma-Separated Value (CSV)** files and store the CSV files on an external storage device. Make the CSV files available so users can report off them.

    b) Make an automated process to archive data older than 18 months into a big object and use Einstein Analytics for reporting.

    c) Create a Microsoft SQL database and archive data into it. Use Microsoft reporting tools to report on the data.

    d) Migrate the data from the **OpportunityHistory** table to a custom Salesforce object and use Salesforce reports to report on the data.

Further reading

*   *Why the Future of Data Storage is (Still) Magnetic Tape*: `https://spectrum.ieee.org/computing/hardware/why-the-future-of-data-storage-is-still-magnetic-tape`

*   *Salesforce Is All About Data*: `https://engineering.salesforce.com/salesforce-is-all-about-data-d6fdf57cc8eb`

*   *Managing Lookup Skew in Salesforce to Avoid Record Lock Exceptions*: `https://developer.salesforce.com/blogs/engineering/2013/04/managing-lookup-skew-to-avoid-record-lock-exceptions.html`

*   *Salesforce Compatibility Considerations for Salesforce Connect—All Adapters*: `https://help.salesforce.com/articleView?id=sf.platform_connect_considerations_compatibility.htm&type=5`

8
Best Practices for General Data Migration

Data migration is a common task that Salesforce admins, developers, and architects are asked to complete. Understanding best practices on how best to approach data migration will ensure that costly mistakes are avoided, and the data migration is complete and accurate.

In this chapter, we will discuss some of the tools available to us for data migration and their advantages and disadvantages. Most of the time, for large and complex data migrations, a third-party tool is used as the standard tools provided by Salesforce may be sufficient but not very efficient in terms of effort.

In the later part of the chapter, we will touch base on the different APIs that Salesforce provides in the context of data migration and integration. You will learn about the general architecture of the APIs as well as ideal use cases for the APIs. Since this book is about data and use cases for large volumes of data are becoming more common, I will be discussing the Bulk API in much more detail compared to the rest of them.

The topics covered in this chapter include the following:

- Assessing data
- The Preparation phase
- The Execution phase
- Tools for loading data into Salesforce
- Understanding APIs

Assessing data

In any business, data is key, and it grows fast, resulting in the use of various databases and data stores that are used to securely store that data. Sometimes the data is in different formats, and it needs to be worked on to bring it into the same format to avoid confusion. But before we go into a deep discussion on data, let's first understand the differences between data migration, conversion, and integration:

- **Data migration**: Data migration is the process of moving data from one system or application to another. This is usually the result of retiring a system to upgrade to a new system that provides improved business functionality. As more businesses move from on-premises systems to cloud infrastructure, they realize that the data must be moved alongside the application for continued business operations.

- **Data conversion**: Conversion is the process of transforming data from one format into another. Each application has its own set of standards it follows in terms of the formatting of data, data types, or the length of fields. For example, in a legacy system, it is possible for the **Stage** field in an `Opportunity` object to be a number field. During the conversion process, we are required to map these number-based **Stage** values to the text-based **Stage** values in Salesforce. This usually entails doing some transformation work in a staging area before the data is loaded into the destination. To avoid confusing data conversion and migration, it is important to understand that the former entails data transformation whereas the latter is geared more towards the processes and the tools used to move the data from one system to another.

- **Data integration**: This involves combining data from different sources to provide a unified view to the user. For example, a business is using Salesforce as its **Customer Relationship Management (CRM)** tool but **Systems, Applications, and Products (SAP)** as the order fulfillment tool. In the absence of any self-service tools where the customer can check the status themselves, sales representatives would need to know the order status so they can keep the customer updated. In this scenario, as the order goes through the different stages in SAP and the status changes, the status can be reflected in Salesforce.

With the definitions out of the way, let's look into the need for assessing data migration.

Components of a data migration assessment

Data migration should not merely be a single line item in the project plan because it is nuanced and requires careful planning and execution. Having it as a minor line item in the project plan is a sure way to run into issues when running the migration into the production environment. Rather, it should be treated as a major component of any project with its own detailed schedule, tasks, and dependencies.

With a proper assessment, you can gauge the landscape and provide realistic time and budgetary estimates that can ensure a quality data migration. Let's discuss some of the integral components of a sound data migration assessment:

- **Volume of data**: This is usually the first thing that most project teams think about during data migration discussions. It is an important consideration since migrating 50,000 records will require a different approach than migrating 100 million records. For example, the choice of APIs, whether to use the **Bulk** or the **REST** API, will make more sense for the latter use case (migrating 100 million records) rather than the former.

- **Type of data**: Another consideration is the type and format of data that you are planning to migrate. For example, migrating leads from the legacy system will be much less work than migrating accounts, contacts, opportunities, and opportunity products. This is because of the potential relationships between these objects in the legacy system and the different data types and formats of the fields. More effort will be required if the **Stage** values, for example, are different in the legacy system than in Salesforce.

- **Number of systems**: What is the number of systems involved in the migration – are we migrating data from one source system or multiple source systems into Salesforce? For example, in a consolidation type data migration, you could have Oracle NetSuite and/or Microsoft Dynamics as the source systems, each with its own data types and standards. Migrating this into Salesforce will be much more involved than, say, simply migrating data from Oracle NetSuite. This may also necessitate that a staging database is introduced in the landscape where de-duplication and transformation can take place before loading the data into Salesforce.

- **Privacy**: With new privacy regulations getting introduced around the world and existing ones getting revised, what are the considerations for data migration during the preparation phase. Can offshore teams have access to it? Where should the infrastructure used during data migration be located – can it be in a country that may not have very robust privacy laws or doesn't enforce them effectively? These are all considerations that could have an impact on the duration as well as the cost of the data migration project. Understanding this and any restrictions in accessing the data, whether they're based on the client requirements or for compliance reasons, will help you plan for and address these requirements properly.

- **Data retention**: Not all data from the legacy system may need to be brought over into Salesforce but the business may have requirements around data retention for compliance purposes. Working with architects and other stakeholders, the project team would need to provide solutions to identify the optimal ways to stay in compliance and provide continued data access to the business.

- **Resource availability**: Data migration is never an exercise in isolation where the data migration team goes away, works on the project, and returns with a finished product that when executed in production will flawlessly migrate data. It must involve business resources who are intimately familiar with the data and can guide the team and validate the data migration as well as the production run. Understanding upfront what the business resource constraints are can help in identifying potential risks and provide the opportunity to put in place an effective mitigation strategy.

- **Current landscape**: This involves assessing whether all systems under consideration are in the cloud or on-premises. Are there any special considerations with respect to access to these systems, and where are the regular planned outage schedules? On-premises systems usually require more configuration because of the need to reach into the internal network. This would also include coordination with any third-party vendor resources whose assistance may be required during the migration.

- **Communication**: A good migration project will always have a solid communication plan that considers the needs of different stakeholders and how they like to be communicated. Depending on the scope, complexity, and the number of stakeholders in the data migration project, the communication plan can be very extensive. That shouldn't deter you from creating a well-thought-out communication plan as it provides a roadmap of how other stakeholders will be kept up to date and what is expected of them during the project.

- **Document data transformations**: Once you have identified your source data and mapped it field by field to the destination's fields, ensure that this is sufficiently documented. Ensure that you have mapped both the tables from the source to objects in Salesforce and the fields from the source table to fields in Salesforce. This document becomes a critical document for any issues down the road that may be due to incorrect field mappings. It also forms the basis for any transformations that are required and can be used by the testing team to validate your test loads.

- **Recurring exercise**: It should be made clear right from the get-go that data migration is a recurring exercise. It means that during the execution phase, multiple iterations will need to be conducted to get to a stage where the team feels comfortable with pulling the trigger in the production environment.

- **Data quality**: Data quality issues are a common problem in today's systems and hardly any system is immune from it. When migrating data into Salesforce, consider the data quality issue of the source systems. This will help you understand how much effort will be required to cleanse the data before it can be loaded into Salesforce. Since data is used for decision-making and, among other things, automating business processes, the data quality of the source systems is of utmost importance during this assessment phase.

The preceding discussion is not intended to be exhaustive but lists some of the more critical aspects of the assessment phase. Each data migration project is unique and properly assessing the requirements and understanding the variables will increase your chances of successful data migration.

Let's now review the preparation phase of data migration.

The Preparation phase

In this phase, you are prepping everything that's needed for the next phase, which is the execution phase. Armed with the trove of information that was gathered in the previous phase, you are set to act on it and prep for successful data migration.

Let's discuss the best practices that apply to this phase.

Best practices

You have developed a sound understanding of the current landscape along with understanding the type of data that is in scope, the source systems and their constraints, and the business requirements of the data migration. Now it's time to put all of this into action by following the best practices described as follows:

- **Analysis**: Carefully analyze the result of the exercise from the assessment phase. Seemingly minor details that are skipped during analysis can cause a lot of rework sometimes down the road. For example, assuming that a legacy system has good data quality; without vetting this assumption with the users or sampling the data to validate it can cause the data cleansing exercise to be a prolonged and expensive effort.

- **Set up data migration environments and tools**: Based on the requirements gathered so far and the analysis performed, set up the environment and the tools that are to be used to migrate the data. This will include any staging databases, data cleansing tools, de-duplication tools, sandboxes, and so on.

- **Test plan**: This is a critical aspect of the preparation phase because you want to have a clear idea of what is going to be tested (the scope of the test and the use cases to test), how it will be tested, and where (tools for testing and applicable sandbox environments), who will do the testing, and what the dependencies for testing are.

- **External IDs**: These are your best friends, so make use of them for easier data migrations. External IDs provide not only a method to keep track of records from the source system but also the ability to leverage the *Upsert* functionality in Salesforce.

- **Respect the loading sequence of objects**: This pertains to ensuring that your parent object is loaded first before the child object can be loaded. This means that if you are using spreadsheets to transform data as a staging area, you need to load accounts before contacts or opportunity records can be loaded.

- **Hardcoding IDs**: Record IDs in Salesforce change by environment and therefore, you should avoid using any hardcoded values in your loads. For example, a record type ID for an opportunity in a sandbox will be different from the ID in the production instance. If you must store IDs, have a configuration type file that is referenced during the runs. This gives you the ability to update the ID once in a centralized place that is then referenceable for all runs. Otherwise, you would need to update the record IDs for individual rows as you move through each environment.

- **Record ownership**: Every record in Salesforce has an owner and this must be kept in mind when prepping for data loads. The system will not migrate data if the record owner is missing or invalid. Your legacy system may have records whose owners are ex-employees and are inactive in the source system. You will want to ensure that if those records are in scope for migration, appropriate record owner names are provided to avoid the records erroring out.

- **Salesforce setup**: Since the next phase will entail running the migration, ensure that the appropriate setup has been completed in Salesforce. This will include things such as role hierarchy, profiles, permission sets, page layouts, and the definition of picklist values. This is an important step. Otherwise, when you run your test loads, you will get bogged down by errors caused not by the data migration process but by an incomplete setup in the destination org.

- **Updates to sandboxes**: As you work on your project, the day-to-day business operations continue, which means that continuous changes in the form of break fixes and enhancements should be made, and other projects will keep getting applied to the production environment. Make sure to take these into account and work with your Salesforce team to coordinate that changes being applied to the production environment also get applied to the project sandboxes. This will prevent any surprises later due to different configurations and code bases when you are running dry runs in a shared environment such as a UAT sandbox.

- **Ability to disable business logic**: You have the option to let your business logic get applied to the data as it's getting loaded in the destination, but this is not recommended. The best practice is to transform your data and apply any business rules outside of Salesforce and load the finalized dataset into Salesforce. This helps with performance and reduces the chances of running into data-related issues. With this approach, though, you would want to ensure that your declarative, as well as code-based, automation logic has built-in disable flags that can easily be disabled at the time of the load. These flags should be built as part of the design when these features are introduced but if they are not there, assess whether it would make sense to include them before running the production run.

- **Go directly to the source**: Whenever possible, read data directly from the source. This is because each intermediary system has its own way of formatting and storing data, and this could lead to data loss while it passes through this intermediary layer. For example, when data is exported to Microsoft Excel from the source system, text fields with numbers may get converted to number fields with decimals or, sometimes, leading zeros in a column may get dropped. This can lead to errors when the data is loaded into Salesforce.

- **Error handling**: When pulling data directly from a source database, it makes rerunning the migration process much easier if, say, the IDs of the new records in Salesforce are written back to the source table. That way, in the next run, you can simply filter on the records that don't have the Salesforce ID column populated and rerun them. Generally speaking, regardless of what the source of the data is, ensure that you have a plan to handle errors and the ability to retry the runs because it is inevitable that retries will be needed.

- **Backup the data**: At this phase, you will also want to make sure that backups of the data are in place and tested procedures are already in place should a data restore be required. Don't underestimate this step as nothing is worse than losing customer data even if it's not your fault. Make sure that the client is aware and has proper backup processes, and has tested those backups in restore scenarios as well.

My experience is that this is often the most rushed phase because we want to get to the execution phase as soon as we can. Make sure that you have enough time allocated for this phase as rushing this phase leads to issues and doing work again.

In the next section, we will look at the meat of any data migration project, the execution phase.

The Execution phase

This is the phase where the rubber meets the road and all the work done in the previous phase gets tested. By this phase, you will have achieved a good understanding of the scope, the type of data, assumptions, and constraints you are dealing with. Let's discuss the best practices that can be applied in this phase.

Best practices

Your mapping document is ready and the tool that you will use along with any staging databases are all set and ready for that moment of truth. You are eager to click the **Run** button and see how the first dry run with some preliminary data goes. To be clear, the execution phase here refers to running your data loads in a sandbox environment and is not limited to production runs. We will discuss specific production environment runs in a later section. Here are some best practices that will increase your chances of success with this phase:

- **Start small**: Start with small loads and iron out any issues before trying large loads. This keeps the effort required to re-validate the batch reasonable as you go and refine your code or tweak the configuration in the migration tool to fix any issues.

- **Follow the steps**: By now, you should have a deployment document that lists the steps required to run the dry runs along with notes on any additional steps needed for the production run. As you test and further tweak your code and the migration too, make sure that the document is up to date. Follow the steps in this document every time you are running a dry run. This will ensure that the document is up to date and develops the document as you get ready for the final full load for UAT.

- **Duplicate rules**: Disable any duplicate management rules that you have set up in Salesforce. These could be out-of-the-box Salesforce functionality you are using or if you are using a third-party solution, rules that have been set up by that tool. You don't want your loads to error out because of duplicate rules and any such concerns should be handled outside of Salesforce before the data gets loaded into it.

- **Disable automations**: Ensure that you have disabled any relevant automations such as triggers, Process Builder, and workflows before you run your loads. Again, any type of transformation to the data should already have been done outside of Salesforce before loading into the system.

As part of the execution phase, there are some specific best practices regarding sandbox testing. Let's review those in the next section.

Sandbox testing

No matter how seemingly *simple* a load looks, I never recommend running it directly in a production environment. Always run it in a sandbox first and get a *feel* for how it may run in production and always validate the results. Here are some best practices related to sandbox testing:

- **Restorable sandboxes**: Data migration is a recurring process, and you will find that you are running multiple test loads to the point you are ready for UAT testing. Setting up a sandbox takes time, especially when considering that Salesforce has limits on how often certain types of sandboxes can be refreshed. For example, if you are using a Developer Pro org, you can refresh it on alternate days. You will be constrained if you need to fix and rerun a test load on the same day.

  To avoid running into these types of constraints and to save time by avoiding having to set up the environment again, use a data backup tool that can easily restore data as well. This will also eliminate the need to rely on an admin with a system administrator in production to do a sandbox refresh. With your admin credentials (assuming you have been granted those), you can easily kick off the restore and have a working environment available to you within a short period.

- **Full-copy sandbox**: When you are ready for UAT and to have the business testing team validate your setup/code, ensure that you have a full-copy sandbox set up for this purpose. Running a full migration in this type of sandbox will give some very good data, for example, how long it would take to run the migration in the production environment. This is because full-copy sandboxes have similar (not the same) hardware and results extrapolated are typically valid for production as well.

  Another benefit is that full-copy sandboxes have the same data as a production environment, so you are working with an environment that very closely resembles a production environment. Of course, if this is a greenfield implementation, then the production environment will not have any data, but in the case of a brownfield implementation, this can be an advantage.

To re-iterate, sandbox testing is a must regardless of how simple or complex the data migration is. For simpler migrations, it seems like an extraneous step, but I think it's worth the time and the effort rather than going back and trying to restore data in the production org in the case of a brownfield org.

Let's now review best practices related to the production run.

Production run

You have conducted multiple dry runs and had business testing validate your results in a full cycle UAT. It's time to press the trigger and run the data migration in the production environment. Some of the best practices for this phase include the following:

- **Production freeze**: Ensure that you have communicated to other stakeholders that there should be a change freeze for metadata in the production environment. This is to avoid running into any issues due to enhancements that were not applied to the sandbox environments. Break-fixes cannot be avoided but if there are any that are not a high priority, it is recommended to postpone them until you have completely migrated your data.

  A change freeze should usually kick in when you move to the full-copy environment and are conducting UAT testing there. To avoid holding up other projects or teams, try to minimize the time between the change freeze and the production run of your migration. I should mention that for simpler migrations, such extensive measures may not be needed but nonetheless, it's a good practice to follow to avoid any unexpected issues.

- **Backup data**: Back up the data before you run your final production run. Ideally, you will have baked in a rollback process if the production run fails but in cases where that's not possible, due to the tool or for other reasons, it makes sense to back up your data before changing any data en masse in production. To be clear, even if you have a rollback mechanism built into your code, it is still a good practice to make a backup of the production data.

- **Timing of the run**: Another factor to consider is the timing of the run. You will have figured out the total time it will take for the migration process when you ran it in the full-copy sandbox. Taking that into account, you would want to minimize any disruption to business users and reduce the amount of time they would need to not use Salesforce. This is not a problem in a greenfield org but is a critical consideration for global brownfield orgs that have users spread out in multiple time zones. In those situations, there is no ideal outage time. You will want to pick a time where the disruption is minimal for users across the different time zones.

- **Validation**: Once the migration process has successfully been completed in the production environment, ensure that you have business users who can validate the data loaded. This can be as varied as sample testing a few records to pre-selecting more strategic records (that is, the latest accounts) along with other methods of validating that data. Ensure that the business team is available and has a clear understanding of what to do when they are called to validate the load.

We have looked at the different phases of a data migration project and the best practices to use for each phase. Now let's look at some of the tools available that could assist with the data migration process itself.

Tools for loading data into Salesforce

Tools are just that, tools, and there are a number of them that can be used to get the job done. Having the right tool for the job will make it smoother and easier to get the job done whereas using the wrong tool will lead to issues and will prolong the job. For example, using the standard **Data Import Wizard** (**DIW**), which is part of the standard CRM, for a complex data migration job that requires extensive transformation and error handling will not work and you will hit the limits of DIW very quickly.

These days, many third-party tools are available that have advanced capabilities such as a retry mechanism, error logging, and others. Modern middleware products usually have an **Extract, Transform, Load** (**ETL**) component to them and can be used to migrate data. In this section, however, we will discuss the standard DIW and the Data loader.

Data Import Wizard (DIW)

Salesforce provides a user interface-based tool called **Data Import Wizard** to import data. This tool is accessed through the **Setup** menu. Some features and limitations of DIW include the following:

- It can be used for accounts, contacts, leads, and custom objects.

- It imports up to 50,000 records at a time.

- It cannot be used to automate the import process.

- A limited number of objects are supported, for example, `Product2` object records cannot be imported using *DIW*.

- It cannot be used to connect directly with the source system to query data.

- It uses Microsoft Excel **Comma-Separated Values (CSV)** files as the input for import jobs.

> **CSV files**
>
> When importing CSV files with special characters, you may see the data imported but with gibberish characters. This is due to the way the file was encoded at the time of saving as a CSV. When saving the file using Microsoft Excel, the encoding is set to the machine-specific ANSI encoding setting. You could also open the file in a text editor and then save it with the CSV extension with the encoding set to UTF-8.

As noted, you will need to split your loads into 50,000 records each as DIW is limited, not to mention the limited number of objects it can support. DIW is ideal for use cases where end users need access to load data into Salesforce and need an intuitive way to do that. For more complex use cases, it's not used or considered.

Salesforce Data loader

This is a client application tool that can be used to import a large number of records. It also supports records from files or database connections. Some of the features and limitations of the Data loader are the following:

- The client application needs to be downloaded and installed.

- It can import up to 5 million records at a time.

- It supports files or database connections for importing data.

- It can be accessed through the user interface or command line.

- It supports the automation of the import process.

- It can be used to load import data into objects that DIW does not support.

- It uses the SOAP API to process records. It also supports the use of the Bulk API for faster processing.

Salesforce Data loader can be used to query data from other sources but only in batch mode, which is further limited by its support for Windows only. Non-Windows users cannot use batch mode and make use of some of the advanced features of the Data loader.

> **Java Software Development Kit (SDK)**
>
> For Data loader to work, Java is required, and it used to be bundled with Data loader. Salesforce has stopped doing that and you need to now install the open source Zulu OpenJDK to ensure Data loader works. Here is a link that will help you install the JDK: `https://help.salesforce.com/articleView?id=installing_the_data_loader.htm&type=5`.

For simpler data migrations, Data loader can be a viable option but anything involving multiple objects that are related via parent-child or lookup can be a hassle as the records need to be manually linked. For this reason, and with the availability of more advanced tools, Data loader is not used for complex data migrations.

In the next section, we will review the backbone of data migrations, that is, APIs that Salesforce provides. There are multiple options for which one to choose and each in its own right is suitable for certain use cases more than other APIs.

Understanding APIs

A salient feature of Salesforce is that it takes an API-first approach. What that means is that Salesforce internal teams focus on building a rich set of functionalities into the API before designing and developing the user interface. The reason this is important is that it gives Salesforce customers the flexibility in using a custom-developed user interface should they desire. This is pretty common in Salesforce Experience Cloud where some customers tend to use the standard templates provided by Salesforce to provide a self-service experience to their customers and partners, whereas others build entirely custom frontends that are powered by Salesforce user interfaces.

Salesforce provides a variety of APIs meant for different purposes, such as manipulating page layouts, deploying code, querying Einstein Analytics data, or general-purpose APIs that are used to manipulate data. In this section, we will discuss the four main APIs that pertain to data manipulation and are considered the core data APIs. I will be showing detailed steps on how to use the SOAP and REST APIs because they are more commonly used than the Bulk or Streaming APIs.

The SOAP API

The **Simple Object Access Protocol (SOAP)** is an industry-wide standard protocol used for data transfers. It uses **Web Services Description Language (WSDL)** to define parameters to access data and supports the XML format. The WSDL is used as a formal contract between the API and the consumer; this API is ideal to use for server-to-server integrations.

Salesforce provides two types of WSDLs to use with the SOAP API – Enterprise WSDL and Partner WSDL. The former is tightly tied to the configuration of the org and should be used for a single Salesforce org. The latter is more generic and can be used to integrate with multiple Salesforce orgs. *Figure 8.1* shows how an external app can access Salesforce resources using the SOAP:

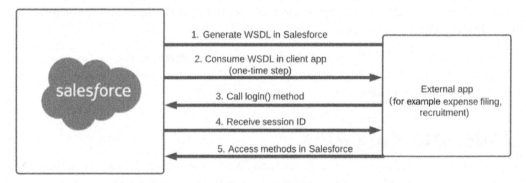

Figure 8.1 – Critical steps to access SOAP resources in Salesforce

As seen in *Figure 8.1*, the WSDL is consumed on the client side and methods in the WSDL are then used to log in and retrieve the session ID. Once the session has been established, other methods can be called to query data or run DML statements in Salesforce.

The Bulk API

This is a RESTful API that is used to query and load large volumes of data. The Bulk API is asynchronous, meaning that data processing only happens when system resources are available. Supported data formats for the Bulk API include CSV, XML, and JSON or binary attachment for ingest operations. For querying data out of Salesforce in bulk, bulk queries can be used that can retrieve up to 15 GB of data.

Bulk jobs can be processed in serial or parallel mode. Serial mode is not optimized because a single batch is processed at a time but operations in parallel mode (parallelism) are optimized, meaning that more than one batch can be processed at any given time. You may think that the more parallelism you have, the more throughput you will get, but that may not be the case. In fact, having a higher level of parallelism can backfire and slow down the process if it's not architected properly. Things such as the tool being used or how well-tuned the code that's running the process is can also affect parallelism.

Designing a Bulk API solution

Although DIW uses the Bulk API behind the scenes, there is no user interface provided by Salesforce to work with the API. You are expected to write your own client program to work with it. This client can be a C++ or Java program, or in another programming language that will then call the Bulk API in Salesforce.

The client creates a Salesforce Bulk API *job* and then batches are created within that job so the data can be processed by Salesforce servers in an asynchronous mode. The client can check for the job status using methods provided with the API. The client application can also retrieve results as batches get completed but the status can also be checked using the user interface on the **Monitor Bulk Data Load Jobs** page. *Figure 8.2* shows the major steps of how a Bulk API operation is processed:

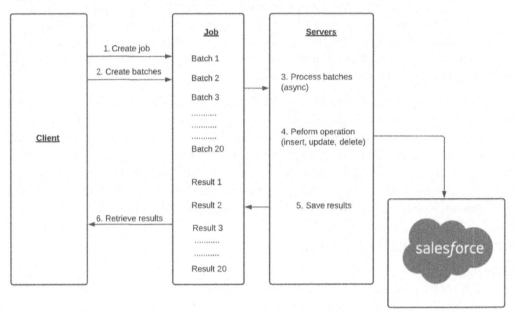

Figure 8.2 – A typical Bulk API operation

Figure 8.2 shows the major steps for using the Bulk API. A job is created, which then has batches created in it. These batches are processed asynchronously by Salesforce and the results are saved. These results can be retrieved by the client application to check on batch statuses.

When deleting data using APIs, a soft delete happens, which means the data remains in the system available to be recovered, if needed. The Bulk API is the only API that can run a hard delete operation, which permanently deletes data from the system. Another consideration is that the Bulk API has its own governor limits, which are different from other APIs.

The Bulk API can also be used to query large volumes of data and sometimes there is a need to query all data from an object. A typical SOQL query will most likely error out because of governor limits but the Bulk API can be used for such a purpose. The Bulk API also has a functionality called **PK (Primary Key)** chunking, which allows querying data from objects in chunks based on sequential primary key IDs. You can specify the record chunk size (the default is 100,000 records) on the job request header and the platform will automatically run the query and return results for each chunk.

It should also be noted that sharing recalculations and Bulk API jobs share the same pool of asynchronous processing threads. If both are running at the same time, it can take a long time for the jobs to complete. Keep this in mind during the design phase as you may need to use the deferred sharing rule calculations feature to avoid any conflicts with the Bulk API process.

Lock contention

Record locking happens when an operation is in progress and has locked the record for data integrity purposes. Bulk API jobs, like other APIs that are used to process data, are prone to locking issues and can cause job failures or reduced throughput.

> **Throughput**
> This is a measure of performance and measures how many records can be processed per second. The higher the throughput, the better the performance of the job is going to be.

There are several reasons why lock contentions may happen and those are discussed as follows:

- **Master-detail relationships**: When an object is in a master-detail relationship with another object, Salesforce locks the master object to ensure referential integrity. If detail records (referring to the same master record) are inserted in parallel processing in different batches, the insert operation would fail due to multiple threads attempting to lock the master record. Locks on this type of relationship can be prevented by ordering the detailed records that belong to the same master records in a single batch. This is because, during parallel processing, multiple batches may try to lock the same master record, thereby causing lock contention.

> **Referential integrity**
>
> Referential integrity refers to the consistency of data within a relationship, for example, an invoice line-item object would have a master-child relationship with the invoice object being the master. Invoice line items each refer to the invoice record 12345. If the record 12345 was deleted, the five invoice line items would become orphaned. Referential integrity prevents these types of scenarios from occurring.

- **Lookup relationships**: These are very similar to master-detail relationships in that if the record being looked up to (the target) is attempted to be locked, a lock contention may arise causing the insertion/update to fail. Use the same aforementioned techniques described for master-detail to avoid lock contention.

  When a lookup is defined, you have the option to select either one of the following:

  i) **Clear the value of this field. You can't choose this option if you make this field required**

  ii) **Don't allow deletion of the lookup record that's part of a lookup relationship**

  This may seem trivial but during large data loads, what you have selected on your lookup definition may cause loads to fail. This is because Salesforce treats the two differently. When the former is selected, that is, **Clear the value of this field. You can't choose this option if you make this field required**, Salesforce just ensures that the lookup value on the target object exists. When the latter is selected, it locks the target lookup record, possibly leading to a lock contention situation.

- **Triggers**: When loading records that fire a trigger, the trigger logic may cause the system to attempt a lock on a record other than the trigger-originating record and cause lock contention. To avoid lock contention, disable triggers or have logic in your trigger code to avoid such situations.

- **Workflow rules**: Salesforce locks the records when a workflow rule triggers a field update and if multiple threads are attempting to lock the same record, lock exceptions can happen; for example, a workflow rule that's attempting to update the same parent record in multiple threads will cause lock contention. To avoid these locks, disable the workflows before loading.

- **Group membership locks**: There are a few operations that cause an org-wide lock. This means that you cannot use parallel processing in this case because once a lock has been acquired on the group membership tables, no other updates can be made unless the lock is released. Some of these operations are as follows:

  - Adding users who are assigned to roles

  - Changing user roles

  - Adding a role to the role hierarchy or territory to the territory hierarchy

  - Adding/removing members from the public or personal groups, roles, territories, and queues

  - Changing the owner of an account to a new owner while this new owner has a different role than the original account record owner. This applies to accounts that have a community role or portal roles associated with them

  Ensure that your code executes in such a way that the lock on group membership objects is minimal and other code is not causing the locks to be prolonged. When group membership type operations are executing, the run must be in serial mode due to the org-wide record locking when these operations are run.

- **Overlapping runs**: Multiple running jobs that overlap can cause unintended lock contention on objects, code, and workflow rules that Salesforce runs as part of the job. Ensure that there is sufficient time between jobs so that the previous one has run completely before the subsequent job.

- **Roll-up summary fields**: When records on the detail side are being updated, the master record is also locked to ensure that the roll-up summary is updated. This can cause lock contention and, if possible, these should be removed before loading data. If that is not possible, then consider using summary reporting on the detail object if it has all the data that's required or a report that spans the master and detail objects. If that is not an option, then order your master object records and avoid having the same master record in multiple batches.

As seen, there are many considerations for efficiently using the Bulk API compared to the other APIs and, usually, the complexities associated with the Bulk API are abstracted by third-party applications that leverage the API. Nonetheless, the Bulk API is the API of choice for data migrations and integrations when large volumes of data are under consideration.

The REST API

The REST API is a web services API that can be used to interact with data in Salesforce. It is considered a lightweight API that uses the request and response framework and is widely used for web and mobile applications.

This API uses the same underlying Salesforce data model for accessing data that the SOAP API uses and unlike the Bulk API (also RESTful based), which has its own limits, the limits for the REST API are the same as the SOAP API.

REST API operations are performed by interacting with **Uniform Resource Identifiers (URIs)** that access **Hypertext Transfer Protocol (HTTP)** methods such as GET, HEAD, and POST. You can use these URIs to perform queries, update records, or run describe operations on objects. *Figure 8.3* shows the critical steps of how a REST-based application interacts and accesses resources within Salesforce:

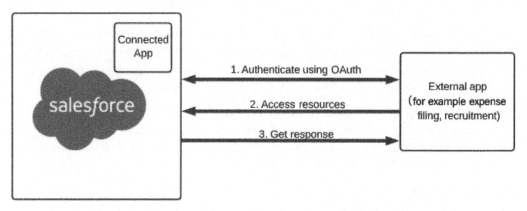

Figure 8.3 – Critical steps to access REST resources using an external application

The REST API is a widely used API that is secure and is used for lightweight applications that are not data intensive. When used with OAuth as the authentication mechanism, it is more secure than SOAP as it eliminates the need to store any credentials and the token in the client app.

The Streaming API

The Streaming API is used for custom integrations or near real-time applications and is not meant for data migrations. This API is based on **Event-Driven Architecture (EDA)**, meaning that data updates are published to a messaging bus. Subscribers to those updates can consume the event on their end. This approach is different than the SOAP or REST API approaches where data is pulled from the system.

In EDA, messages or events are published to a central location; in this case, it's the **Enterprise Messaging Bus** (**EMS**) and systems that are interested in those events subscribe to it. Whenever an event is published, it is published on the bus and all consumers that subscribed to it can use it. This type of architecture decouples systems that produce these events from systems that consume these events, leading to a scalable architecture. *Figure 8.4* shows how EDA works:

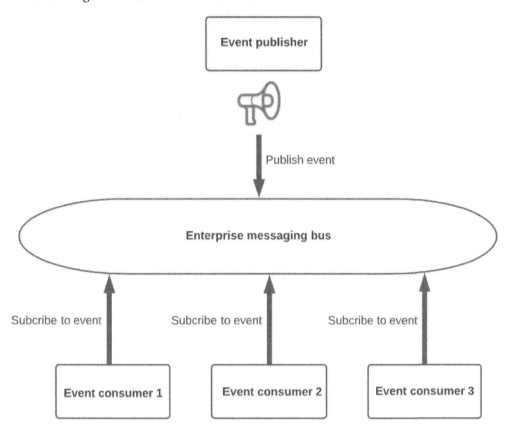

Figure 8.4 – Event-Driven Architecture

The enterprise messaging bus is part of the technology on which the Streaming API is based. This is called **CometD** and uses the messaging bus to publish and subscribe to events. The Streaming API has multiple flavors; two of the most commonly used ones are **Platform Events** and **Change Data Capture** (**CDC**). The earlier flavors of the Streaming API were **Generic** and **PushTopic**, both of which required code for publishing or subscribing to an event. With Platform Events and CDC, there is more flexibility as they are supported both by code and other declarative features in Salesforce, such as Salesforce Flow or Process Builder.

> **CometD**
>
> Visit the CometD website at `CometD.org` to learn about the features and detailed documentation about CometD.

In this section, we reviewed the four most commonly used APIs from a data perspective, learning about optimal use cases for them and how they work. We discussed in detail the Bulk API because that is the API of choice when dealing with large volumes of data, a topic that we covered extensively in *Chapter 7, Working with Large Volumes of Data*.

Summary

Data migration is an exciting topic because regardless of whether you are migrating 1,000 records or 1,000,000 records, there are certain things that you must keep in mind for smooth data migration. Best practices related to the different phases of data migration that you learned will help you to conduct a successful migration without running into any major obstacles. The key thing is to spend time doing proper analysis before jumping into the execution phase of the data migration. That will save you a lot of headaches and wasted effort down the road.

You also learned about the standard Salesforce tools available to us for data migration along with their constraints. As mentioned earlier, for simple migrations, these may be sufficient, but for complex migrations, more sophisticated third-party tools are available that make the job much easier and smoother.

We concluded the chapter by discussing APIs that are provided by Salesforce. Although there are a lot of other APIs that Salesforce provides, we covered the ones that are pertinent to data migrations and integrations. You learned about the general architecture of each API and how to use them, alongside a detailed discussion on the Bulk API. We also covered EDA during our review of the Streaming API and how the Streaming API supports scalability and near real-time integrations.

Congratulations on getting through the last chapter! I hope that you had fun reading it while also learning new concepts and techniques that you can use to add value to your organization.

Questions

1. **Precision Printing (PP)** has recently acquired another company and is looking to migrate CRM data into their main Salesforce instance and decommission the legacy CRM system. The legacy system has 7 million records. What API should be used to load this data into Salesforce? (Select one answer)

    a) REST

    b) Streaming

    c) SOAP

    d) Bulk

2. The Salesforce team at Centauri Logistics is looking to integrate an external text messaging-based notification system with Salesforce. A text message will be sent to the customer as the shipment is received at a location. Drivers scan a location-specific barcode as they arrive at the location. The team anticipates other systems in the future may be interested in this data as well. Which API should be used for this integration? (Select one answer)

    a) Streaming

    b) Bulk

    c) SOAP

    d) Metadata

3. The team at PP has been hard at work and has designed a solution to load 7 million records into Salesforce. They start the run but immediately run into failed records with locking errors. The team is confused because the API is being run in parallel mode. What can the data architect suggest to fix these errors? (Select one answer)

    a) They should run the load in serial mode.

    b) They should ensure that parent and child records are in the same batch.

    c) They should switch over to use the SOAP API.

    d) They should open a case with Salesforce requesting that support allocates more CPU and memory resources to the server.

Further reading

- *Lightning Platform API Basics,* `https://trailhead.salesforce.com/en/content/learn/modules/api_basics/api_basics_overview`

- *Bulk API 2.0 and Bulk API Developer Guide,* `https://developer.salesforce.com/docs/atlas.en-us.api_asynch.meta/api_asynch/asynch_api_intro.htm`

Assessments

This section contains answers of questions from all chapters.

Chapter 1 – Data Architect Roles and Responsibilities

Answers

1. The answer is c.
2. The answer is False.
3. The answer is d.

Chapter 2 – Understanding Salesforce Objects and Data Modeling

Answers

1. The answer is a.
2. The answer is c.
3. The answers are a and c.

Chapter 3 – Understanding Data Management

Answers

1. The answer is c.
2. The answers are c and d.
3. The answer is b.

Chapter 4 – Making Sense of Master Data Management

Answers

1. The answer is a.
2. The answer is a and c.
3. The answer is c.

Chapter 5 – Implementing Data Governance

Answers

1. The answers are b, c, and d.
2. The answers are b and c.
3. The answers are b and c.

Chapter 6 – Managing Performance

Answers

1. The answer is c and d.
2. The answer is d and e.
3. The answer is b and c.

Chapter 7 – Working with Large Volumes of Data

Answers

1. The answer is c.
2. The answer is a and d.
3. The answer is b.

Chapter 8 – Best Practices for General Data Migration

Answers

1. The answer is d.

2. The answer is a.

3. The answer is b.

`Packt.com`

Subscribe to our online digital library for full access to over 7,000 books and videos, as well as industry leading tools to help you plan your personal development and advance your career. For more information, please visit our website.

Why subscribe?

- Spend less time learning and more time coding with practical eBooks and Videos from over 4,000 industry professionals

- Improve your learning with Skill Plans built especially for you

- Get a free eBook or video every month

- Fully searchable for easy access to vital information

- Copy and paste, print, and bookmark content

Did you know that Packt offers eBook versions of every book published, with PDF and ePub files available? You can upgrade to the eBook version at `packt.com` and as a print book customer, you are entitled to a discount on the eBook copy. Get in touch with us at `customercare@packtpub.com` for more details.

At `www.packt.com`, you can also read a collection of free technical articles, sign up for a range of free newsletters, and receive exclusive discounts and offers on Packt books and eBooks.

Other Books You May Enjoy

If you enjoyed this book, you may be interested in these other books by Packt:

Becoming a Salesforce Certified Technical Architect

Tameem Bahri

ISBN: 978-1-80056-875-4

- Explore data lifecycle management and apply it effectively in the Salesforce ecosystem
- Design appropriate enterprise integration interfaces to build your connected solution
- Understand the essential concepts of identity and access management
- Develop scalable Salesforce data and system architecture
- Design the project environment and release strategy for your solution
- Articulate the benefits, limitations, and design considerations relating to your solution
- Discover tips, tricks, and strategies to prepare for the Salesforce CTA review board exam

Mastering Apex Programming

Paul Battisson

ISBN: 978-1-80020-092-0

- Understand common coding mistakes in Apex and how to avoid them using best practices
- Find out how to debug a Salesforce Apex application effectively
- Explore different asynchronous Apex options and their common use cases
- Discover tips to work effectively with platform events
- Develop custom Apex REST services to allow inbound integrations
- Build complex logic and processes on the Salesforce platform

Hands-On Low-Code Application Development with Salesforce

Enrico Murru

ISBN: 978-1-80020-977-0

- Get to grips with the fundamentals of data modeling to enhance data quality
- Deliver dynamic configuration capabilities using custom settings and metadata types
- Secure your data by implementing the Salesforce security model
- Customize Salesforce applications with Lightning App Builder
- Create impressive pages for your community using Experience Builder
- Use Data Loader to import and export data without writing any code
- Embrace the Salesforce Ohana culture to share knowledge and learn from the global Salesforce community

Packt is searching for authors like you

If you're interested in becoming an author for Packt, please visit `authors.packtpub.com` and apply today. We have worked with thousands of developers and tech professionals, just like you, to help them share their insight with the global tech community. You can make a general application, apply for a specific hot topic that we are recruiting an author for, or submit your own idea.

Share Your Thoughts

Now you've finished *Salesforce Data Architecture and Management*, we'd love to hear your thoughts! Scan the QR code below to go straight to the Amazon review page for this book and share your feedback.

`https://packt.link/r/1801073244`

Your review is important to us and the tech community and will help us make sure we're delivering excellent quality content.

Index

N